more praise for **waking up white**

"*Waking Up White* is a brutally honest, unflinching exploration of race and personal identity, told with heart by a truly gifted storyteller. Much as Irving's family sought to shield her from the contours of the nation's racial drama, far too many white Americans continue to do the same. For their sakes, and ours, let's hope Irving's words spark even more truth-telling. They certainly have the power to do so."

—Tim Wise

author of *White Like Me: Reflections on Race from a Privileged Son*

"*Waking Up White* is engaging, challenging, and action-oriented! It's a must read for anyone exploring issues of racism, power, privilege, and leadership."

—Eddie Moore Jr.

founder of the White Privilege Conference

"*Waking Up White* is a wake-up call for white people who want to consciously contribute to racial justice rather than unconsciously perpetuate patterns of racism. With honesty and humility, Debby Irving shares her own story of transformation—a journey of opening herself to learning about the realities of racism and the unintended impacts of white privilege. By confronting her own fears and mistakes, she gleans many useful lessons and tips that can help move others from confusion and avoidance to constructive engagement, authentic connection, and courageous action."

—Terry Keleher

Thought Leadership and Practice Specialist, Race Forward

"Debby Irving's *Waking Up White, and Finding Myself in the Story of Race* is a courageous, insightful, and critical contribution to awareness of race in the United States. A virtual one-woman Truth and Reconciliation Commission, Debby's journey from an 'aha' instant to consciousness is a journey for all Americans."

—Thomas Shapiro

author of *The Hidden Cost of Being African American*
and Director of the Institute on Assets and Social Policy

waking up

white

AND FINDING MYSELF IN THE STORY OF RACE

debby irving

ELEPHANT
ROOM
PRESS

**Debby is available for keynotes, discussion forums, book talks,
and book group discussions via Skype or in person.
Visit debbyirving.com to contact her.**

Library of Congress Control Number: 2013958088

ISBN, print: 978-0-9913313-0-7
ISBN, ebook: 978-0-9913313-1-4

Printed in the United States of America

If I love you, I have to make you conscious of the things you don't see.

— James Baldwin

CONTENTS

INTRODUCTION

NOT SO LONG AGO, if someone had called me a racist, I would have kicked and screamed in protest. "But I'm a good person!" I would have insisted. "I don't see color! I don't have a racist bone in my body!" I would have felt insulted and misunderstood and stomped off to lick my wounds. That's because I thought being a racist meant not liking people of color or being a name-calling bigot.

For years I struggled silently to understand race and racism. I had no way to make sense of debates in the media about whether the white guy was "being a racist" or the black guy was "playing the race card." I wanted close friends of color but kept ending up with white people as my closest friends. When I was with a person of color, I felt an inexplicable tension and a fear that I might say or do something offensive or embarrassing. When white people made blatantly racist jokes or remarks, I felt upset but had no idea what to do or say. I didn't understand why, if laws supporting slavery, segregation, and discrimination had been abolished, lifestyles still looked so different across color lines. Most confusing were unwanted racist thoughts that made me feel like a jerk. I felt too embarrassed to admit any of this, which prevented me from going in search of answers.

It turns out, stumbling block number 1 was that I didn't think I had a race, so I never thought to look within myself for answers. The way I understood it, race was for other people, brown- and black-skinned people. Don't get me wrong—if you put a census form in my hand, I would know to check "white" or "Caucasian." It's more that I thought all those other categories, like Asian, African American, American Indian, and Latino, were the real races. I thought white was the raceless race—just plain, normal, the one against which all others were measured.

What I've learned is that thinking myself raceless allowed for a distorted frame of reference built on faulty beliefs. For instance, I used to believe:

- Race is all about biological differences.
- I can help people of color by teaching them to be more like me.
- Racism is about bigots who make snarky comments and commit intentionally cruel acts against people of color.
- Culture and ethnicity are only for people of other races and from other countries.
- If the cause of racial inequity were understood, it would be solved by now.

If these beliefs sound familiar to you, you are not alone. I've met hundreds of white people across America who share not only these beliefs but the same feelings of race-related confusion and anxiety I experienced. This widespread phenomenon of white people wanting to guard themselves against appearing stupid, racist, or radical has resulted in an epidemic of silence from people who care deeply about justice and love for their fellow human beings. I believe most white people would take a stand against racism if only they knew how, or even imagined they had a role.

In the state that is somewhere between fear and indifference lies an opportunity to awaken to the intuitive voice that says, "Something's not right." "What is going on here?" "I wish I could make a difference." In my experience, learning to listen to that voice is slowly but surely rewiring my intuition, breaking down walls that kept me from parts of myself, and expanding my capacity to seek truths, no matter how painful they may be. Learning about racism has settled inner conflicts and is allowing me to step out of my comfort zone with both strength and vulnerability in all parts of my life. Racism holds all of us captive in ways white people rarely imagine.

As my white husband said to me recently, "It couldn't have happened to a whiter person." And if I, a middle-aged white woman raised in the suburbs, can wake up to my whiteness, any white person can. Waking up white has been an unexpected journey that's required me to dig back into childhood memories to recall when, how, and why I developed such distorted ideas about race, racism, and the dominant culture in which I soaked. Like the memoir by the guy who loses two hundred pounds or the woman who overcomes alcohol addiction, my story of transformation is an intimate one. In order to convey racism's ability to shape beliefs, values, behaviors, and ideas, I share personal and often humiliating stories, as well as thoughts I spent decades not admitting, not even to myself.

As I unpack my own white experience in the pages ahead, I have no pretense that I speak for all white Americans, not even my four white siblings. Never before have I been so keenly aware of how individual our cultural experiences and perspectives are. That said, all Americans live within the context of one dominant culture, the one brought to this country by white Anglo settlers. Exploring one's relationship to that culture is where the waking-up process begins.

For white readers I've included short prompts and exercises at the end of each chapter to help you explore the themes in depth and in relation to your own experience. To get the most out of them, I suggest using a journal and taking the time to write out your thoughts. I've found the act of writing to be a great excavator of buried thoughts and feelings.

My waking-up process has been built largely on the collective wisdom from people of color throughout the centuries who've risked lives, jobs, and reputations in an effort to convey the experience of racism. It can be infuriating, therefore, to have the voice of a white person suddenly get through to another white person. For this reason, throughout the book I've included the voices and perspectives of people of color to highlight the many ways they have tried to motivate white people to consider the effects of racism.

I can think of no bigger misstep in American history than the invention and perpetuation of the idea of white superiority. It allows white children to believe they are exceptional and entitled while allowing children of color to believe they are inferior and less deserving. Neither is true; both distort and stunt development. Racism crushes spirits, incites divisiveness, and justifies the estrangement of entire groups of individuals who, like all humans, come into the world full of goodness, with a desire to connect, and with boundless capacity to learn and grow. Unless adults understand racism, they will, as I did, unknowingly teach it to their children.

No one alive today created this mess, but everyone alive today has the power to work on undoing it. Four hundred years since its inception, American racism is all twisted up in our cultural fabric. But there's a loophole: people are not born racist. Racism is taught, and racism is learned. Understanding how and why our beliefs developed along racial lines holds the promise of healing, liberation, and the unleashing of America's vast human potential.

Racism is not the unsolvable, mysterious tug-of-war I once thought. There is an explanation for how America got so tangled up with racism. Ironically racism, the great divider, is also one of the most vital links we share, a massive social dysfunction in which we all play a role. Perhaps the greatest irony for me has been the discovery that after all these years of trying to connect with people I was taught to see as different and less-than, I've learned that the way to start is to connect with parts of myself lost in the process of learning to be white. I invite you to use my story to uncover your own, so that you too can discover your power to make the world a more humane place to live, work, and thrive.

Thank you for reading.

CHILDHOOD IN WHITE

A man's character always takes its hue, more or less,
from the form and color of things about him.

—Frederick Douglass

Lessons my mother couldn't teach me.

"WHATEVER HAPPENED TO ALL THE INDIANS?" I asked my mother on a Friday morning ride home from the library. I was five years old.

The library's main draw for me had always been a large, colorful mural located high on the lobby wall. It featured three feathered and fringed Indians standing with four colonial men on a lush, green lakeshore. The colonists didn't hold much interest, perhaps because these were images familiar to me, a white New England girl with colonial ancestors. The dark-skinned Indians and their "exotic" dress, on the other hand, took my breath away. The highlight of my library excursions was sitting in a chair and gazing up at the Indians on the wall as my mother chatted with the librarian checking out our family's weekly reading supply.

About a year earlier, my mother, amused by my interest, had suggested I check out some books about Indian life. Lying on my bedroom floor back at home, I had pored over the images. Colorful illustrations of teepees clustered close together, horses being ridden bareback, and food being cooked over the campfire added to my romanticized imaginings of the Indian life. Children and grown-ups appeared to live in an intergenerational world in which boundaries between work and play blurred. Whittling, gardening, cooking over the fire, canoeing, and fishing—these were enough for me. I wanted to be an Indian. I collected little plastic Indian figures, teepees, and horses. For Halloween my mother made me an outfit as close to the one in the mural as she could.

Eventually, my infatuation led to curiosity. If I had descended from colonists, there must be kids who'd descended from Indians, right? I wondered if there was a place I could go meet them, which is what led me that Friday morning to ask the simple question, "Whatever happened to all the Indians?"

"Oh, those poor Indians," my mother said, sagging a little as she shook her head with something that looked like sadness.

"Why? What happened?" I turned in my seat, alarmed.

"They drank too much," she answered. My heart sank. "They were lovely people," she said, "who became dangerous when they drank liquor."

I could not believe what I was hearing. *Dangerous?* This would have been the last word I would have applied to my horseback-riding, nature-loving friends. "Dangerous from drinking?" I asked.

"Yes, it's so sad. They just couldn't handle it, and it ruined them really."

This made no sense to me. My parents drank liquor. Some friends and family drank quite a bit actually. How could something like liquor bring down an entire people? People who loved grass and trees and lakes and horses, the stuff I loved?

I must have pressed her for more because my mother, who along with my father sought to protect my siblings and me from anything upsetting, went on to tell a tale in vivid detail about children hiding under a staircase, in pitch blackness, trying to escape the ravages of their local friendly Indian now on a drunken rampage, ax in hand. They were all murdered.

"Well, what happened to the Indian?" I asked, my heart beating in my chest.

She paused, thinking. "You know, I don't know," my mother answered sincerely. We both went silent.

I never questioned this narrative's truth or fullness despite its dissonance with the peaceful images in my books. My mother, full of kindness and empathy, told it to me. I don't question that she believed it. She told me a version of a story as she had heard it from someone else, who also likely believed it. I had no other, more complete historical context in which to place this story about a nearly extinguished culture now neatly tucked away on isolated reservations I didn't know existed. I had minimal knowledge of how Native peoples had long flourished in their own cultures before white Europeans decimated them with theirs. It makes me wonder how many lies and half-truths I've swallowed and in turn inadvertently passed along in my lifetime.

Stereotypes, I've learned, are not so much incorrect as incomplete. It's true that alcohol was a factor in the waning of indigenous people. But there's infinitely more to the story. What my mother didn't tell me was that the white colonists had purposefully introduced alcohol to Native Americans, using it to weaken, subdue, and coerce them into signing over land and rights. She didn't explain how disease brought by our ancestors had infected and killed Indian men, women, and children, in some cases killing

90 percent of a Native nation's population. Nor did she tell me that those who survived disease found themselves in dehumanizing federal programs designed by white men to "civilize" Indians, separating them from one another and stripping them of the languages, customs, beliefs, and human bonds that had held them together for centuries.

She didn't help me understand what it might have felt like, for people as attached to their families and homes as I was to mine, to be torn from theirs. She didn't turn and gently ask me to imagine what it might be like to lose nine out of ten of my closest friends and family. She didn't tell me that today indigenous people use words like "invaders" and "terrorists" and "genocide" to describe the Pilgrims and their actions. She didn't explain that the English coming to America was part of a larger historical pattern of white Europeans invading countries, exploiting resources, and "civilizing" people they considered to be savages, all in an entangled quest to dominate through Christianity and capitalism. She couldn't tell me any of these things because she herself had never learned them.

The question I asked that Friday morning was typical of a young child trying to make meaning of the world around her. Unfortunately, my mother's own upbringing had left her lacking the necessary knowledge and life skills to connect me to my world through historical truths and critical analysis. Instead I got hand-me-down snippets that never added up and left me feeling confused and upset. Neither my mother nor I understood that moment as one of many in which she was racializing me. Without ever once mentioning the words "race" or "skin color," my mother passed along to me the belief that the two were connected to inherent human difference.

Without meaning to, on that day or any other, my mother gravely misled me. She didn't do it because she was evil or stupid or had upholding racism on her mind. My mother was warm, compassionate, and bright. She told me the versions of events as she knew them, errors and omissions included. Just as she had once done, I used my scant information to construct a story about humanity. Over the course of my childhood the media confirmed my idea of Indians as "savage" and "dangerous." I came to see them as drunks who grunted, whooped, yelled, and painted their faces to scare and scalp white people. What a tragedy that over time my natural curiosity, open mind, and loving heart dulled, keeping me from confronting wrongs I never knew existed.

That Friday morning was the first and last time my mother and I spoke of the Indians' fate. Shock gave way to disappointment. My little collection of plastic Indians lost its luster and ultimately got boxed up and put in a dark corner of the attic. Out of sight meant out of mind. First, though, I separated out the horses and built a barn of cardboard for them, using oatmeal for shavings and packing straw for hay. As I deconstructed the Indian world according to my wants and needs, and parceled out its parts to new roles and hidden spaces, I had no idea of the parallel playing out between my actions and those of white people over the centuries.

As stunning as my mother's version of events is for its incomplete portrayal of indigenous people, equally powerful to me is the subtle and indirect way it contributed to the ongoing portrayal of white people as the superior race. The story whispered to me the idea that Indians were somehow "other," like a whole separate and inferior species. Indians were drunks, so white folks must not be. Indians were dangerous, so white people must be safe. Indians lacked self-control, so white people must really have their act together. Indians weren't good enough or tough enough to survive, but white people sure were, even when they drank liquor. Like drops of water into a sponge, moments like these saturated me with the belief that I was of a superior race and wholly disconnected from other races—except as a potential victim.

On top of all of this is another critical point. Embedded in her incomplete story was a message that just one piece of information, drawn from a single perspective, was good enough to form a conclusion. Neither my mother, nor the media, nor my schooling encouraged me to dig deeper, to find indigenous people and ask how they told their own history. My mother passed along to me not only incomplete information but also an intellectual habit of not questioning authority, not pursuing other dimensions of a story, and not having the interest or stamina to grapple with complex issues. As a result, I came to view history as something set in stone, printed in books, painted in pictures, and taught by teachers who delivered facts. I took it all at face value, constructing for myself a one-dimensional world in which people were right or wrong, good or bad, like me or not.

Q   What stereotypes about people of another race do you remember hearing and believing as a child? Were you ever encouraged to question stereotypes?

The making of a belief system.

THE PHOTO ALBUMS OF MY CHILDHOOD read like a stroll through the Norman Rockwell Museum. Skating and skiing on the ponds and hills of New England. Holiday gatherings with food-laden tables and exuberant faces. Men on the golf course. Women knitting in rocking chairs next to children playing games by the fire. The vacation-bound family station wagon crammed with children, dogs, and sporting equipment. And everyone, everywhere, white. These iconic visions of a life of comfort and frolic, however, are but the tip of the iceberg. The real story begins beneath the waterline, where the beliefs I adopted over the course of my childhood informed my choices and behaviors.

When I arrived in March 1960, my white parents, Bob Kittredge and Jane Pierce Kittredge, had been married fifteen years and produced my four older siblings, ages six to fourteen. My parents made their home in Winchester, an almost exclusively white Boston suburb set in a leafy green, pond- and lake-filled area north of the city. With excellent public schools and plenty of green space to play in, it provided a clean and safe world in which my mother could take care of the five of us while my father enjoyed an easy commute to his job as an investment lawyer in Boston.

Today, my father would probably be called a workaholic. Long days at the office were often topped off with volunteer board or committee work for the bank, hospital, and country club. I hovered around him when he was at home, playing blocks nearby while he worked. Saturday mornings he worked from his favorite easy chair, his briefcase open in his lap, a pencil between his teeth. The sound of the briefcase snapping shut usually indicated the start of a family project: household jobs that gave me not only a number of skills but also an unshakable work ethic. Under the direction of both parents, the whole family raked, shoveled, mowed, weeded, pruned, and fertilized. We built a backyard patio ourselves, following a guide from the hardware store about how to lay bricks with the help of a level. I did most of this willingly, just to be a part of the group and spend time with the father I adored.

My father's family was only minimally present in our lives. My dad's mother came from a big Boston Irish Catholic family who owned Doyle's, a bar where word had it Boston's Irish Catholic body politic made backroom deals. The family had also, according to lore, made sure no cronies went thirsty during Prohibition. Unfortunately, relations were fraught on my father's side, in no small part because of my grandmother's choice of a husband in the 1920s. My grandfather, a Protestant farm boy from northern Vermont, never measured up in the eyes of my grandmother's family. For one, he was on the wrong side of the Protestant-Catholic divide at a time when that particular culture clash raged in Boston. For the last fifty years of her life, my grandmother burned with anger at her family for the rejection she felt, even contending that she'd been shortchanged in a cleverly manipulated family will.

In her anger, my grandmother put the kibosh on the Catholic Church and raised her two sons Protestant. She also worked overtime to make sure her children proved her family wrong by becoming the superstars she needed them to be. It worked. My father, through a series of scholarships, excelled his way through prep school, Williams College, and Harvard Law School, making him a worthy match for my mother, a Smith College graduate from an esteemed New England family.

The heart and soul of the family culture in which I was raised came from my mother's family, a large, close-knit clan of interwoven clans of old, white, Massachusetts and Maine families with whom we spent holidays and summer vacations. By the time I came along, my father's Irish Catholic and poor-farmer roots had been so thoroughly extinguished I knew little of them until I was in my twenties. I identified 100 percent as a New England WASP, with parents and an extended family who bore all the trappings of the social elite and an extensive network of like-looking and like-minded family and friends with whom to preserve our Anglicized, Yankee culture.

Like many New England Yankee families, our roots went back to the *Mayflower* and other early boatloads of English settlers. (If you're related to one settler, you're related to a dozen or so: after all, they were each other's only mates for the first hundred years.) Families like mine had had ample opportunity to accumulate and merge land and wealth, creating a sense of perpetual abundance and stability.

It has perplexed more than a few friends of mine who are not of Yankee descent why on earth people with so much wealth also embody that famous Yankee frugality. Despite mortgage-free houses, private educations, and ever-growing financial investments, families like mine drove cars until the engine's last breath, patched up the elbows of old sweaters to extend their wear, and reused their morning teabags throughout the day. To me it made perfect sense. These visible expressions of my culture aligned seamlessly with family teachings that money was mostly for accumulating, waste showed carelessness, and flashiness—well, there was almost nothing more evident of poor breeding than flashiness.

Frugality must have been a carryover from the Puritan days, as were restrained emotions and extreme modesty about the body. These three values weighed heavily in my understanding of the world. I wonder, though, at which point exuberance, joy, and humor worked their way into my family's culture, for these were highly prized traits that put the party in the Puritans, at least in my family's case.

Like many old New England families, we had a shared vacation home at which we all soaked up and reinforced these values for one another. Ours was, and still is, in northern Maine, where in 1807 a land grant led a branch of my family to help settle a border town. Well over a century later, a log cabin set on a crystal clear, mountain-ringed lake occupied by my family for generations provided the ideal setting in which to unleash the rowdy (but still frugal) family spirit in all its glory.

Full of successful lawyers, bankers, and businessmen who married spirited women, the extended family lived by the motto "Work Hard; Play Hard." Even on vacation we rarely sat still. We spent a month of each summer at the lake, where early-morning flotillas of small boats ferried children, adults, and dogs to the lake's tiny island for campfire breakfasts. Boating, swimming, horseback riding, and tennis competitions filled the days, and raucous multigenerational card games on the screen porch echoed over the lake late into the night. At evening's end, boats and cars would rumble away from the dock and driveway, signaling the children to scamper to their sleeping porch cots to rest up for the next day. People in northern

Maine still joke: "It's black flies in June, mosquitoes in July, and Pierces in August." I am a Pierce. These are my roots. This is the group whose heritage and cultural traditions I made my own, from whom I took my identity.

From a young age I internalized the idea that accomplishment for anyone was simply a matter of intention and hard work. Family gatherings inevitably included stories about our New England ancestors overcoming challenges. Only recently have I come to understand the impact these stories had on me. Tales of *Mayflower* settlers and other early American ancestors suggested to me that America provided a kind of neutral template on which anyone could design the life they chose. Not only did these stories affirm my place in American history; they translated into a sense of confidence and ability that took hold from an early age. Like my siblings and cousins, I could hold my own by age ten at most any family sport or game, organize an overnight camping expedition, or sew and bake all my Christmas gifts for friends and family. Little did I know how each skill was developing in me the kind of strategy, efficiency, productivity, and confidence so valued in American classrooms and corporate offices.

Being accomplished and staying busy were signs of good character, I believed, in part because they offered ways to show my forebears my gratitude. I would rather have been labeled homely than lazy. Somehow, without anyone ever saying it directly, I felt immeasurably beholden to my long-lost ancestors, pioneers who impressed me with their drive, high morals, and hard work. Because they endured great sacrifice in reaching their goal to establish a new nation, I felt it my duty to carry the torch they lit on New England's shores.

Our good fortune and long line of self-sacrificing forebears led me to another belief: complaining about anything was out of the question. Physical and emotional hardiness were parts of the same whole. Unrestrained emotion was seen as a weakness, unless of course it came in the form of a happy yelp at a notable golf shot or tennis slam. Displays of anger showed poor rearing; pride was gauche; sadness, anger, jealousy, and fear were just plain pitiful—all worthy of being shunned with silver-clinking-on-china silence or a swift change of subject. A "good attitude" was highly valued and rewarded. I learned to stuff down my negative feelings and to buck up with expected chipperness. Each cultural norm motivated me to fit in while judging others who didn't. I learned to become deeply uncomfortable around people who exhibited any of the disapproved emotions, especially anger.

How could I live a life of stifled emotions? Simple: it was all I knew. Later in life I would pay a steep price for my emotional numbness, but at the time the focus on the positive served as my North Star. I'll get into this conditioning more later, as it has huge implications for racism. For now, just know that it is no coincidence that one of the things my white mother could not teach me was to honor feelings of outrage. "The point of life is to enjoy it!" she used to say, in a declarative kind of way, raising her fist in the air. When she said it like that, I liked it. So I went with the program.

A reluctant homemaker, my mother thrived instead on athletics, creative projects, and the general chaos of neighborhood kids running in and out of her house and yard. Our house in Winchester was a six-bedroom, Tudor-style home with big first-floor rooms perfect for spreading out our blocks, train tracks, coloring books, and board games. We were allowed to tear around on tricycles, rolling over the worn rugs and by the antiques handed down through generations of New England ancestors. My mother set up the house to run more like a summer camp or after-school program than a typical suburban home. Even if it were just a closet, my mother named various parts of the house for the activity they were meant to inspire—the sewing room, the sports room, the costume room. She taught us to sew, bake, and create plays, backyard fairs, and around-the-block parades. She encouraged us to build elaborate forts of tables and sheets. This household atmosphere of endless possibility surely engrained in me the belief that if I could envision it, it could be done.

On most days we were expected to spend at least some of the time outdoors being active and getting fresh air and sunshine. In addition to having a big yard to play in and a summer home to retreat to, we belonged to the Winchester Country Club and the Winchester Boat Club, where we could swim, play tennis, golf, and sail. Both were just a bike ride away. In the colder months my mother bundled us up in hand-me-down jackets and hand-knit hats, mittens, and scarves to share with us her love of sledding, skiing, and skating. Each November, my father built a backyard skating rink on which the figure-skating girls timed their twirls between the puck slaps of the hockey-playing boys. I had more activities to choose from than I had time to do them.

Being the youngest of five, I spent my entire childhood trying to catch up, figure things out, and not get left behind. "Last but not least," my father used to smile in recognition of my efforts. This status as youngest created in me a lifelong sensitivity to people—especially children—who feel "less-than" in any way, shape, or form. Despite all the riches, all the fun, and all the internal confidence I developed, I also struggled with feeling left out and left behind. My older siblings always seemed to have more important people to be with and more important things to do. My entire family went to the 1964 World's Fair in New York City and left me, age four, behind with a babysitter to watch it on TV. I've never forgotten my sense of being a second-class citizen as a result of their choice. It was a silent and stuffed-down suffering, for I had learned young that complaining was for losers.

Q What values and admonitions did you learn in your family? Think about education, work, lifestyle, money, expression of emotions, and so forth. Try making a list of ten principles, values, and unspoken beliefs. Siblings and cousins can be good resources for thinking about this. Now consider what conclusions you drew about people who did not appear to follow your family's belief system.

Everyone wants to know:
Which one is the real issue?

BEFORE I CONTINUE, I have to call out what could potentially become a distraction. By now you've noticed that I am not only white but a white Anglo-Saxon Protestant (WASP), from a family with plenty of socioeconomic advantage. I worry that some white readers will quickly conclude: *This story has nothing to do with me. My family wasn't wealthy or WASPy. We immigrated here and made it from nothing.*

Let me first acknowledge that your relationship to American culture may well be different from mine. With the exception of indigenous people, who have been on this continent for thousands of years, every American has a unique coming-to-America story and a unique location in our social landscape. Yet not to be overlooked is the fact that the vast range of white-skinned ethnicities have one critical factor in common: namely, that ever-visible white skin and the perks (whether acknowledged or not) that come with it. Also crucial is the fact that just as white people tend to look at other racial groups as a group, loading them up with stereotypes and judgments, the same thing happens with the white race. Understanding whiteness, regardless of class, is key to understanding racism.

Likewise, you might find yourself thinking, *Wait a minute—this is about class, not race.* I've often heard people debate the entangled relationship between race and class. "Which one is the real issue?" people ask. "Is it race or class?" I've wondered myself how much my socioeconomic advantage versus my skin color advantage shaped my life and skewed my worldview. I've come to believe it's not an either/or issue. Both are real, and both matter. Trying to determine which one is the "real" issue does a disservice to both. Concluding class is the real issue would give me permission to avoid thinking about race. Similarly, assuming race is the more significant issue overlooks the complications faced by white people caught in a vicious cycle of poverty. Both can trap people in a kind of second-class citizenship. If you can't get the education you need to get a job to pay for healthy food, medical care, transportation, and a home in a neighborhood with good schools, then you can't educate your children in a school that will prepare them for a job that will . . . and so on. Any cycle that traps someone in a state of perpetual disadvantage is the real issue for the person experiencing it.

And yet race and class are inextricably linked. Because class has long been easier for me to understand than race, this book focuses on the more elusive role skin color has had in my life. In grappling with whiteness, I've tried as much as possible to tease out and examine the race factor. Two stories stand out as ones that helped me understand skin color's potential to carry advantage or disadvantage across the socioeconomic spectrum.

A white man I met at a conference shared a story about his 1970s adolescence in poverty. His father had lost everything as a result of a double addiction to alcohol and gambling. Desperate to get a college education, the son shoplifted to pay his way. In all his years of sneaking electronic equipment out of stores, he got nabbed only once. For that, he was told to hand over what he'd stolen and not come back to the store. A young black man trying the same tuition-funding strategy very likely would have been followed around the store by a suspicious employee and arrested if caught.

On the other side of the equation is a story told by John Hope Franklin, an African American man revered for his contributions as a US historian, educator, and author. In 1995 President Clinton awarded Dr. Franklin the Presidential Medal of Freedom. In celebration of the honor, Dr. Franklin hosted a small dinner at Washington, DC's, exclusive Cosmos Club. That evening, a white club member handed Dr. Franklin—who was dressed in a tuxedo—a coat check tag and asked him to fetch her coat. Nothing like this has ever happened to me or any white people I know.

Unlike poverty, skin color is visible and fixed, forever and always. In both stories I see skin color translating to an expectation on the part of onlookers. White skin can erroneously bring high expectations and the message "You belong"; dark skin can erroneously bring low expectations and the message "You don't belong."

Until I understood the impact skin color can have on one's life, I wasn't able to consider racism in combination with other factors that influence one's culture. The cultures that shape people are breathtakingly complex when you consider all that goes into them. Era, geographic location, language, level of education, ethnic heritage, race, gender, sexual orientation, income, wealth, religion, health, family personalities and professions, birth order, hobbies, and sports provide multiple variables that mix and match to create a unique culture in each and every family and each and every person. To further complicate matters, each element is a cultural carryover from prior generations. When it comes to culture, the only thing we all have in common is that we have one, and it shapes us.

Each of the above variables creates elements of shared experience that spawn shared beliefs and values. People in certain parts of the country, for instance, develop strong identities as Southerners, Californians, or in my case New Englanders. The same can be said of every variable, including race and class. Yet race stands apart from the variables listed above. Not only is race visible and permanent; it's come to act as a social proxy for one's value in American society. White has long stood for normal and better, while black and brown have been considered different and inferior. Social value isn't just a matter of feeling as if one belongs or doesn't; it affects one's access to housing, education, and jobs, the building blocks necessary to access the great American promise—class mobility.

So there we are, full circle, back to racism and classism and how they interact with each other. A discipline within the study of race, intersectionality, examines the myriad ways cultural differences intersect with one another to create unique life experiences and perspectives. That's another book. For now, consider this one story. An acquaintance of mine is a middle-aged white woman from the Midwest. Comparing notes one day, she talked about how her parents were working-class folks struggling financially. They were overtly racist as they spoke and acted from a deep fear that black people were going to move in and take their jobs or buy a house in their neighborhood and lower the value of their home. In contrast, my parents' upper-middle-class world insulated them to a point where they felt little threat. Their lack of fear allowed them to pass along to me a sense of responsibility to help the poor. An element of class you'll notice in my story is the persistent sense of needing to "help" and "fix." These characteristics are considered by many to be trademarks of the dominant class.

You may also notice that I often conflate racism and classism. Though at times it may sound as if I think all white people are loaded and all black people are downtrodden, I know it's not that cut-and-dried. But I need to start somewhere, and this book is the story of the *beginning* of my racial learning journey. As much as I tried to untangle and hold separate the racial thread, at certain points I couldn't. I'm getting better at it as I go, but it's a long, slow process of distancing myself from the embedded beliefs I internalized throughout my young life.

I hope that the fact my story is loaded with socioeconomic privilege doesn't prevent white readers from finding their own connection to race and racism. Every white person can awaken to the impact the ideology and practice of whiteness has on our brothers and sisters of color. Despite our cultural differences, what's crucial to grasp are the ways in which our shared social system ultimately connects all our stories into a single collective narrative. My story is just one point of entry into our shared history.

Q Class is determined by income, wealth (assets), education, and profession. Betsy Leondar-Wright, program director at Class Action, suggests these categories as a way of thinking about class:

Poverty

Working Class

Lower-Middle Class

Professional Middle Class

Upper-Middle Class

Owning Class

How would you characterize your parents' class? Your grandparents' class? Your class as a child? Your class now? What messages did you get about race in each?

The downside of perpetually looking on the bright side.

IN CONSIDERING THE CULTURAL INFLUENCES that shaped me, I've thought a lot about how optimism infused itself into my very being. I used to think it was something I inherited, a kind of hardwired chipper trait. Recently, however, I came across a description of Baby Boomers as a "postwar generation of opportunity and optimism." *Ha!* I thought. *There it is again, me attributing something to myself when it actually is as much about my culture as my character.* It was yet another moment in this unending journey of coming to see the ways in which I soaked up and enacted larger social forces.

The year I was born, 1960, marked the fourteenth year of the postwar baby boom—generally defined as 1946–1964. With their oldest child born in 1946 and their last in 1960, my family embodied the national fertility phenomenon resulting from the sudden influx of men in their early to mid-twenties returning from World War II. My father and uncles were just a handful of the millions of GIs who returned home to women awaiting marriage. Making things even rosier, the US government stood poised to inject cash into the GIs' dreams to settle down, pursue careers, and start families. Known as the GI Bill, this federal program allowed men, like those in my family, to pursue higher education on the government's nickel and buy homes with low-rate, government-backed mortgages.

The bill funded an economic and housing boom that created a vibrant suburban sprawl and a culture to go with it. New suburbs popped up around the country, while established suburbs burgeoned. Free from burdensome loan payments, suburbanites consumed and accumulated in grand proportions. Across America, families like mine purchased once-rare commodities at exponential rates. The sale of televisions, cars, and single-family homes exploded. Ads and television shows promoted goods while projecting images of the suburban ideal onto the popular psyche, promising a world of happy nuclear families, clear gender roles, manicured lawns, throngs of children on shiny new bikes, and neat driveways harboring stylish new cars. Suburban life and all it entailed became a norm for millions of American families. By the time I was born, the newly defined American dream had become an attainable reality for millions of white families. It turns out that the culture of achievement, security, and optimism I so thoroughly internalized was part of a larger pattern.

Being born and raised in the post–World War II baby boom era exposed me to a particularly potent brand of optimism that mixed like a gin punch cocktail with the New England Yankee can-do spirit that had been defining my family for generations. Not having experienced the Great Depression or World Wars I and II, I believed optimism was a given and achievement and security were available to all who bucked up and kept their nose to the grindstone. Optimism seemed not only a realistic mindset, but necessary for achievement. After all, people who complained or moped were unlikely to get far in life. Upbeat was the attitude of the successful.

The 1960s media-delivered world of white people confirmed my understanding of life as pretty comfortable. Ozzie and Harriet could have been my parents. Beaver Cleaver could have been my neighbor. The world was jovial, problems were surmountable, and people got along. Life was comfortable. Normal was a house or two, a car or two, a pet or two, a TV or two. The social issues of my TV world were limited to squabbles and misunderstandings between family and friends and could be solved in thirty minutes or less. And everybody was white.

History lessons further reinforced the world as I knew it. At home and in school I learned about my country's history exclusively through the lens of white European Americans, the kind of people I'd heard about in my own family history. The guys in the history books looked a lot like the guys in the portraits at the Winchester Savings Bank. I used to squint and imagine them without their wigs and goofy old-fashioned clothes, turning them into people I might bump into on the street. The black-and-white photos of former and current hospital presidents hanging in the Winchester Hospital lobby looked a lot like the men I knew. My father was even one of them. Everywhere I looked I saw a world I wouldn't have described as white. I would have told you it was just the world. These were the guys who ran things. I knew and liked them. They felt familiar. Life was friendly, and I belonged. Of course I was optimistic.

My parents spoke often of their commitment to making our childhoods worry-free. They never argued, at least not in front of us. They never spoke ill of anyone else. They didn't let us watch the news. They didn't speak about world events unless they were cheerful events, like Neil Armstrong landing on the moon or Mark Spitz winning seven gold medals. I wish they were still alive so I could ask them what their thinking was. How much was their impulse to protect us in reaction to the hardship they'd experienced in their own young lives? I imagine that fifteen years of economic depression and family and friends fighting in world wars must have made for tense households. I can't know their intentions, but I can say that the impact was to leave me both programmed to look for hope in dire circumstances and ill prepared for a world far more complex and multidimensional than the one I knew. (It's not lost on me that this tension led me to this book.)

As I've swapped childhood stories with people of color, I've learned the ways in which many parents of color prepare their children for a hostile world. Trying to protect children by providing a worry-free childhood is a privilege of the dominant class—a white privilege. Many parents of color teach their children to keep their hands in plain sight if a police officer is near and to avoid white neighborhoods in order to avoid being questioned simply for being there. In the same way I was trained to make myself visible and seek opportunity, many children of color are trained to stay under the radar and avoid suspicion.

Another thing that kept family conversations light in my house was the ability to avoid sharing disturbing history and current events. Watching the documentary *Cracking the Codes: The System of Racial Inequality* gave me a glimpse into how much more difficult such avoidance must be for families of color. Just trying to pass down family history would inevitably lead to upsetting truths. In the film, a black woman describes a childhood conversation she had with her mother. It begins when the young girl asks her mother why neighborhoods in her hometown, Washington, DC, look so different. Question by question and answer by answer, the mother and daughter ease the conversation all the way back to slavery. The daughter, struggling to understand the concept, presses her mother, just as I had pressed mine about the Indians. "What do you mean? They had them doing a lot of chores?" the girl asks. Her mother tries to explain slavery. "Oh no sugar, uh-uh, they couldn't be married, they couldn't keep their children, they didn't have their own souls, everything was taken from them, and you know your grandfather? His father was a slave. That's why he has that African name, Osi." The girl is stunned. "Well, why did the people let themselves be slaves?" she asks.

Her mother answers, "Oh Ericka, it wasn't like that. The whole government supported it."

I had no awareness of girls like Ericka or mother–daughter conversations about history not told in textbooks. The image of young Ericka trying to take all that in shook me. I imagined having a conversation about a topic so tragic with my own children. It felt unbearable to me to have to taint a young heart and mind with such injustice. Yet I don't believe that avoiding all potentially upsetting conversations serves anyone. There is no painless or easy way to convey truth to our children.

I remember the day Dr. Martin Luther King Jr. was assassinated. I was sliding down the banister when I heard our sitter, an older white woman with blue-collar roots, scream in the TV room. I ran in to see why she was making such a fuss. Her hand was over her mouth, her eyes were glued to the TV, and tears flowed down her cheeks. "King's been shot," she said in monotone, more to the TV than to me. I had just turned eight.

"What king?" I asked.

"Dr. King. Dr. Martin Luther King," she answered without looking at me. "What will become of America?" she asked no one in particular.

I still remember climbing those stairs for another ride down the banister, surprised that no one had ever told me America had a king, let alone one who was also a doctor.

Toward the end of his life, my father, out of the blue, said to me, "I think maybe your mother and I made a mistake by trying to protect you kids so much." The more we talked, the more I understood that as he watched the marriages of three of his five children fall apart, and his four daughters' struggles to balance work and family, he questioned how the sheltered life of comfort, innocence, and ease he'd conspired to create may have played a role. "I don't think we did our job in preparing you for the real world," he said. He wasn't in a contemplative mood; he was deeply distraught.

Invoking the optimism so prevalent in our family, I think I said something with a lighthearted laugh to comfort him. "We could have turned out a lot worse, Dad." Though that is what I felt at the time, the more I understand the world, the more I think he was right. By pretending the world was virtually problem-free, my family culture left me grossly underprepared to solve problems. Oh, I could fix a flat tire or jury-rig a spent boat rope, but messes created by difference of opinion or lifestyle? Those left me high and dry, as I looked on with no tools to understand the situation, de-escalate tension, or navigate toward a solution. In my case, my protected childhood only made for years of stress and confusion about real-world issues. If I had been introduced to some holes in the illusion of perfection, I might have been able to peek through and see the many sufferings and contradictions in the world around me. I might also have understood earlier in life how to connect to the world beyond mine.

Q What were some of the major economic, political, demographic, and pop culture trends from ten years before your birth until age twenty? How did they show up in your life? How do you think they influenced your beliefs?

The exclusive world of thriving people raising thriving children.

FOR MUCH OF MY LIFE, the word "exclusive" brought warm, fuzzy feelings. An *exclusive* resort, *exclusive* club, or *exclusive* school meant top-notch quality. It felt good to know I was a part of an exclusive place or group of people because it made me feel that I too was exclusive, meaning of top-notch quality. But doesn't "exclusive" actually mean people are being excluded? How did it ever become okay with me to exclude someone? In the same way I hadn't given much thought to the implications of "race," I hadn't given much thought to the concept of "exclusivity." I took on the word, and I took on the lifestyle, without thinking through the implications.

For me, part of the waking-up-white process is acknowledging that I'm a recovering lemming. Of course I did things like live in Winchester, play at the Winchester Country Club, and ski at the "exclusive" ski club to which we belonged, because that was the life into which I was delivered. I simply went along to get along. I never considered that the space I was taking, or the resources I was using, might be being withheld from another to make it all possible.

I also had no idea of the valuable and coveted social network I was forming. I never imagined that the life that felt so regular to me could perpetuate my good fortune and ensure my corner of the market. As I moved about in a world where CEOs were just dads and board chairs just friends and family, I developed a wealth of social capital, a network of people and a cultural affinity with them, that would later add to my own success by employing me or supporting my fundraising efforts. It's impossible to fully quantify the accumulated and compounded advantages that came simply from living day in and day out with a small group of people connected to each other and to untold resources.

Beyond Winchester my parents' well-established New England network of white friends and family immersed me in a monocultural world. If we traveled, we stayed with people who lived in homes a lot like ours, belonged to country clubs a lot like ours, attended schools like ours, and had similar cars, TV sets, artwork, and antiques. My exceptionally sheltered world felt familiar and easy to navigate everywhere I went.

The social rules remained constant. I remember being shocked when my mother asked me to change up my language and say "Yes, ma'am," to my Southern aunt. I looked at my mother as if she had two heads. *I don't say "ma'am,"* I thought. *That's not the right way—that's just weird.* She gave me the hairy eyeball enough times that, for the course of the trip, I conformed to this Southern convention. That's about as multicultural as I got. Right through my senior year of college, life exposed me mostly to other versions of myself and the customs and traditions I considered normal.

My friends and I took our socializing seriously, often acting like miniature versions of our parents, reinforcing for one another the expected responsibilities and rewards as descendants of people we believed to be New England's "first people" (overlooking the fact that indigenous people were actually the real "first people"). Catchy little phrases such as "Blood is thicker than water" and "Don't air your dirty laundry" reminded us to stick together, show our excellent breeding and rearing, and set an example for others. I tried to buck the system here and there (which you'll read about later) but eventually conformed to the demands of the strict social code of upper-middle-class life. At country clubs and other likely gathering places where intersecting clans of WASP families met and mingled with the assurance of practiced square dancers, I mastered every step.

Being with people a lot like me allowed me to avoid any serious cultural clashes. Not only were family and friends similarly raised; a key social code included avoiding conflict by keeping social interactions light and cheerful. "Never discuss politics or religion" served as an explicit conversation guideline. The rest were implicit—learned by feedback. If I stuck to conversation within my culture's conversational norms, I'd get a laugh or a follow-up question. If I said something outside the norms, the tension, silence, or swift change of topic would tell me I'd made a misstep. If there'd been a handout on conversation principles, it might have said: *Don't discuss* religion, politics, money, negative emotions, fears, resentments, vulnerabilities, or bodily functions. *Do discuss* weather, hopes and dreams (as long as they're none of the above), travels, who you know, who's doing what where, commuting routes and times, consumer products you've tried and do or do not like, where you go/went to school, sports, and music. *Remember*, it might have said: *problems are private.*

Perhaps this is why the civil rights movement seemed so removed from my life until two decades after landmark protests and policy changes shook the country. Only recently, in a family conversation about my awakening, did my two oldest sisters tell me of their involvement in the movement. As Smith College students, both had traveled to the South. One sister spent a week at the predominantly black Benedict College in South Carolina and followed up by arranging to have a renowned Benedict professor speak at Smith. The other sister traveled to North Carolina to register voters, staying with a black host family. Why did I never hear of their efforts? Perhaps the answer lay in the fact that my parents had asked at least one sister not to mention anything to our aunt and uncle living in South Carolina, who they presumed would not approve. Did they intentionally not say anything to me in an effort to prevent a chatty four-year-old from spilling the beans? Or was it a way to avoid the risk of bringing a potentially contentious conversational topic to the dinner table? In either case, the omission contributed to the ignorance that now makes me burn with regret.

People of all colors have been incredulous about just how sheltered my childhood was. "Didn't you see pictures of the civil rights movement in the paper?" they ask, trying to imagine how the images and stories of the era could have escaped me entirely. Here's the embarrassing truth: until I was a teenager, the only parts of the paper I ever saw were the sports and comic sections. The paper landed on our front porch every morning but was gone before I could sit down for breakfast. Each day, when my father left at exactly 7:03 to catch the 7:18 train to Boston, he folded the paper and snapped it into his briefcase, along with his peanut butter and jelly sandwich and train fare, which my mother placed on the kitchen table. The paper left with my father, who joined all the other commuting men striding down the street in their gray suits and fedoras, each carrying a briefcase as they headed to buildings in Boston's financial district, where they would meet and mingle with friends and colleagues from other exclusive, walled-off towns and neighborhoods.

In the absence of larger social concerns, my childhood was filled with the excitement of days ahead, of a time when I would step into the roles I watched the adults in my life play. I studied them deeply out of both affection and a desire to emulate them. Saturday night dinner parties at our house, when I'd weave through the crowd handing out appetizers, gave me the ideal opportunity to examine my parents' friends. Standing around the room in a smoke-swirled haze in their V-neck sweaters and pearls, swishing ice in their cocktail glasses, and throwing their heads back with laughter, they made being a grown-up look wonderful to me.

Until the age of twenty-two, when I graduated from college, this was my world. I was surrounded by similar houses with similar families of children with homemaker mothers and commuting suit-and-tie fathers. Now I can see they were *white* children with *white* homemaker mothers and *white* commuting fathers. That white-skinned people were the only ones I knew never struck me as anything other than perfectly normal. They weren't white people to me—just people. And this, I assumed, was the American experience.

If I could turn back time and rewrite the script for those years, my parents would be deft at sharing with me the realties of American history and current events, especially the civil rights movement. They would explain to me the movement's ideals and the strength and courage of the resistors. Instead of protecting me from what they may have perceived as frightful events fit only for adults, they would point out the courage of people on different sides of the racial divide coming together to encourage America to live up to its ideals. They would help me imagine what it must feel like to hold your ground at a lunch counter or in your town's first integrated high school. They would explore with me the similarities and differences between the way my ancestors risked their lives to free themselves from English rule and the way black Americans and their white allies were now risking their lives to free themselves from segregation. My heart aches to think of the lessons I lost in being "protected" from this powerful and poignant chapter in American history.

As it was, I was left to imagine myself imitating the only world I knew. My parents trained me well to succeed in a world I would ultimately find too constrained. Did I sense on some level that injustice was in play? Or was it the sick, sad feeling that came over me when I was asked to tamp down feelings and steer conversations away from authenticity and toward a narrow definition of politeness? Whatever it was that drove me to pursue the life I did, in the mix was a need to find out what existed beyond the walls so I could make sense of what was happening within them. I never anticipated having to challenge my belief that everything I had was earned or inherited from people who'd earned it. The big houses, the private educations, the clubs, the optimism—all of these I believed were earned through nothing other than hard work and high ethics. For most of my life the idea of unearned privileges remained unheard of, an unfamiliar concept from an unknown American reality.

Q How connected to or disconnected from the larger world was your family, your school, your town? How much did you understand about conflict and struggle in your world or beyond? How did you make sense of people who had material wealth and people who didn't? What was your family's attitude about the people in power?

MIDLIFE WAKE-UP CALLS

Education is learning what you didn't
even know you didn't know.

—Daniel J. Boorstin

The course that changed the course of my life.

ONLY WHEN I MOVED, shortly after college, to the city of Cambridge, Massachusetts, did I start to see racial disparities that signaled something was terribly amiss. From 1984 to 1994 I worked in arts administration, where I developed a passion for connecting arts organizations to "inner-city" schools and neighborhood centers, disproportionately populated by kids of color. Because of my family's connections to Boston's corporate and foundation gatekeepers, raising money came fairly easily, and I truly believed my efforts to bring arts to inner-city schools would help "the disadvantaged" experience something positive that would bring lasting change. I had no idea what I was up against or how supremely ill equipped for the task I was.

Once I had children of my own, I shifted my focus exclusively to urban schools, first as a volunteer and eventually as a classroom teacher. I became increasingly disturbed by the racial divide I observed, as well as by my ongoing inability to explain it. Buildings seemed to be shiny and new and full of white kids, or dilapidated and old and full of black kids. In my children's Cambridge elementary school, where students of multiple races actually coexisted, the white kids appeared happier and performed better academically than their peers of color.

Looking for answers, I worked on diversity committees, went to diversity forums, and participated in outreach efforts to include and welcome students and families of color. The more I tried to understand and "help," the more confused I became. The fact that my efforts lacked traction mystified me. The persistent worrying about doing or saying something wrong perplexed me. Worst of all, over time I started to wonder if I might be doing more harm than good. Lurking in my consciousness was a haunting sense that I was missing something.

In the winter of 2009, at age forty-eight, I began coursework for my master's degree in special education at Boston's Wheelock College. The class

"Racial and Cultural Identity" offered the only opening for me, a late registrant. Though the decades since college had stripped away some of the naiveté left by my sheltered white childhood, nothing had prepared me for the dose of reality I was about to get. I expected the course to teach me about "other" races and cultures so I could better help students of color. I suppose I thought I'd get some tips, some do's and don'ts that would keep me from offending students and parents. Much to my surprise, however, the course asked me to turn the lens on myself. I had never thought to look within for solutions to a problem I imagined as outside of myself, and what I found shocked me.

In the first class the professor explained that we would be examining our own cultural and racial identities deeply, "deeeeeply," she'd said a second time, slowly, for emphasis. *Huh? I thought. Racial what? Racial identity?! What am I going to do?* Not thinking I had a race, the idea of asking me to study my "racial identity" felt ludicrous. On top of that, I reasoned, the subject of race was not new to me. After all, I'd had a twenty-five-year run of creating opportunities to bring together different cultural groups and to serve underserved populations. I'd raised money and developed programs for inner-city youth and families, disproportionately black and poor. I'd attended every diversity workshop that would have me. My teaching job in the Cambridge public schools brought me face-to-face every day with young children and families from an array of racial and cultural backgrounds. I saw difference as just difference, not better or worse. I was nice and kind to people of all races and cultures. I believed every person could make it in America, if just given the opportunity. Typical of a long-standing pattern of thinking I knew more than I actually did, I felt skeptical that examining myself could further my understanding of others.

I suppose in that "we're going to examine ourselves *deeply*" moment, I was about 90 percent sure this was the wrong approach and 10 percent curious. I also felt drawn to the professor and her candid way of speaking about racial difference. Fortunately I kept my mind open just enough to get drawn in, bit by bit, each class wedging in enough new information to erode old understandings and leave me questioning assumptions. It didn't take long for me to bump up against the limitations of my knowledge of American history, despite the fact that I had majored in history in college.

As my understanding of America's history broadened, isolated bits of disconnected data found their logical place in a tapestry carefully woven over time. The dilapidated and isolated inner-city neighborhood, the phone call that landed me my first job, the diversity initiatives that fell short, the way my white students consistently rose to the top, my mixed feelings about affirmative action, friendships with people of color that felt stilted—suddenly they all became united in a single narrative. It was as if I'd been examining the world through a telephoto lens, zooming in on events, communities, and individuals without putting each in context or connecting one to the other. As my lens retracted, more of the tapestry came into view, revealing the interplay between various scenes. Racism wasn't about this person or that, this upset or that, this community or that; racism is, and always has been, the way America has sorted and ranked its people in a bitterly divisive, humanity-robbing system.

Q The late historian Ronald Takaki referred to the history taught in American schools as "The Master Narrative," the version of history told by Americans of Anglo descent. Think about what you did not study. Did you learn about Lincoln's views on enslaved black people? Anti-immigration laws of the nineteenth century? America's laws regarding who could and could not gain citizenship? The Native Americans who had once lived on your town's or school's land?

Discovering the meaning of unearned privilege.

RETURNING TO WHEELOCK week after week to study the history of industry, immigration, law, policy, education, and scientific and social beliefs from a variety of perspectives added multiple dimensions to my worldview. Some classes left me with a sense of relief, an *Aha, that explains that feeling.* Other classes hit me like a ton of bricks, a *Damn, this cannot be true!* reaction. There was no moment more profound or life altering, however, than the night I learned about the GI Bill.

On April 9, 2009, I raced into class, arriving just in time. I took a deep breath, relieved to see a television set in the corner of the room. *Great—we get to watch a movie,* I thought. About a half hour into the film, *Race: The Power of an Illusion,* the focus turns to the GI Bill. I remember thinking, *Hmm, my father and uncles talked about that bill, about how great it felt to win the war and come home to free education and a housing loan.* My father's law school education had been paid for by that bill. My parents' first home had been subsidized by it. In 1975, when Vietnam vets came home to a cruel reception, my father expressed his outrage by contrasting it to the enthusiastic welcome he'd gotten in 1945. He pointed to the GI Bill as proof.

But all of a sudden, the film starts talking about the bill not being accessible to black Americans. An elderly black couple, Mr. and Mrs. Burnett, appear on the screen, speaking about the day half a century earlier that they'd excitedly driven out to a New York suburb, Levittown, to look for a home. Mr. Burnett, a returning GI, and his wife drove through a neighborhood and toured a house, imagining themselves living there. They were convinced: this was the lifestyle they wanted. When Mr. Burnett approached the realtor, expressing his interest and inquiring about the purchase procedure, the realtor sheepishly told him he couldn't sell to Negroes. "It's not me," he explained. The Federal Housing Authority (FHA) had warned the town's developers that even one or two nonwhite families could topple the kind of values necessary to profit from their enterprise. The Burnetts were crushed.

The chilling reality is that while the American dream fell into the laps of millions of Americans, making the GI Bill the great equalizer for the range of white ethnicities in the melting pot, Americans of color, including the one million black GIs who'd risked their lives in the war, were largely excluded. The same GI Bill that had given white families like mine a socio-economic rocket boost had left people of color out to dry. I'd been reaping the benefits of being a white person without even knowing it. I felt duped and alarmed.

Watching this film was like driving by a grotesque car crash—trans-fixed, I couldn't turn away, yet what I was taking in was literally making me nauseated and short of breath. My thoughts raced with the notion that racism was frightfully bigger and more sinister than I'd ever understood—and hardest for me, that people like my own family and friends, people in charge, must have understood this to a certain degree, if not had a hand in its orchestration. This was intentional. This was manipulative. This was not freedom for all.

Though black GIs were technically eligible for the bill's benefits, in reality our higher education, finance, and housing systems made it difficult if not impossible for African American GIs to access them. On the education front, most colleges and universities used a quota system, limiting the number of black students accepted each year. There were not enough "black seats" available to allow in the one million returning black GIs. In addition, many black families, already caught in a cycle of poverty from earlier discriminatory laws and policies, needed their men to produce income, not go off to school. In the end, a mere 4 percent of black GIs were able to access the bill's offer of free education. Meanwhile, the bill allowed my father to go to law school without paying a dime, assured that his white parents could retire comfortably with the aid of the Social Security program, an earlier government program tilted heavily in favor of white people.

On the housing front, it got worse. A set of policies created by the FHA, and implemented by lenders and realtors, mapped out neighborhoods according to the skin color of residents. This national housing appraisal system, commonly referred to as "redlining," deemed skin color as much a valuation indicator as a building's condition. Neighborhoods inhabited by blacks or other people of color were outlined in red, the color in the legend next to the word "Hazardous" (investment). Towns like Winchester, far from Boston's redlined neighborhoods, would have been outlined in green and noted as "Best." The higher the rating, the lower the interest rate on the loan, and the greater the appreciation in home values.

Bluelined ("Still Desirable") and yellowlined ("Declining") areas attracted realtors eager to fill their pockets by leveraging the notion of "marginal" neighborhoods. Going door to door, these fear-inciting sales-men promoted the idea of black residents as dangerous for neighborhood values. In a practice known as blockbusting, the strategy was to scare white homeowners into selling their homes quickly at fire-sale prices before black folks moved in and dragged down property values. Then realtors would turn around and sell that same home at an inflated value to a black customer, who had effectively just bought a home in a neighborhood about to lose its value because of their purchase.

Not only was blockbusting a moment of sordid greed on the realtors' part; it was the catalyst for a racial wealth and trust divide that contin-ues today. Home values in black neighborhoods plummeted, while those in white-only areas rose, with an FHA and lending-institution color-coded map spelling out exactly which was which. On top of leaving black people owing years of mortgage payments on a declining asset while funneling white people into homes whose equity grew steadily over time, the twin terrors of redlining and blockbusting fueled white fear and resentment of black people, who could "destroy" a neighborhood just by moving in.

As houses were bought and sold according to skin color and loans were rated and made based on skin color, black folks were left to make do with the remains of city housing, under assault by another federal effort, the Urban Renewal Program. Dubbed by James Baldwin as the "Negro Removal Program," it involved demolishing entire neighborhoods in part to make room for ramps and highways to provide car-owning, professional, white suburbanites easy access to and from the city. The program's promise to replace the razed neighborhoods with new and improved housing never materialized. With 90 percent of low-income housing destroyed, what remained were rental properties—housing without pride of ownership or equity-building opportunity. This critical juncture in American history created a housing footprint that fossilized our communities into skin-color-coded haves and have-nots, reaffirming segregation and provoking increased mistrust between the races.

Between 1934 and 1962 the federal government underwrote $120 billion in new housing, less than 2 percent of which went to people of color. America's largest single investment in its people, through an intertwined structure of housing and banking systems, gave whites a lifestyle and financial boost that would accrue in the decades to come while driving blacks and other minority populations into a downward spiral. Discriminatory practices among colleges, universities, banks, and realtors created an impenetrable barrier to the GI Bill's promise, turning America's golden opportunity to right its racially imbalanced ship into an acceleration of its listing. From the perspective of Americans excluded from this massive leg-up policy, the GI Bill is one of the best examples of affirmative action for white people.

I saw myself in this story. I saw Winchester, my house, my parents' giddy parties with only white people. I saw the stretch of towns between the nearest black neighborhood and mine. I saw my father's law degree, neatly framed above his desk. I saw my isolation. I saw the redlined neighborhoods' isolation. I thought of the house I live in now, partially paid for with money my parents accumulated through their GI Bill–subsidized education and purchase of "Best" white real estate. I thought of how the leg-up the government gave my family had compounded into wealth my parents had passed on to me and my white siblings, a phenomenon duplicated in white families coast to coast. Though I would go on to discover many more similarly divisive laws and policies throughout US history, this was the first one I came to know, and it hit me hard. I felt overcome with emptiness that my parents were no longer alive, because more than anything, I wanted to ask them, "Did you know?" I thought of my father's plea to us at the end of his life, as he gave us his funeral and estate preferences. In a rare display of anger and disgust he admonished us, "Don't use a realtor. Find another way to sell this place. A sealed bid, anything. Realtors are low-lives."

When the class ended, I called my husband, Bruce.

"I need to drive around for a while," I told him. "Can you get the kids to bed?"

"Are you okay? You sound terrible."

"It was an upsetting class." I couldn't put words to what I was feeling. My head spun and my chest burned. "I'll tell you more when I've had a chance to collect my thoughts."

I shook as I drove through the manicured neighborhoods of Belmont, Lexington, and Arlington, the white towns I'd lived in and around most of my life. I drove out to Winchester and parked in front of my childhood home. My life here had felt so innocent, the world such a safe and joyful place. My house stood before me, no longer as a symbol of my happy childhood but as a sinister representation of a social-engineering scheme in which I'd been an unwitting player. I couldn't shake the duped feeling— duped and infuriated to have inherited a legacy that contaminated me with injustice. I felt overcome with a sense of participation and responsibility. For the first time I understood that a tragedy had been staged under my nose, a tragedy in which I played the part of a deluded and unknowing beneficiary.

Prior to the Wheelock course, my attempts to make sense of racism had been akin to trying to understand a game just by watching the players. I made guesses based on what I could see. In contrast, the course asked me to study the rules—centuries of law and policy—to see how players had gotten into their present-day positions. Suddenly every player appeared in a new light.

The game, it turns out, offers different rules and different starting points for different people. It's a drastically uneven contest in which I am among the more advantaged players. Advantage in the game can take several forms: male trumps female, straight trumps LGBT, able-bodied trumps disabled, Western religions trump Eastern religions, higher class trumps lower class, and so on. But nowhere, as far as I can see, is any advantage as hard-hitting and enduring as skin color. My white skin, an epidermal gold card, has greased the skids for a life full of opportunities and rewards that I was sure were available to everyone. My notions that America offered a level playing field disintegrated. I thought of how hypocritical my belief in small government was, now that I understood how well big government had served me through programs and policies such as those entwined in the GI Bill.

I ruminated on this question: If my childhood of racially organized comfort and opportunity had made me feel like the master of my own destiny, full of confidence, and certain of a bright future, what did this imply about people on the flip side of the coin—people who'd been shut out of a world of comfort and opportunity? How does one construct dreams about the future under those conditions? How can one bear to watch TV shows depicting lives of comfort and ease for people with a skin color you don't share?

When I got home that night, Bruce was in bed reading. He put down his book and took off his glasses.

"What the hell's going on?" he asked. "Are you okay?"

I sat down on the bed next to him. "What do you know about the GI Bill?"

"Um, that was the policy after World War II that helped guys coming back from the war. Free education, low-rate mortgages, maybe down payments? Right?" He looked unsure about why I was asking.

"Who do you think was eligible?" I asked.

"Anyone who'd served. Where is this going?"

I told him about what I'd learned and about how shaken up I was. Bruce, one of the smartest people I know, knew nothing of the GI Bill's inequities.

"Are you sure? That can't be true," he said, getting out of bed to retrieve his laptop. I guessed from his expression that the idea of a twentieth-century federal policy screwing black people seemed as unimaginable to him as it had been to me. I looked around our bedroom and thought of how my parents had helped us with the down payment for our house. I thought of the subsidized housing community two blocks away, full of financially struggling people, mostly people of color, whose parents had no money to lend. Suddenly, it felt criminal to feel comfortable in my own house.

"Holy shit, Deb. This is amazing." A quick Internet search had turned up article after article about the subject.

We looked at each other. This wasn't history locked up in a drawer somewhere; this was public record.

"This changes everything," I said, before laying my head on the pillow for the first of many sleepless nights, wondering, *What else don't I know?*

Q Have you ever uncovered a family secret or piece of information
about a person or place that countered your previous perception?
Once you learned the new information, were you able to look
back and see clues that had been there all along but that you didn't
recognize as evidence of a narrative you didn't yet know about?

The day I learned race is more of a social construct than a biological certainty.

I GREW UP BELIEVING that all black people were great athletes and had a gift for rhythm. My father, a college athlete and accomplished musician himself, frequently pointed out the athletic and musical talents of black people. I assumed him to be an expert. Quick little sound bites such as, "Boy, those Negroes can run!" or "Look at how easily these Negroes jump!" made an impression on me. When it came to jazz, he'd stand in the living room, listening to music, snapping his fingers, tapping his foot, and shaking his head in admiration, "Just listen to that timing. Those Negroes have rhythm like no one else." To this day, I am always a little shocked when I see a white person with rhythm.

For all I know, my father was trying to impart into the household positive images about black people. He most certainly never said a disparaging word. But whatever his intent, the impact was to create in my mind the belief that skin color signified inherent difference. So along with my pencil case and notebooks, I brought to my Wheelock course a deeply embedded constellation of unexamined beliefs about each race having its own special assortment of talents and handicaps—except for the white race, of course, which seemed to be free of built-in handicaps.

The news that racial categories are not in fact the neat, biologically ordered classifications I'd long imagined came to me through another segment of the same film in which I'd learned about the GI Bill's differential accessibility, *Race: The Power of an Illusion*. In this segment the film documents a racially mixed class of high school students learning about what mitochondrial DNA can and can't teach us. As the film starts, students are asked to guess which classmates might have DNA close to their own. Each looks around and points to people who look the most like them. The film then jumps to a later class, when the students get back their DNA results. Much to their surprise, and mine, in every case the closest matches were classmates with *different* racial and/or ethnic backgrounds. I learned that night that, genetically speaking, humans have the least intraspecies genetic variation, and the greatest variation occurs *within* ethnic groups.

I stole glances around the room. Were my fellow students as flabbergasted by this as I was? As we discussed the film later, it became apparent that our class was split. There was cold comfort in knowing I was not alone in holding such an antiquated belief. Though science has never been my strong suit, it seemed to me that a misperception of this magnitude should be against the law: Shouldn't people be randomly stopped on the streets, given a pop quiz about racial categories, and then issued a citation for failing to answer correctly? Shouldn't billboards line our highways and byways in an all-out effort to clear up this kind of gargantuan public relations error? Shouldn't public service announcements lace every television and radio station with the news that race is not what we once thought? Repeat: *not* what we once thought.

For weeks I scoured the Internet for more information. Hundreds of websites supported what the film had conveyed. No one argues that human beings don't come in different packaging. Anyone can see that skin color, eye shape, and hair texture look different among various populations. Yet whereas scientists were once limited to measuring skulls and studying nose shape to try to understand these differences, they can now collect, study, and compare blood and DNA sequences. No science supports the idea that genetic makeup follows the neat racial lines white people have created. No science links race to intrinsic traits such as intelligence or musical or physical abilities.

In the midst of getting my understanding of racial categories shaken up, I started thinking, *What if, instead of categorizing people by skin color, hair color was the guiding physical attribute?* To compare it to the way race works in America, I loaded up categories with narrowly defined assumptions. I imagined a world where redheads were perceived as smart and powerful, black-haired people as artistic, brunettes as able to work long grueling hours, and blonds as lazy. Also, to hold the analogy constant, I imagined entire families sporting a single hair color.

Then I imagined myself in this scheme, born to a brunette family. How would this shape my identity and life? Wouldn't my destiny be somewhat set? I'd be on a hair-color track, the brunette track. Family members would be laborers. Those would be the people I hung out with. That would be the world I knew, and the one to which society told me I belonged.

How would I interpret those who had power? Wouldn't I wonder what special quality redheads had that made them extra smart? Mightn't I fear I'd come up short if I stepped out of my box and tried to be like a redhead? Wouldn't redheads scrutinize my every move to see if I were some kind of exception? Or would I be labeled just a typical brunette who'd gotten a little too ambitious, a little too uppity? What if I had brunette friends and family counting on my success to pave the way for other brunettes to break out of their assigned role? Would I crumble under that kind of pressure? If I couldn't hide my hair color, everyone would see I wasn't a redhead and wonder why I thought I could do a redhead's work. I'd be under constant scrutiny. If I tried and failed, maybe I'd fight to maintain my status by bad-mouthing those lazy blonds.

Whether the whole hair-color ruse had begun as an earnest belief or not, the fact is, by the time I came along, years after its initiation, the scheme would have taken on a life of its own, and my place in it would seem natural, not engineered. Unless someone told me the hair-color scheme was based on some antiquated theory, I'd believe it, wouldn't I? Everything about me, my identity, my view of myself in relation to others, and even my personal and professional aspirations would be "hairified." Could I have survived this brand of demoralizing, boxed-in socialization? My brunette identity would be something that had been created for me, shaping my understanding of myself and my ranking among others. Maybe I'd have ended up taking a course called "Hair Color and Cultural Identity" in order to properly educate children from different hair-color groups.

In March 1960, America's four-hundred-year-old skin color sorting and ranking scheme landed me in the redhead equivalent, the white skin category—the dominant, top-of-the-heap group. As easily as breathing in the air around me, I spent my days soaking up unspoken beliefs about white people versus everyone else. By looking at who ran offices and who entertained in the form of sports and music, I concluded that white people were especially smart and capable and black people were good athletes and musicians. Given my ignorance about the backstory behind the creation of racial categories and their assigned roles, it was a logical conclusion. I fit my observations to my accumulating belief that skin color meant differing abilities.

The biggest problem with America's idea of racial categories is that they're not just categories: they've been used to imply a hierarchy born of nature. Regardless of how racial categories came into being, Americans have been cast in racial roles that have the power to become self-fulfilling, self-perpetuating prophecies.

Q How have you understood racial difference? In terms of biology? Culture? Have you given it much thought? Why or why not?

How white people decided white people were the best people of all.

AS I CONTINUED TO LEARN about the history of racial categories, I repeatedly came across the description of race as a "social construct" and a "human invention." If the idea of race was human-made, it begged the questions, *What person made it up? When? And why?* I also started to hear and see the terms "whiteness" and "white superiority," both of which made me cringe with defensiveness. Not wanting to be associated with either, I searched for validation that I was not a part of what I was beginning to sense might be considered a "white problem." In reading about long-ago events I felt comfortably removed, but as I found in myself traces of rusty old ideas, I could no longer deny the fact that I'd bought into the very social construct I now sought to take apart.

The story of how the idea of race was invented speaks volumes about how human beings struggle to make sense of the world around them, and the way those in power are the ones whose interpretations get broadcast to the culture at large. Be it scientific conclusions, business practices, government policy, popular literature, or art, the folks at the top are the ones whose ideas get heard and valued. This is not a history book, so I'll keep it short, but history buffs, if you haven't delved into the history of race, whiteness, and racism, this is a fascinating area of study.

The first attempt to categorize humans by skin color seems to have been made by a white Frenchman named François Bernier, who in the mid-1600s traveled throughout the Middle East in his role as physician for a Persian emperor. In his view, the world's people sorted into four categories: white, yellow, brown, and black. By publishing his observations, Bernier put the idea of racial categories on the radar of his white European readership.

Five years later, another white Frenchman cranked up the concept of whiteness by adding glowing subjective judgments to the category "white." Jean-Baptiste Chardin, a jeweler traveling through the Middle East in search of precious stones, put forth his ideas about the beautiful, naked, light-skinned women he saw in the Caucasus Mountains, a region bordered by what are now Chechnya and Georgia. Chardin's take on skin color, as featured in his writings, added a flavor of eroticism and beauty into the white category, further capturing popular European imagination. By the 1720s pale skin had become a beauty ideal for white people, making its way into European art and literature.

During these same years, white European colonization of Asia, Africa, and the Americas was gathering speed, fueling ideas of white dominance and superiority. In contrast to the ancient traditions and practices valued by indigenous peoples, white Europeans' long-standing wealth-accumulation culture had them busy hustling the globe, using ever-advancing technologies such as the steam engine and the gun to exploit other continents' natural resources, while using native populations to do the grueling work.

Entangled in all of this were white European missionaries bringing Christianity to far-flung parts of the world. Core to their work was the belief that the white, Christian way was the superior way and that "taming the heathens" in order to save their souls required a full-on conversion to Christianity. In this case, the white way was not only better in this world but a requirement for entrance to heaven.

This being the Age of Enlightenment (aka Age of Reason), a time when science first emerged as a legitimate discipline, scientists jumped into the ring as well. White anthropologists and physicians measured skulls and wrestled with human variables such as eye and nose shape, skin color, hair type, blood type, and even fingerprints in search of correlations proving racial differences in terms of intelligence, temperament, and physical ability. As classifications and theories changed, the only constant remained the idea of white as an immutable category, distinct and superior.

Today's social sciences are exploring how culture—separate from biology—contributes to human variation. We now understand that the preponderance of Chinese students' outstanding musical and academic accomplishments has a lot to do with a culture in which parents push their children to achieve, replacing play dates and TV time with math drills and four-hour piano practice sessions. Likewise, the rise of Kenyan runners in the marathon community can be largely explained by their highly focused running culture, diet, and lifestyle.

I found myself passing harsh judgment on those who'd begun the cycle of whites revering whites. And then, with no small amount of horror and shame, I realized I'd been doing the same thing. I'd long "othered" people of color, wanting to help and fix them. My thinking definitely fell along the lines of If only they could be more like me. Wasn't I sorting people into different groups according to race? And didn't wanting to help and fix imply my way is better? Just how far from the "taming the heathens" mindset was I really? When I got honest with myself, I had to own up to the fact that I'd bought into the myth of white superiority, silently and privately, explaining to myself the pattern of white dominance I observed as a natural outgrowth of biologically wired superior white intelligence and ability. Like a fish unable to recognize its surrounding waters, I'd never noticed the culture of white superiority in which I now understood I'd been soaking.

In fact, not only is there no clear skin color correlation to athleticism, intelligence, or any other ability-related attribute, there is more genetic variation within racial groups than across racial lines. In complete contrast to my childhood beliefs, I've learned that the chances are high that I have more in common genetically with a darker-skinned person on the other side of the world than I do with the white woman who lives next door. Whiteness, it turns out, is but a pigment of the imagination.

An indication of the fallacy of racial categories is the way they have shifted through time and across human-made geographic boundaries. Because in America so many children were born to enslaved black women impregnated by white slave-owners, and because lives were made or destroyed according to race, courtrooms across the country filled with cases attempting to define what made a human "black" or "white." Every state had its own standards, so someone could be considered black in one state, step across the state line, and be white. Even today, a person can be considered black in America and white in Brazil, where there are 134 skin color classifications. As immigrants came to the United States, ideas of racial categories also got tested and retested. The US Census over time has gone from attempting a few simple categories, determined by door-to-door census takers looking at and sizing people up, to today's complex form in which people self-identity their racial category and are allowed to choose more than one. If sorting out racial categories has proven so elusive, perhaps sorting was never a smart idea.

Particularly interesting to me as a white person is the origin of the term "Caucasian." Using the highly subjective term first suggested by the jeweler Chardin after he was wowed by the light-skinned women of the Caucasus Mountains, German philosopher Christoph Meiners promoted the term in 1785 by using it in his publication The Outline of the History of Mankind.

Ten years later, a colleague of Meiners, German physician Johann Friedrich Blumenbach, reinforced the term and concept by publishing his theory that humans divide into four categories: Caucasian, Mongolian, Ethiopian, and American. A few years later he added a fifth, Malayan. By the end of his career, Blumenbach had offered up twelve competing racial schemes and encouraged readers to pick the ones that made most sense to them. Despite his shifting ideas about race, two things stuck: (1) the term "Caucasian" and (2) its ranking as number 1. While Blumenbach's other racial labels faded into obscurity over time, "Caucasian" endures.

Suddenly, the idea of calling myself a Caucasian felt ludicrous. It reminded me of the way my mother could never let go of the word "Victrola," despite changes in technology. "Turn that Victrola down!" she'd yell over a blaring radio. Were she alive today, I'm guessing she'd marvel at iPods: "Just look at that little red Victrola!"

When I came out of class the night I'd been introduced to the idea of race as a human invention, my fifteen-year-old daughter was waiting for me for a ride home.

"What's up?" she asked, wondering why my jaw was slack and I was shaking my head.

"I just found out race isn't even real the way I thought it was. I mean, 'real' as in based in biology," I clarified.

"You didn't know that?" she looked at me with shock.

I stopped short, put my hand on her arm, looked at her, and said, "You did?"

Using a tone usually reserved for the word "duh," she said, "Yeah. It was the first thing we did in bio this year."

"What do you mean the 'first thing you did'?"

"We studied the biology of skin color. You know, melanin and the way skin colors adapted to climate as people migrated."

No, I hadn't known. I wonder if some day humanity will look back on people's belief in racial categories in the same way that I shake my head at the olden days when people thought the world was flat.

Q Prior to reading this chapter, what did you know about the history of naming the races? How do you now feel about the term "Caucasian"?

Thinking for the first time about who could and could not melt into the pot.

"TONIGHT WE'RE GOING to talk about 'white ethnics,'" my Wheelock professor said one evening. I couldn't imagine what a "white ethnic" could be, let alone imagine that I might in part be one myself. It turns out "white ethnics" refers to light-skinned people immigrating to America from non-Anglo countries like Ireland, Italy, Russia, and Germany. Between 1820 and 1920, 17.3 million people immigrated to the United States from these countries. I learned that my Irish ancestors had been considered racially and culturally inferior by America's established WASP population and had faced stereotypes and discrimination that limited not only social acceptance but job opportunities. This brought new understanding to the phenomenon of immigrant families shedding native language, dress, and even names in order to adopt Anglicized versions of each. Even my O'Doyle ancestors dropped the O'. For those who had escaped a homeland in pursuit of survival or the American dream, assimilation—the idea of adopting the dominant culture's norms—became a norm unto itself, one utterly unattainable unless one is white.

I'd always loved the idea of America as a melting pot. *Wasn't it great, I thought, that anyone could come to America and start life anew?* I felt proud of America's role as a safe harbor, a land where hopes and dreams come true. By the time I was forty-nine years old, I'd met countless first-, second-, and third-generation white Americans with stories of relatives coming to America with a few dollars in their pocket and little command of the English language yet rising to middle-class status and lifestyle in a generation or two. But once again, I found myself stunned as I learned the role white skin had played in these stories. What I didn't know was that while millions of white immigrants, including my own Irish ancestors, did in fact overcome initial desperate circumstances and ethnic discrimination, the very same rights and resources that allowed their socioeconomic mobility were denied to darker-skinned immigrants—and, of course, to the indigenous people who had been here before everyone else and to the African Americans brought here against their will in America's earliest days.

I now understand that acting like a white American wasn't just a "When in Rome do as the Romans do" cultural sensibility, but a matter of survival. In policy after policy, act after act, the United States has reaffirmed its commitment to being a melting-pot society adhering to Anglo-Saxon standards, as opposed to a mosaic nation built on the diversity of multiple cultures. Be it Europeans' initial assumption of the right to invade in the 1600s, the Indian Removal Act in the 1800s, or the English-only acts in the 1900s, the white settlers established and the white government of the United States has enforced a model of dominance and assimilation that elevates those who can fit the prescribed mold while excluding and destabilizing those who can't.

Though part of this thinking may have resulted from the conviction that it is more practical to have one culture to which all can subscribe, there's no doubt in my mind that it also stemmed from a deeply entrenched belief that the superior Anglo culture should be spread far and wide because everyone would benefit by being more like the English. Again I saw in myself traces of this ideology. I remember thinking, *Uh oh, don't I bring to the classroom the unspoken, maybe even subconscious, belief that my English ancestry somehow made me a more capable teacher? "I really know how to be an American! They're lucky to have someone like me. Wasn't I charitable to choose such a do-good vocation! If I can teach these children to be more like me they'll be better off."*

This deep, subconscious wiring is what makes finding new ways to think about race and racism so hard. If rethinking were just a matter of getting real about some comments made by my parents in my childhood, the task would be far easier. What makes reexamining my racialized ideology so arduous is that its roots run so deep. English attempts to save others by imposing their culture on them can be traced back to their twelfth-century invasion of Ireland, home to people they considered inferior and savage. English conquest of North America was part of a much larger expansion effort that took them to South America, Africa, and Asia. Seven centuries after that first invasion of Ireland, with ideas of white superiority and dominance embedded in US culture, the US government embarked on an expansion of its own. Complete with a brand name, the mid-nineteenth-century quest called "Manifest Destiny" sought to spread

American democracy, capitalism, and Christianity westward to the coast (including Mexican land) and eventually throughout the world.

Though it's tempting to point to the arrogance of such an attitude, I can imagine that in the minds of early Anglo Americans, belief in their mission to civilize the world felt justifiable if not noble. After all, isn't this a close cousin of what I was doing in my work to "help" and "fix" children of color? The last thing I felt I was doing was imposing my culture on students. I thought I was being helpful. This is one of the many horrors of whiteness—the ease with which good intentions can instead perpetuate one's attachment to racial roles.

Like the tiniest Russian nesting doll, I looked a lot like my family, who looked a lot like the prescribed America ideal, which looked a lot like the generations of European Americans before it, which looked a lot like centuries of Europeans before them. Though there are myriad traits from my culture for which I am grateful—perseverance, optimism, and the ability to be tough when I need to be—imposing my culture on others is not one I embrace.

I've lost my appetite many times on hearing stories of well-intentioned efforts to reform people from nondominant cultures only to inflict irreversible damage. In 1879 Richard Henry Pratt established the Carlisle Indian School in Carlisle, Pennsylvania. In this brutal assimilation-through-education project, Native American children from different tribes around the country were kidnapped from the reservations on which they'd previously been sequestered by the US government. Once brought to the school, already traumatized, they were stripped of all remaining shreds of culture and dignity. Scrubbing them with kerosene, chopping off their hair, assigning meaningless English names, cloaking them in English clothing, and forbidding any language other than English, Anglo teachers plunged Indian children into a traditional English course of study, including the study of Christianity. Speaking in their native language earned children a mouth washed out with lye or even a snip to the tongue.

As a teacher and mother I can hardly imagine the terror these kids felt. I try to fathom their shock as they found themselves stolen from their homes, in a foreign world, stripped of their cultural symbols, each correlating to a deeply held belief. In many American Indian traditions, long hair has spiritual significance, cut in some nations only when mourning the death of a close relative. I think of how it might feel for one of my Catholic friends to have the cross yanked from around her neck and discarded, its meaning fundamental in her old world but regarded as shameful in her new one. Or what it would be like for me to have the clothing my mother had carefully sewn for me tossed out by someone who didn't know her or care about the hours I'd sat with her as she'd crafted it. I can only imagine the devastating impact of having all the ways in which I connect to my home stripped from me. No parents, no siblings, no English; none of my favorite food, music, or clothes; no familiar routine—all the while being forced to worship an unfamiliar God and practice a perplexing set of new symbols and rituals deemed superior by my oppressor. If I close my eyes and imagine my own children enduring this kind of radical cultural over-haul, I cannot bear the anguish and fury I feel. I find myself asking, *Who are the real "savages" in this picture?*

The Carlisle school eventually inspired 150 similar Indian boarding schools around the country, all intended to civilize Indian children so they could participate in the new, dominant American culture, albeit as servants or laborers. The schools' intent was to completely transform people, inside and out, including "language, religion, family structure, economics, the way you make a living, the way you express emotion, everything," says Tsianina Lomawaima, head of the American Indian Studies Program at the University of Arizona. Parents faced punishment if they resisted the removal of their children.

Though it sounds downright abusive today, I have to remember the power of internalized superiority to enable one to believe good intent ensures positive outcomes. When Mr. Pratt described the school's mission to "kill the Indian and save the man," I imagine he felt good and moral as he advocated for the Indian peoples' survival in their new world and salvation in the next. Like all of us, he was a product of his culture and of his time.

Thick in the cultural waters of the time was the ongoing scientific effort to make sense of human difference. Elaborate texts such as the 1854 *Types of Mankind*, a 738-page best-selling book, attempted to rank various racial groups as inferior or superior based on skull size and other physical obser-vations. Scientific theories seemed to be a national obsession. People flocked to the 1904 World's Fair in St. Louis to see exhibits of "Real Uncivilized People." The fair, showcasing America as the World's Number 1 Empire alongside an elaborate display of those deemed inferior, reinforced com-mingled beliefs in white superiority and American dominance.

Not yet under consideration was the possibility that much about human difference could be explained by environment and culture. It seems no one imagined that the idea of biological superiority could be just that, an idea. The debate around the potential benefit of Indian boarding schools, therefore, never weighed the pros and cons of dismantling a child's culture but focused instead on the extent to which this breed of people was "fixable."

The Indian boarding school movement tore apart families and communities, creating wounds still fresh today. Referred to as agents of cultural genocide and terrorism by Native people, Indian boarding schools were institutions where children died from illness, abuse, and even homesickness. Without their native language and cultural understandings, those who graduated found themselves unable to function back in their home communities. Despite having adopted the cultural trappings imposed on them, Indian schoolchildren had no control over the internalized beliefs held by the white people awaiting them in the outside world. Unlike the millions of white ethnics who were able to "melt" into the pot, indigenous children could not shed the physical attributes that marked them as different and inferior. No longer Indian, unable to be white, these young adults ended up belonging nowhere.

For much of American history, people who couldn't pass for white lacked not only social acceptance but also access to citizenship, the legal status needed to reap the full rewards of the American dream. Individuals without citizenship can't vote, run for public office, own land, or work in the higher-paying jobs of America's economic machine. Whiteness didn't just earn normalcy or a sense of belonging; whiteness was nothing short of a lifeline. In the 175 years between the Naturalization Act of 1790 and the Immigration and Nationality Act of 1965, American courts used a vague definition of skin tone as a primary qualifier for who could and could not be a citizen. Despite America's ideological commitment to freedom as a natural right for all, through most of US history, white skin has acted as a free pass, while dark skin has impeded freedoms and rights.

This new awareness about melting-pot privilege forced me to face the reality that while my white-skinned family used its free pass to grow in health, wealth, and self-image through the generations, dark-skinned people had encountered roadblock upon roadblock. How would my family's traits of perseverance and optimism have held up were we dark-skinned? I imagined my father in the shoes of Hawaiian businessman Takao Ozawa, who in 1922 petitioned the Supreme Court, arguing that beliefs and behavior, not skin color, should determine citizenship eligibility. Mr. Ozawa, of Japanese descent, additionally pleaded that based on skin color alone, the courts should consider that his skin was as white as any Caucasian's. Like my father, Mr. Ozawa had a sense of dignity and a family to care for. Wouldn't my father also have longed for equal rights? Would he have settled for a lesser lot in life to avoid conflict, or would he have fought back? Would he have gone so far as to petition the Supreme Court?

"My honesty and industriousness are well known among my Japanese and American friends. In name Benedict Arnold was an American, but at heart he was a traitor. In name I am not an American, but at heart I am a true American," Mr. Ozawa wrote. The court ruled against Mr. Ozawa, saying he was not white because he was not Caucasian. Commenting on this case, historian Mae Ngai said, "He did everything right. He learned English, he had a lifestyle that was American, he went to Christian church on Sunday, he dressed as a Westerner, he brought up his children . . . as Americans."

But here's where things get really weird. A few months later an Asian Indian man, Bhagat Singh Thind, in response to the Ozawa ruling, appealed to the court on the grounds that according to scientific classification at the time, he qualified as a Caucasian. The court responded by declaring that whiteness would, from that point forth, be determined using "the common understanding of the white man," and noting that "it is a matter of familiar observation and knowledge that the physical group characteristics of the Hindus render them readily distinguishable from the various groups of persons in this country commonly recognized as white." In other words, white men would decide who was white and who was not. Though this is no laughing matter, when I learned about this case, The Gong Show came to mind. These decisions made by white men felt so arbitrary. Gong, you're in. Gong, you're not.

Even for white ethnics such as Irish and Italians, the US government questioned each new immigrant population's place in the American hierarchy. No country, no group was spared scrutiny by the government or popular consensus. White-based judgments about skin color and cultural norms were used to determine whether citizenship should be granted. My Irish ancestors at one point, I learned, were deemed a distinct race, the missing link between apes, Africans, and English. Jews were judged to be greedy and of low intelligence. Italians, also assessed as a distinct race, were ridiculed for being oversexed and overly emotional. Held against the singular cultural norms of the English, no one else seemed, well, normal. No one else quite measured up. I have to wonder if my grandmother's falling-out with her Irish Catholic family, or my father's lack of interest in mending it, had to do with an impulse to distance themselves from their "inferior" Irish heritage and play up the WASP connection.

Unlike those with melting-pot privilege, my Japanese American neighbor spent her preteen years in a World War II internment camp. In response to the 1941 Japanese attack on Pearl Harbor, President Franklin D. Roosevelt authorized the military to round up my Japanese American friend and 120,000 others like her. Families were separated, forced to leave their homes and jobs, and subjected to the controlled life of a government camp. Though efforts were also made to intern American people of German and Italian descent, it is the Japanese internment camps that gathered the most people.

What were internment camp proponents thinking? Where did the fear of Japanese Americans come from? Why would Japanese Americans be more likely to turn on their country than other Axis country descendants— German and Italian Americans? How much of it had to do with the easy-to-identify Japanese physical traits versus the blendability of their white German and Italian counterparts? How much easier was it psychologically to trust someone who looked the part of the American prototype?

Rethinking assimilation has challenged me to the core. I crave the efficiency and practicality I used to think came with it. No question it would be easier for those in the dominant culture if everyone came around to their way of thinking and acting. It reminds me of how I spent the first ten years of my marriage highly irritated that my husband wasn't coming around to my way of thinking and acting. Of course it's easier when we don't have to negotiate difference. But forcing this vision, it seems to me, hurts us all, because we cannot all do it. We cannot all assimilate because we do not all share one single heritage, one look, or even one common American experience. Isn't the more intelligent choice to create a culture built around difference?

Though today skin color cannot be used to withhold citizenship, the legacy remains. For many people struggling to earn acceptance or American citizenship or both, the ultimate test often has to do not with their efforts to assimilate, but with the dominant group's regard for their racial group. As a member of the dominant group, I can tell you how exceptionally easy it is to be ignorant of the racial forces that have shaped my life and views, and how effortless it was *not* to make the connection that much of my comfort has been built on the backs of enslaved Africans, Chinese railroad workers, and other people of color, who, for much of history, were brought here or allowed here to work their tails off fueling America's growth yet not be considered full Americans.

In the film *Race: The Power of an Illusion*, sociologist Eduardo Bonilla-Silva comments: "[The] melting pot never included people of color. Blacks, Chinese, Puerto Ricans, et cetera, could not melt into the pot. They could be used as wood to produce the fire for the pot, but they could not be used as material to be melted into the pot." Without an understanding of this crucial fact, my head was filled with racial stereotypes, not an understanding of the skin-color-coded policies that had created them.

Q Think about your ethnic heritage. If you are white and know little about it, why do you think that is? Do some ethnicities in your mix get played up and some down? What family stories have held fast through the generations? How have they shaped your understanding of America as a meritocracy—a society in which everyone succeeds or fails on their own merits?

How I finally came to understand systemic racism.

DESPITE THE FACT that the term "systemic racism" spills off the tongues of antiracists the way "disease" might roll off a physician's, I struggled to understand what it meant. Explanations like "It's the way racism is systemic" or "It's the way racism shows up in our institutions" or "It's structural" did little to enlighten me. I think I now understand why it so confounded me. Like "headwinds" and "tailwinds," the terms I now use to characterize systemic racism, there are many factors in play. Until one understands each factor, it's tough to imagine how they interact. On its own, each element might not look like a big deal. The momentum takes hold when they work together.

Here's one way I've come to think about it. Think about three basic elements:

1. skin color symbolism: using skin color to imagine innate levels of intelligence, athleticism, aggression, and so forth in oneself and others
2. favoritism: the idea that one is the best
3. power: the ability to make decisions for and/or distribute resources to people

> skin color symbolism + favoritism + power = systemic racism

Take away any one of these three factors, and the kind of racism that makes and breaks lives would not exist. Until I got the power piece, understanding racism as something more than prejudice eluded me. It started to come together when a black woman at a workshop offered this perspective to those of us struggling with the concept: "All racial groups have problems with people in other racial groups," she said. "White folks have not cornered the market on that. The difference between white folks and everybody else is that they have the *power* to turn those feelings into policy, law, and practice. White folks run everything in this country." I realized that while power is an age-old issue, attaching it to skin color is not.

Once I got clear about the power differential, I went back to the drawing board, trying to understand the word "systemic." I made myself think about what a system is. In its simplest form, I realized, a system is a procedure, a way of doing something. Language is a system. Banking is a system. But even those stymied me, because I immediately tried to bring race in, and then I got all confused. So I had to start even smaller. I have a garbage system at my house, for instance. We put food down the disposal, and everything else in either the trash or the recycling under the kitchen sink. When they're full, I harass my children until one of them takes it out. That's our system.

Now let's throw a barrier—a divider—into the system, something that allows some to benefit from the system and others not to. Because taking the garbage out involves going down a flight of stairs, if someone in my house had a physical disability, they would be unable to participate in the Irving family garbage system. In the case of garbage, this might be considered a joy, but what if taking out the garbage earned you $1 every time you did it? The family member with a disability would no longer be able to benefit from the system.

Okay, so that's a simple system with an easy-to-understand barrier. If someone in my family had a disability, and participating in the garbage job was important to them, we'd come up with a different system. Because we all know and care about each other and the barrier would be obvious, we'd figure it out so everyone would be served by the system.

But what about when systems are designed for big groups of people? What about when the barrier is less obvious? In his book *Outliers*, Malcolm Gladwell writes about the unintended consequences of Canada's youth hockey system, a big deal given how central hockey is to Canadian lifestyle and identity. The way the system is structured, kids have to be a certain age as of January 1 to enter their age class. So in the same grouping, you could have a kid 8 years 360 days old (January 5 birthday) with someone 8 years 5 days old (December 28 birthday). At age 8, that's a big difference in physical and cognitive development. The January kid is a full 12 percent more developed than the December kid.

So how does this play out? Coaches select the bigger, better players (disproportionately the older kids) for all-star teams. Not only does that boost the all-star kids' confidence and deflate the rejected kids, but the all-star kids go on to get better coaching, play with increasingly stronger players, and practice two to three times as often as those who didn't make the cut. Compound that over the years, and what do you get? Professional hockey teams with disproportionate numbers of players with January to March birthdays who rode the tailwind of birth-date advantage. Those born later in the year are more likely to face a headwind of insurmountable system-induced challenges that prevent a professional hockey career; it's not impossible, just far more unlikely. It would be so easy to look at the individual hockey star and ask, "Wow, what is it about that kid, or his family, that gave him those hockey superpowers?" Much harder is untangling the invisible system that played a significant role in the outcome. The birth-date cutoff acts as a divider between those who benefit from the system and those who do not.

In American society, racism acts as a barrier, a divider, allowing white people to benefit from the system in ways people of color do not. Skin color itself is not the barrier; it's the beliefs attached to it. And beliefs, compared to birth dates or other more tangible barriers, are harder to pinpoint and also much harder to change.

My biggest aha moment in understanding how the skin color barrier plays out happened while watching an ABC News *Nightline* video, *The Color Line and the Bus Line*. By the end of the report, I understood not only how systemic racism worked but the mechanics of it in my own life. The film starts off with Ted Koppel describing a tragic yet simple story. In 1995 a Buffalo, New York, black teenager named Cynthia Wiggins was hit by a truck while crossing the road. She died from her injuries. The driver didn't see her; it was by all accounts an accident. As it turns out, however, it was a preventable accident.

As the film unfolded, I watched Buffalo's black residents speak out about the racial injustice of Cynthia's death. In turn, white people accuse them of "playing the race card." Though I wouldn't have used the term "race card," I too was at a complete loss as to how this could have anything to do with racism—until the film walked me step by step through the issues, making visible what I couldn't see on my own. Cynthia's death, it turned out, resulted in no small part from a series of decisions on the part of white businessmen as they set out to develop a new mall on the white side of town.

Buffalo, like many US cities, is segregated along racial lines: black residents live on one side of the thruway, white residents on the other. The white side of town, manicured and full of stores and businesses, offers not just better education and housing but jobs in those stores and businesses. The black side of town, rundown and far from commerce, offers substandard education, shabby housing, and few, if any, job opportunities. For Buffalo's white residents, avoiding black folks seems a matter of staying on the white side of town. For black folks wanting a job, avoidance of white people isn't possible.

This pattern of segregation and avoidance, so common across America, is a critical piece of this story. Avoidance allows an irrational fear of "the other" to take hold, which is exactly what happened in this situation. Fearing that black customers would scare off white customers, the white mall developers worked with city transportation officials to redirect Buffalo's bus routes, making it extremely inconvenient to get from the black part of town to their new mall. No one actually said, "You can't come to our mall, black folks." They just made getting there unwieldy.

This didn't stop Cynthia from pursuing the job she wanted. Thrilled to be hired by a vendor in the new mall's food court, Cynthia remained undaunted by the long and convoluted commute, a ninety-minute trip with multiple bus changes. At one connection, not only were there no sidewalks or crosswalks, but you had to make a run for your life across seven lanes of traffic to get from one bus to another. On-ramps and off-ramps to the nearby highway added to the precariousness. On a cold day just before Christmas, Cynthia was hit and killed as she made the crossing on the way to her job.

Whoosh, I saw it: an isolated outcome connected to an entangled and entrenched system invisible to the eye. A wave of horror rolled through me as I realized how frightfully easy it is for white folks to make decisions that don't just maintain but strengthen racism's hold on communities. It didn't even take evil, just ignorance. My mind flashed to the beginning of the film, when the confident white interviewees had been tsk-tsking, accusing the black folks of "playing the race card" and "crying wolf." Suddenly it felt ironic that white people had spent centuries questioning black people's intelligence. White people must look so stupid to black people who find themselves again and again in the position of thinking, *C'mon, white people, how can you not see this?*

Without setting out to perpetuate racism, the white mall developers did just that. All they had to do was what most business people do: put protecting an investment ahead of weighing the impact on people you don't know. How many millions of conversations like those of the mall developers have played out at conference tables surrounded by white decision makers?

Imagine if even one of the decision makers in this situation understood systemic racism and was aware of racial bias. Might he have questioned the idea that black clientele would create such pandemonium that white customers would stay away? Might he have understood that white fear had been built on years of media reporting the crime stories but not the everyday moments of socializing and patronage at "the black mall"? Might he have done the research that showed that the mall frequented by black folks had no higher a rate of crime than Buffalo's white areas? What about the bus system's decision makers? What about the store owners at the mall? What if a handful of these people had stood up and said, "I think we can both make a profit and make some positive social change"? What if someone, anyone, had dared to put some skin in the game of racial change? How can anyone be expected to do that, if they have no understanding of how racism works?

Without understanding systemic racism, it is easy to blame the victim and say, "She shouldn't have been crossing the street," or "She must not have looked where she was going," or "It was her parents' fault she was living in that far-off dilapidated neighborhood in the first place." Easy, but unfair and profoundly flawed. Just as easily, someone could look at my teenage life and credit my parents and me for making such excellent choices, when in fact they were practically tossed to me like candy from across the room.

Because of the white town I lived in and my parents' resources, I had a choice of work opportunities. Downtown Winchester was rich with profitable little clothing and hobby shops, a large grocery store, and two department stores. The town was small enough that a quick phone call from a parent to a store owner could get a kid a job. Transportation was a snap, thanks to an old Buick that became mine when my grandmother died. I had wheels. I had options. Because I loved horses, I opted to work at a barn through my high school years. I also babysat regularly, my wages paid by parents with spare change. By the time I graduated from high school, not only did I have a top-notch education and a wealth of social connections, but I had a couple thousand dollars (a lot in 1979) in the bank, work experience, and letters of recommendation. Yes, I was willing to work hard, but that tailwind sure helped.

The thing of it is, I didn't just experience tangible benefits like easier-to-get jobs, a home near a vibrant town center, fully stocked classrooms, and hassle-free transportation. I received a whole host of intangible benefits. In addition to developing a sense of optimism and confidence, I developed an unshakable faith in the idea that anyone could make it with hard work, in the freedom that comes with choice, and in the thrill that comes with high expectations. And I developed a sense of trust in American institutions and the belief that the future was mine for the taking. My life had been built on more than a diploma, a paycheck, fresh fruit, or medicine when I needed it; it had been cemented with a sense of access, belonging, and optimism.

The racially divisive belief barrier shows up in all American institutions: in medical policy, in emergency rooms, in education reform, in classrooms, in corporate hiring policies, in workplaces, in lending policies, in banks, in urban planning, on city streets, in policing practices, in courtrooms, in federal policies, in state policies, and in municipal policies. Racism lives in individuals' hearts and minds; those in power embed it into institutional policies and practices. Systemic racism touches every aspect of every American life, and skin color determines how.

Imagine if the Canadian hockey birth-date barrier operated not only in the hockey system but in other systems. What if housing went first to those with January, February, and March birthdays? What if hiring practices and medical care gave preferential treatment to folks based on birth-date preference? As the April through December citizens struggled to catch up or keep up, imagine the media highlighting what losers they were while never pointing to the birth-date system working against them. Imagine what might happen if the disadvantaged people organized to register their dissatisfaction. Would they get blamed for playing "the birth-date card"?

Suddenly my pride in my ability to work hard and carry the torch of my sacrificing forebears felt mixed with fraudulence. My ancestors did sacrifice and work hard, and I am a diligent worker. But no longer could I deny that my life had been borne on the wings of whiteness. I've had an unfair advantage since before I was born. Just as time has compounded disadvantages for people living on the downside of systemic racism, it has compounded the advantages I and other white people enjoy. My life is built on family members able to get citizenship status without a fight, land grants for free, GI Bill benefits, low-rate loans, good education, and solid health care. Each generation has set up the starting point for the next, perpetuating the illusion that white people are more successful, not beneficiaries of an inequitable system. As Jim Hightower said about President George W. Bush, and one could say just as easily about me, "[He] was born on third base [but] he thought he had hit a triple." Unacceptable is the counterpart to that: the kid who hits and hits and still gets nowhere, ultimately coming to believe in his own inferiority.

The more I came to understand systemic racism, the more I longed to be able to talk about it with white friends and family. The one question that stopped me in my tracks every time was this: "If that's true, then how do you explain people like Oprah and Chris Rock and Tiger Woods?" I now see it would be like someone, in response to an attempt to describe the Canadian hockey system birth-date barrier, saying, "If that's true, then how do you explain [fill in the blank with a fall birthday player]'s career?" What I've learned is that the system doesn't make achievement impossible for someone affected adversely by the barrier, but it makes it harder. In the case of racism, which relies on an invisible belief-system barrier and has compounded over hundreds of years, I would say it makes it not just harder, but exponentially harder.

Averages, not outliers, tell the story, and the numbers regarding who is and is not achieving in school, attaining employment, enjoying good health, being incarcerated, and living in poverty have only grown further apart. Data, however, is only as good as the knowledge of the person interpreting it. As Tom Shapiro, author of *The Hidden Cost of Being African American* and coauthor of *Black Wealth / White Wealth*, said to me, "[The numbers gap] is like a racial Rorschach test. You see what you want to see."

Without understanding systemic racism, one could easily see a 2011 headline like "Wealth Gaps Rise to Record Highs Between Whites, Blacks and Hispanics," and think, *Man those black and brown people just can't pull it together. They are really dragging our country down.* The story emerging for me, however, tells a tale of black and brown people being been held down so long that white folks have come to believe they got there on their own. The removal of legal barriers that once separated the races has done little to change the distorted belief system that lives on in the hearts and minds of millions of individuals. At this point, the only thing needed for racism to continue is for good people to do nothing.

Q Consider each of these tangible and intangible aspects of your life: work, sense of belonging, social connections, choice, education, healthy food, legal protection, housing, transportation, medical care. How easy or hard has it been for you to attain each?

We don't see things as they are,
we see them as we are.

—Anaïs Nin

Seeing is believing, or is it the other way 'round?

ONE OF THE BREAKTHROUGHS I had during the Wheelock course was understanding the degree to which I tend to align what I see and hear with my underlying beliefs. Recently I watched an episode of I Love Lucy that perfectly illustrates this capacity for self-reinforced thinking. Lucy, wrapped up in a murder mystery book, begins to see and hear everything Ricky does as part of a plot to kill her. The viewer, privy to both Lucy's paranoia and the true circumstances behind Ricky's words and actions, can see the logic of both interpretations. Lucy's fears begin when she overhears Ricky say on the phone, "I've finally made up my mind. I'm gonna get rid of her." Though he's talking to his manager about letting go of one of the female performers in his act, she uses this first piece of perceived evidence to fuel her suspicion. Lucy's perception grows increasingly narrow as she sees and hears everything Ricky does and says in ways that fit her distorted storyline— hence the episode's title, "Lucy Thinks Ricky Is Trying to Murder Her."

It's one thing for Lucy, a character on a TV show, to be caught up in a deluded slant on her husband's words and actions, or even for just me, an individual, to hold distorted beliefs about the meaning of skin color; but an entire culture filtering what it sees and hears through a fractured belief system built on missing information is a setup for misunderstanding, mistrust, resentment, and violence. It also creates a self-fulfilling, self-perpetuating cycle of outcomes.

When I was a child, I thought the term "culture" referred to the ballet or the symphony. I had no idea that I lived in a culture or that with every breath its underlying beliefs shaped the way I understood myself and the world around me. I've come to think of culture this way: culture is to a group what personality is to an individual. It's a collective character that describes a set of beliefs and behaviors that identify the group. Though individuals in the group vary, these common beliefs and behaviors hold the group together. Whether as small in number as a street gang or church choir, or as large as a Fortune 500 company or a country, each group has its own code of acceptable behavior driven by underlying beliefs.

Sociologist Kenneth Cushner explains culture by dividing an iceberg into two parts: the 10 percent above the waterline and the 90 percent below. Above the waterline are the things we can see and hear: spoken language, body language, clothing, material possessions, job titles, foods, and traditions, for instance. Below the waterline and invisible to the eye are the beliefs and values one adopts because they are the norms of one's culture. This metaphor helped me understand the phenomenon of self-reinforced thinking and how my interpretations about race and racism got so off track.

One of the basic beliefs I adopted was the idea that in America people failed or succeeded based on individual skill and effort. Therefore, logic told me, the people who succeeded most must have superior skill and have exerted extra effort. Collecting evidence in support of this was effortless. I could see that the white folks were living in the best houses and running America's institutions—government, schools, hospitals, banks, corporations, and media. I assumed white people were in charge because they were more capable.

In stark contrast, when we went to our home in northern Maine each summer, I saw Maliseet people (the indigenous people in the area) picking through white people's trash at the dump. This observation bolstered my storyline that indigenous people couldn't keep up with white people. When we replaced the screens on our cabin's front porch one summer, my parents had us carefully roll up and bind the old screens and set them off to the side "for the Indians." Acts of charity for people I was taught to see as inferior fed right into my belief that the white race was not only better at achieving but an exceptionally generous and moral breed on whom others depended. Missing from my storyline was the part about how the land grant my family used to settle the town had been a catalyst for the demise of Native peoples.

Like a personal information processor, my cultural iceberg stores biases and beliefs as hard data, whether or not they are reliable. The good news is that as we get more complete and accurate information, our ability to interpret what we observe can evolve and improve. Until I understood that present-day Native American culture reflects the ongoing effects of genocide and deculturalization (being stripped of one's culture) at the hands of white Europeans, I attributed the Maliseet people's need to scavenge to a race-wide genetic flaw.

Just as important, until I understood the way white Europeans had established beliefs, customs, and a government favoring their own kind, I attributed my own white European family's success and generosity solely to personal merit. Without understanding the white Europeans' role in contrast to the indigenous people's role, I couldn't connect my family's outcomes to the advantages gained by being members of the dominant group. Nor could I connect my advantage to the Maliseet people's disadvantage.

Culture and identity invisibly and continually interface, shaping who we are and what we think as individuals and groups. They're inextricably linked in a chicken-and-egg kind of way. We create our culture, which in turn creates our identities, which create our cultures, and so on. Though some of my cultural norms had been taught explicitly, like always saying please and thank-you and making sure you look people in the eye when you speak, most of what I'd learned happened implicitly, by quietly interpreting what I could see and hear. Over time I internalized what I'd been taught as right, so that it didn't just feel right—it felt normal, like the only legitimate way to think and act. Anyone who followed a different code of behavior was not only different but weird, or perhaps even rude.

For example, my family believed that if you don't have anything nice to say, you don't say anything at all. The resulting behavior showed up as silence or a swift change of topic in mid-conversation. People who "pushed" the conversation were thought of as poorly raised and ignorant. Being socialized not to seek out or listen to perspectives that might conflict with mine set me up to shut out and shut down the experiences of people of color as told by people of color. Meanwhile, throughout my life the image of happy, thriving white people set against struggling people of color repeated itself in books and media. The imbalance fed and fed again my misinterpretation of white as normal and superior.

Paramount to my growing understanding of racism in America has been the concept that wrapped around each stereotype is a much larger and more complex context that went missing for most of my life. Indians as savages? That belief changed when I realized they were fighting for their families' survival, for land, and for a way of life being stolen from them. Wouldn't I too become savage and violent? How about my stereotype of

Chinese people as good launderers? Did I actually think Chinese people had a laundering gene that led to their role as America's premier clothing cleaners? Missing from my understanding was the fact that in the 1800s, Chinese immigrants, prevented by US policy from owning land or gaining citizenship, filled a crucial yet unpopular societal need—laundering—in order to make a living. That Chinese people in China worked as farmers, doctors, teachers, and lawyers never made it to my radar.

Then there are ideas I picked up about what was normal in terms of physical appearance. The size and shape of various people's various body parts were always measured in relation to prototypical white body parts. Not until this waking-up journey did I learn that my white lips might be considered thin, my white ass flat, my white skin ghostly, or my white self smelly. As my learning about American history slowly broadened, what emerged was the less articulated story of the impact white people had on everybody else by declaring what makes for "right, good, and beautiful."

The more I understood how off-base my judgments had been, the more I began to understand the racial divide. Surely, if I were internalizing a false sense of racial superiority, indigenous children, black children, and Chinese American children were internalizing something too. And it sure wouldn't be superiority. How would my sense of self have developed were I a child of color? How would it have felt to see my race depicted in silly and violent and insulting ways? If I didn't know the story of race and racism, would I have interpreted all those media images as confirmation that people like me weren't fit to achieve? Would I have wondered what special gene the white folks had that made them so capable? How would that influence my dreams for my own future? If I did know the story of race and racism, how would I deal with the unfairness I witnessed my parents, siblings, aunts, uncles, and cousins enduring? I'm not sure which would be worse, knowing or not knowing. No matter what happens above the waterline, little will change until our belief systems get a twenty-first-century tune-up.

Some of the most compelling descriptions of how different life is on either side of the racial divide are in stories from mixed-race families who find themselves with a foot on each iceberg, stretched over the ocean of racism that connects the two. In spring 2011 I attended a traveling exhibit, *Race: Are We So Different?*, at Boston's Museum of Science. Oddly, amid all the science, a single anecdote printed on an exhibition panel was the most striking to me. It relayed the story of a black woman who'd gone to the corner store one Sunday morning to pick up some odds and ends. When she went to pay with a check, the clerk told her they only took cash. Leaving her items at the store, she dashed home to get cash. When her white husband asked her what was going on, she repeated the clerk's explanation that they didn't take checks, only cash. "They take checks from me all the time," he said, confused. It hit them hard when they realized it "wasn't the bank account but the color of the hand writing the check" that mattered.

If Americans of different races are processing contrasting life experiences through grossly different belief systems, no wonder racial conflict hasn't dissipated. It gets refueled every day. Imagine if the black and white individuals in the above story weren't spouses, for instance, but coworkers? How might I (before waking up white) have interpreted the comment, "The corner store doesn't take checks"? In my experience the corner store takes my checks all the time. If her experience didn't align with mine, I'm guessing I would have wondered to myself, *Hmmmm, she must have cashed a bad check there once,* or *I can't believe she thinks that—it says "please make checks payable to . . ." right there on the cash register.* Judging or not believing her would have been easier than having to shake up my entrenched belief that the world was fair and the playing field level.

What makes this issue of divergent narratives so serious is that it goes far beyond an isolated experience. I think about Frederick Hoffman, who in his role at Prudential Life Insurance suggested that African Americans were genetically headed in the wrong direction, toward extinction. As a statistician examining mortality rates, he concluded that the black population's higher rates of death and disease were a result of genetics, not an outcome of hundreds of years of minimal rights and resources. So Mr. Hoffman took his preexisting beliefs and institutionalized them in his 1896 publication *Race, Traits and Tendencies of the American Negro,* a source then used by other white people in power to conclude that investing resources in the black population was pointless, if not wasteful.

When I put together Hoffman's work with the discriminatory housing and lending practices that shaped the GI Bill's investment in America's white families fifty years later, I begin to see how racialized ideas get handed along like a relay torch. Ideas create outcomes that, if unexamined, reinforce old ideas—America's oldest idea being that the white race rules. White folks don't just control America's institutions; they control the narrative. And the narrative, I believe, controls just about everything else.

Q Think of a time you grossly misinterpreted a person (of any race) or situation. What information was missing that allowed you to draw incorrect conclusions? What in your belief system contributed to your misinterpretation?

Out of sight, out of mind.

WORKING IN LOCKSTEP with the iceberg phenomenon, in which we see what we already believe, is another phenomenon: inattentional blindness, also known as selective seeing. To raise awareness of this problem the Wheelock curriculum included not only copious amounts of reading and viewing material but assignments designed to examine how we made meaning of what we were reading and viewing. We were pushed hard to be cognizant of what we did and did not notice. And most importantly, why?

One day, while cueing up a video for us, the professor said, "Okay, once this starts, you're going to see two teams of people. Pay close attention because I want you to keep track of how many times the people in the black shirts pass the basketball to the people in the white shirts." *Fun!* I thought. *I love little tests like this.*

The video started, and six people—three of each shirt color—began mingling around, at a walking pace, tossing basketballs to one another. I was rapt. I counted, counted, counted. "Fifteen!" I said shooting my hand up in the air.

The professor smiled. "Did anyone see the gorilla?"

"What gorilla?"

"Are you kidding?"

Six of us refused to believe we'd missed seeing the gorilla that the professor and the six other students swore up and down had just been on the TV screen.

"This time," the professor said, "instead of concentrating on the ball, look for the gorilla." Shortly after the second viewing began, I saw it: a person in a big furry gorilla suit, entering stage left, shuffling around a bit, *waving at the camera*, and exiting stage right. How had I missed a giant, furry gorilla on center stage?

This exercise, meant to demonstrate inattentional blindness, got my attention. What was my real-world corollary to counting basketball passes? What was I so busy keeping my eye on that I hadn't noticed my white privilege? Keeping myself and my family fed, getting myself and my kids to where we needed to be on time, making sure there was enough money in the bank, paying the bills on time, keeping in touch with friends and family—these were the things that occupied my attention in a way that allowed the rest of the world and other people's problems to remain background noise.

I began making an effort to slow down, look around, and notice how other people might be experiencing the world. One fall evening at the grocery store I noticed a woman straining to reach an item from her wheelchair—not an unusual sight, but one on which I usually would not have ruminated. My norm would have been to get through my list and home in time to whip up a family dinner. Even if I'd paused to help her, a kind of tunnel vision would have set me right back to my task. This time I made an effort to think about this woman's reality. Had she taken a car or subway here? Was there a curb cut where she needed it? Half of the items at the store lay beyond her reach. How did she negotiate that? A simple trip to the grocery store suddenly became an endless series of obstacles I'd never considered because I had the able-bodied privilege of not having to.

In the following days I found myself noticing things that I could do that the woman in the wheelchair could not. *Ah*, I'd think, *I couldn't get into this store*, or *Wow, I'd have a hard time grabbing this deposit slip*. I was starting to recognize my able-bodied privilege, which in turn helped me imagine the challenges faced by people without it. I thought about the day in, day out frustrations of trying to move about in a world designed by people who hadn't considered my reality, my needs.

But how could I imagine the experience of a person of color? Without any understanding of systemic racism's ability to produce drastically different life experiences and outcomes along racial lines, I had assumed my daily experience was basically universal. People were mostly friendly, I felt mostly safe, and those with authority encouraged and supported me. Making visible the privilege of white skin is key to racism's undoing, and antiracists coast to coast are continually looking for new ways to help white people see the phenomenon as real and operating 24/7 in their own lives.

In 1988 Dr. Peggy McIntosh, a white Wellesley College professor, documented her own effort to wrap her head around her invisible white-skin privilege. She pushed herself to compile a list of privileges enjoyed by her but not, she had learned, by her black colleagues. So elusive were the examples she sought to identify that most of them came to her in her sleep, requiring her to keep a notepad and pencil by her bed. In her essay "White Privilege: Unpacking the Invisible Knapsack," Dr. McIntosh laid out the forty-six seemingly benign privileges she dislodged from her subconscious. I say "benign" because they don't seem like big deal until their opposites—the lack of privileges, the discrimination—are considered. Here's a sampling.

I can go shopping alone most of the time, pretty well assured that I will not be followed or harassed.

I can be sure that my children will be given curricular materials that testify to the existence of their race.

I can swear, or dress in second-hand clothes, or not answer letters, without having people attribute these choices to the bad morals, the poverty or the illiteracy of my race.

Whether I use checks, credit cards or cash, I can count on my skin color not to work against the appearance of my financial reliability.

I am never asked to speak for all the people of my racial group.

I can criticize our government and talk about how much I fear its policies and behavior without being seen as a cultural outsider.

I can choose blemish cover or bandages in "flesh" color and have them more or less match my skin.

Privilege is a strange thing in that you notice it least when you have it most. I'm never more grateful for the privilege of good health, for instance, than when I'm sick. It's the old "You don't know what you've got till it's gone." But with skin color's permanence, we only get to experience what we've got. As a white person, whether or not I know it, whether or not I admit it, I've got white privilege, an advantage that both is born of and has fed into white dominance.

In an effort to make visible white advantages, Diane Sawyer did an investigative report for ABC's *Primetime Live* called "True Colors." When I watched it for the first time, I felt as if I were watching a *Twilight Zone* episode. In the video, made in 1991, she sends two twenty-something guys—equal age, education, dress, and so on—to St. Louis for two weeks. John (white) and Glenn (black) are given the charge to "begin a new life" in this new city. They set out separately, hidden cameras in tow, to buy clothes, find an apartment, buy a used car, and find a job.

The contrast in treatment at every turn is stunning. John is given hearty handshakes, welcomed to the community, invited into stores, encouraged by the employment office, offered a car for less money than Glenn, and offered an apartment to rent. Conversely, Glenn is ignored in stores, harassed on the street by a car full of white guys, warned by the employment office not to screw up, charged more for the very same car, and turned away from the very same apartment John ended up getting, *after* Glenn had been told it was no longer available.

If I hadn't watched this with a racially mixed group of workshop attendees, I might have underestimated the film's validity in the year 2010. As soon as the lights came up, however, the people of color shook their heads and looked at each other in camaraderie, while the white participants sat wide-eyed and incredulous. I broke the silence: "But that was 1991. It must be better now." The people of color in the room quickly set me straight. "Debby, I don't feel like I can even go out to get the paper on my front lawn in my bathrobe. There's so much scrutiny around me *all* the time. This is no secret in my circle of friends," a black man said.

I felt gut-punched by this unveiling of a parallel universe, until now out of sight and out of mind. Once I'd seen it, though, I started to hear people of color report incident after incident just like those in the film. Like learning a new word and then hearing it everywhere, I couldn't believe how pervasive these stories were. Why hadn't I heard them before? Or had I?

There's an interesting circularity to this learning. The more I understand the privilege side of the equation, the more I understand the discrimination side, and vice versa. Until I have a clear idea of what racial discrimination looks and feels like, I can't imagine how the lack of it affects my life. Discrimination and privilege are flip sides of the same coin. What must make it so infuriating for people of color is the double whammy that white folks, unaware of their skin color advantage, pose: To really get racism, a white person must get both pieces. It's not enough to feel empathy toward people on the downside; white people must also see themselves on the upside to understand that discrimination results from privilege. You can't have one without the other. Like a seesaw, the upside and downside are joined together.

Seeing and feeling one's privilege proves a much harder task than seeing and feeling discriminated against. In a workshop titled "Reproducing Whiteness" I listened while a white man aired his frustration about the lack of privilege awareness that so often comes with being white in a white-dominated society. "I just don't see it unless someone else points it out to me," he said, "and then I feel like, 'Duh, why couldn't I see that on my own?'"

"Maybe it's because you don't *want* to see it," a black man sitting near him said, his arms crossed, his annoyance barely cloaked. "I'm sick of white people saying they can't see it. I think they can't see it because they don't *want* to see it."

For a moment, I felt personally attacked. How could he not believe it when so many white people had just been talking about how hard it was? Then the irony hit me. Before waking up, hadn't I questioned the validity of people of color's experiences? It's hard to imagine something you don't experience firsthand, especially when it is so counter to your own experiences.

As I've spoken with longtime friends of color about what I'm learning, most have nodded their heads in recognition. What restraint and grace these friends have shown not to grab me by the shoulders and try to shake me awake earlier. Most have been followed in stores, harassed by police, given higher interest rates when applying for loans, mistaken for an employee when in fact they are a customer, mistaken for an orderly when in fact they are a doctor, not challenged as students, not listened to as parents—and the list goes on.

At another workshop, led by Crossroads Antiracism Organizing & Training, the facilitator asked for a white person who'd taken out a loan recently to describe the process. The woman who volunteered spoke about filling out a form while chatting with the banker, giving some references, being thanked for her business, and being approved within a couple of days. The facilitator looked around the room and asked, "Sound like what you've experienced, white folks?" White heads, mine included, nodded. This sounded like the loan process to me.

She then asked for someone from a racial group other than white to volunteer to share a recent loan application story. The black woman who volunteered stood and described this: "I don't just fill out a form. I fill out form after form. Documentation this and documentation that. There's no chitchat." She turned to the room, "Chitchat? What, are y'all kidding me?" The room filled with laughter, temporarily breaking the tension. "No one thanks me; that's for sure. More like, 'I can't guarantee the outcome here, ma'am,'" she said, mocking the cold tone of a bureaucrat holding a customer at arm's length. "Then it takes *weeks*, sometimes *months*, for the loan to get approved. That's what it looks like in my world," she concluded, sitting down, while the black and brown workshop participants nodded their heads in silent recognition. The facilitator let us sit there for a few minutes, with the white people quietly taking in the alternate universe we'd just heard described.

The way America's lending and housing systems have partnered to create a segregated housing footprint plays a massive role in maintaining the alternate universe syndrome. Segregation enables avoidance, which enables denial, which creates the illusion that white privilege doesn't exist. But just because I didn't see my skin color advantage didn't mean it didn't exist. As a white person, I don't have to do *anything* to have skin color advantages conferred on me without my permission, without my awareness. I can choose to write and speak against it, but at the end of the day, as long as our racial system is intact, there's nothing I can do to give away my privilege. I've got it, whether I want it or not. The question is what will I *do* with it.

Q Watch parts 1 and 2 of "True Colors" online, a total of eighteen minutes. (See Notes on Sources for the URL.) Write ten words that describe how Glenn (black) is treated. Write ten words for how John (white) is treated. Which customer service experience feels more like yours?

The discomfort of trying to cross racial lines.

THE FACT THAT THE PLAYING FIELD is not level means that life experiences are not merely different, but unequal and unfair. Not understanding this basic reality made me unaware of how people of color experience America, and more than that: it set me up to be skeptical and judgmental when a person of color tried to explain it. I've had people question me when I've tried to convey a painful experience—it's infuriating and alienating. Not being believed, especially about an experience that is painful to begin with, is salt in the wound. It drives a wedge in a relationship, creating mistrust and disrespect. I now understand that the signals I was sending out to people of color were alerting them to keep quiet, since my ignorance might render their comments fodder for accusations of oversensitivity or paranoid imaginings. My oblivion acted like a wall, a warning of danger, between us.

The charged barrier that makes crossing the racial line so fraught reminds me of the electric fencing systems people use to train their dogs to stay in the yard. Wearing a collar that interfaces with the "fence," the dog gets zapped by an electric current each time he attempts to stray beyond the boundary. It's a great way to train a dog to stay in its safe zone, away from a busy road and in the yard close to home. It doesn't take many startling Zaps for the dog to know exactly where the line is and retreat back to safety. Eventually, the collar isn't even necessary. It's a form of conditioning.

For decades, the racially charged Zap, also invisible, sent me scampering back to my comfort zone like a well-trained dog. Rather than examining the source of the social tension I felt around people of color, I retreated to my social comfort zone—other white people. While I had been conditioned not to see race at all, people of color had been conditioned not to bring up race to white people. The resulting elephant in the room helps maintain segregation, avoidance, and racially socialized behaviors. While friends and acquaintances of color bottled up accumulated racial pain, I maintained a degree of racial oblivion that made me a poor listener for their tender and charged words.

I now understand that my exchanges and friendships with people of color were cautious ones. As nervous as I was about saying something wrong, my racial counterparts likely felt equally apprehensive that I would judge them or perhaps expect that they teach me about racism, putting them in the weary role of educating yet another white person, a white person who registered disbelief at every revelation. Looking back, I can see now that my few friends and colleagues of color had in fact made attempts to share the burden of racism with me, only to have their worst fears realized. As I openly or silently judged and questioned their stories of discrimination with words and body language that said, "Really? Are you sure she meant it that way?" they must've thought, *You don't have a clue, do you?*

Without knowing terms like "segregation" and "avoidance," I stuck to my white-dominated world and ideas. I did what felt easiest. And true to any self-perpetuating system, the path of least resistance served to maintain the system. As I further immersed myself in a monocultural world, the playing field continued to look level, and opportunities to raise my racial awareness stagnated. Like living in a hall of mirrors, I constructed and reconstructed my reality based on the same old views, shielding myself from the knowledge that my friends of color lived in an alternate universe about which they couldn't tell me because I couldn't hear it.

Had I known then what I know now, I would have understood that I had the power to defuse that Zap line. Had I known that learning about systemic racism, understanding whiteness, and practicing the art of cross-racial conversation lay in wait for me, perhaps I would have taken the plunge years earlier. Instead, my ignorance acted like a charger cord for the cross-racial Zap factor, setting me up to avoid, avoid, avoid and perpetuate, perpetuate, perpetuate.

I had my first experience with feeling the Zap and sensing it for what it was one night at Wheelock. Pamela, a black classmate in her late fifties, and I often were the first to arrive in the classroom. On this particular night we started chatting about the recent inauguration of President Barack Obama. As I was speaking, I referred to him as "Obama." Pamela literally flinched, took a breath, and said, "I don't think that's right, you calling him 'Obama.'"

"What do you call him?" I asked.

"President Obama—that's what he is. He's our *president*." She didn't look one bit happy with me.

The first thing I thought was, *That's not right. I've called all our presidents by their last name. And so did my parents.* Had I not been in a class about racism, I might have changed the topic right there, further affirming for me a vague idea that black people were overly sensitive about race. Fortunately, given the setting, I forced myself to stay with the conversation.

"But I've called all the presidents by their last name," I said, trying hard not to sound as defensive as I was feeling.

"Are you sure?" she asked. "I doubt you called President Bush 'Bush.'"

I thought for a minute. Truth be told, I believe I called President Bush something much worse than "Bush," but I kept my mouth shut. *This might be one of those cases where racial realities and belief systems are clashing,* I thought to myself. I felt all stirred up and was trying to figure out what to say just as the professor walked in and class swung into action. *Saved by the bell,* I thought, though my insides churned with the feeling of an unhealed upset.

About fifteen minutes into the class, I was still trying to make sense of our conversation when Pamela offered another insight, this time to the whole class. We were talking about cross-cultural misunderstanding. I was worried Pamela might use her minutes-old example with me. Instead, she offered a fresh one. Pamela had put each of her four children through one of Boston's most elite private schools. She told us about a night, years earlier, when she'd driven out to a wealthy, white suburb to pick up her daughter from her friend Alison's house. As they were leaving, Pamela noticed that her daughter said good-bye to Mary, the housekeeper. Once in the car Pamela turned to her daughter and asked, "What do you call Alison's parents?"

"Mr. and Mrs. Smith," she answered.

"Then why do you call Mary by her first name?" she'd asked.

"Because everyone in the house does," her daughter explained.

"Well, not you. From now on I want you to refer to her the same way you do the parents. She's your elder, and she deserves your respect as much as any elder. Find out her last name, and use it."

As I sat in my sweatpants that night listening to the impeccably dressed Pamela, I thought of how differently we valued formality. I viewed it as an obstacle to connecting with people; Pamela viewed it as a sign of respect. I grew up in a household where proper manners and attire were the standard.

Somewhere in the twenty-five years between college and Wheelock, I began to want to shed the formality, feeling that it alienated me from new friends and colleagues by marking me as an "other," a snob. I could still do the small talk, corporate dinner, country club thing, but I loved nothing more than the informality and casual dress that passed for normal in my circle of Cambridge friends—white friends. It felt like the pressure was off, and I could just be me. I suppose I ended up equating informality with authenticity.

Bruce and I consciously created an informal atmosphere around our home, encouraging our children's friends to call us Bruce and Debby and letting our kids pick out their own clothes as soon as they expressed interest. We encouraged respect toward others but not in a stiff, scripted way. I prided myself in my lack of concern about appearances, often going out in sweatpants with my hair done up in a quick and sloppy twist and thinking, *This is what I love about Cambridge. No one cares how I dress.* I didn't see that having the choice to be more casual was a privilege that came with my skin color. Unlike my friends of color, I didn't have to counterbalance a narrative that told the world I was less-than. Like a too-tight skirt that I could put on or take off at will, I chose when and when not to be formal and felt totally entitled to do so.

Sitting next to Pamela that night, I felt like a baggy gray insult. I thought of all the times I'd casually introduced my children to adults of color using the grown-ups' first names. I thought of the way I took the liberty of calling adults of color I didn't know all that well by their first names and wondered what impact it might have had on them. Did my casual tone impart the authentic spirit I meant or an indication of disrespect? Using first versus last names meant something entirely different for Pamela from what it meant to me.

I've long known that cross-cultural mismatches lay thick on the ground. But I thought culture clashes only applied to interactions with people from different countries, in which looking at someone in the eye is respectful in one culture and an insult in another. A touch may be a sign of sympathy in one culture, a sexual advance in another. But in my own country? I was beginning to see how different people's beliefs and behaviors could be based on the way their race positioned them within a single dominant culture. I thought of the Golden Rule, the set-in-stone belief I'd been raised on, that one should always treat others the way you yourself would want to be treated. The limitations of this adage in the realm of race relations struck me like a thunderbolt.

In the years since Pamela opened my eyes, I've heard countless stories of how white people's casual ignorance about skin color privilege has insulted and alienated people of color. Part of the power differential is that white people have the choice, the power, to ignore race and racism. I can choose not to have a single cross-racial relationship. I can choose not to talk about race. And I can choose not to learn the beliefs, customs, traditions, and values of racial groups other than my own.

Not so for people of color, who can't escape knowing what life looks like in White Land. White life is everywhere—on TV and billboards, in movies, magazines, and newspapers. For survival purposes people of color must learn the dominant culture, the white culture, in order to survive. Knowing how to act in a white-run classroom, a white-run office, or a white-dominated public space is essential. What's more, people of color often report they have to act more white than white people because of the scrutiny they're under. It reminds me of how, as a child, I quickly learned the names of the kids in the upper grades and how, as an adult, I swiftly learned the ways of the people at the top of the ladder in my workplaces. It seems a fairly natural survival tactic to study those on whom one depends to survive socially or otherwise.

The worst part of the cycle of segregation and avoidance is that it happens at the institutional level, with the consequences ranging from social discomfort to lack of access to survival basics. White people are more likely to hire white people. White teachers are more likely to understand and gravitate to white students. White police are more likely to trust and support white citizens. White doctors are more likely to relate to and appropriately treat white patients. White bankers are more likely to make speedy, low-interest loans to people who look and act like them. The Zap factor doesn't just hurt feelings; it limits possibilities in a way that affects people of color's ability to access life-sustaining resources such as education, wealth, and health.

The more I understood that my aversion to social discomfort was replicated millions of times over by millions of white people, including those leading America's educational, medical, finance, and housing systems, the more I understood how oppression can be held in place by good, but ignorant, people. If the people with less power, in this case people of color, try to convey the way the dynamic disempowers them, they risk being seen as ungrateful, paranoid, weak, irrational, and unworthy. The fact that people

of color still find the strength to continue trying to be heard tells me something about their resilience and fortitude.

Crossing the charged racial line, as uncomfortable as it was at first,
allowed me both to learn about life on the other side and to reexamine my
own from a new vantage point. As I replaced ignorance with understanding,
the cross-racial conversational playing field leveled. As I spoke freely of my
white privilege and shock at not having understood systemic racism until
recently, people of color began to open up about their own experiences. We
used our contrasting exposures to racism to explore them as related experiences. As I moved from segregation and avoidance to contact and connection, I slowly transformed what had once been a charged barrier to a
beckoning bond.

In year three of my journey, a black woman approached me after a
meeting. "Did you say your maiden name was Kittredge?"

My parents had been gone for over five years, and I longed for moments
when someone might say, "I knew your mother," or "I worked with your
father."

"Yes," I answered, eager to see where she was going.

"Do you have an older sister Diane?"

"Yes," I answered, wondering if they'd been college classmates or professional colleagues.

"Well, how about that," she said. "I went to high school with Diane."

"In Winchester?!?" I blurted out, unable to hide my shock that there
had been even one black person in the town during my life there.

She laughed. During the meeting she'd heard my open confession of
not understanding racism or white privilege until recently. "Honey," she
said smiling, "there's a whole lot I'll bet you don't know about Winchester
and the history of black folks living there."

She told me of how Winchester once had hundreds of black families
working for white families. She put a new spin on the postwar era, explaining that hand in hand with suburban expansion came an appliance boom:
dishwashers and laundry machines replaced household help, a machine-for-
people swap that drove families like hers out of Winchester. She described
her family's resolve to stay in the town that had been theirs for three generations, to continue to give their children the top-notch education the town
delivered.

"My mother trained us well," she said. "She told us, 'This is where the good schools are, and if you want to make the most of it, you need to stay away from drugs.' You know what else she told us?" She paused. "'White kids who do drugs go to college; black kids go to jail.'" She leaned closer and whispered, "That's still happening today you know, more than ever."

I had a revelatory moment this year as I was writing down the word "ignorance." Interesting that the word, which implies a passive state of being, shares the same root with the word "ignore," which implies an active choice. How much of my not crossing the color line earlier had to do with not seeing, and how much was it my choice not to go in search of it? This is a question I am not yet able to answer. It felt passive, but I know too well these days how understandings like this can change with time and reflection.

Cross-racial relationships are essential to racial healing. The kind of contact and connection they engender is indeed the antidote to the centuries-old pattern of segregation and avoidance. But it doesn't work without understanding and braving the Zap factor, an important step in the process of building trust.

Q Have you ever had anyone doubt, dismiss, or minimalize an experience that was formative for you? How did it feel? How did it affect your feelings about that person?

The effect of swallowing one-sided stories.

ONE OF THE MOST POWERFUL TOOLS of racism is stories. I used to think stories were neatly crafted tales—each with a beginning, a middle, and an end—packaged in books or speeches or told for fun around the campfire. But along with expanding my understanding of just about everything over the past few years, I've expanded my understanding of what stories are and how they function in our lives. Stories feed our belief systems. True, false, or somewhere in between, they are narratives we use to entertain and/or instruct ourselves. We all tell stories all the time. They can be written, drawn, filmed, or spoken aloud, or they can even incubate silently in our imaginations.

I had an ongoing story in my head, for instance, about my husband, Bruce, in which he hadn't been raised as well as I had, hadn't learned that complaining was a sign of weakness, hadn't learned that constant work exemplified a life well lived, hadn't learned that not wiping the counter clean after doing the dishes meant he might as well have not done the dishes at all. My story about him came less from who he was than from my interpretation of him, as informed by my childhood values regarding right and wrong. My ideas created my story, and my story created my ideas. This cycle included a tendency to collect evidence in support of the storyline and overlook the multiple facts that didn't fit. Bruce unknowingly had been cast as a character in a role he didn't identify with at all, one that prevented me from seeing him in his truest light. This in turn put him on the defensive and made it hard for him to be his best around me.

It's no coincidence that the word "story" is contained in the word "history." Either way, we're talking about human-constructed narratives used to describe people, values, places, eras, and events. Stories are a primary way we connect to those around us and before us. But if my story about my dear husband was so susceptible to selective seeing and processing, wouldn't this mean the possibility existed that I'd taken in other stories in an equally distorted way? And if I did this, did others too? If we all do, where could I find reality? Whose "truth" defined the truth?

Each year my three sisters, one cousin, and I gather on the first weekend of April to hole up in a hotel and just visit. We love our family stories. In recent years we've spent time shaking our heads at how differently we remember them. If there are five of us, there will be five renditions, each of us absolutely sure her own is the accurate one.

Last year we were nearly kicked out of a restaurant for laughing uncontrollably as we tried to reconstruct the tale of the time my aunt's dachshund, Maudy, peed through a knothole in the upstairs floor of our family's Maine cabin, delivering a stream of urine onto the head of my unsuspecting uncle relaxing by the fire on the first floor. The story is legend. Everyone in the family knows it. But between the five of us we had different relatives in the room, different reasons the dog was upstairs; one sister even had Maudy's gender wrong.

So what does this mean about the family stories I've relied on to shape my understanding of who I am and where I come from? If stories in my lifetime run the risk of being misremembered or distorted, how reliable are older family stories? A favorite of mine has always been the tale of my forebear Lydia Trask Putnam, who, in 1805, finagled to get a land grant to establish New Salem Academy in northern Maine. Because land grants were available only to white men, she did all the legwork and had the men sign on the dotted line. At least that's how the story goes.

She spent months hacking her way though brush and timber and crossing streams and bogs, through inclement weather, family in tow, their possessions on their backs. After months and months of trudging, they settled along Maine's eastern Canadian border. Lydia was in her sixties. Once established, she traveled the northern Maine woods on horseback as a midwife, bags of herbs and natural medicinal concoctions hanging off the saddle of her trusty horse, who, according to lore, would cross any stream or leap any felled tree. Lydia traversed the uncompromising terrain not only to aid mothers in childbirth but to tend to whatever ailment she encountered along the way. I love Lydia. I love this story.

More important than this story as I originally heard it, however, is the story it generated in my head and the way I used it to connect to the world around me. In the same way my education, elementary through college, taught me US history in a sugarcoated way, my family told the story of Lydia in a romanticized way. It reminds me of the way funerals rarely point to the deceased's flaws but instead send the person, surely as complex as the next person, off to rest with a set of immaculate stories.

Despite the fact that my story of Lydia may be incomplete, inaccurate, or flawed, I internalized both its content and all it implied. The story about Lydia told me women are strong, have great ideas, can be leaders, are resourceful, and can work until late in life. It told me my love of horses is in my blood. It told me I owe it to my rugged Yankee ancestors not to complain and to work tirelessly. It told me education was worth hacking your way through a forest to make happen. It told me that if she could persevere and do great things, so could I. It made me feel special to be a part of this narrative. Believing I have the blood of this pioneering woman in my veins has served as a building block in my identity formation. Even if all or part of that story were disproven or somehow called into question, the fact would remain: this story is part of what made me who I am today. Like removing the forms from poured and hardened concrete, the shape remains even when what shaped it is removed.

What if instead of a glorified history of family members connecting me to a glorified history of the United States, I'd learned a more balanced history in which humans and their endeavors are both imperfect and ever-changing? What if, at a young age, because of a more balanced narrative told through history classes, I could have tied the story about Lydia and the land grant to the harsh reality that there was no such thing as "free land" to be given away, that land grants were parcels of land stolen from indigenous people who'd lived on them for tens of thousands of years? What if I could have learned how one person's windfall can be another person's downfall? Would I have suddenly rejected my country? Would Lydia have lost all merit in my eyes? I doubt it.

The story of race is at the center of racism's entanglement. The very idea that the world's many peoples could be categorized by something called "race" is a story, one that has created a system of dominance for its storytellers. The story of race has become a self-fulfilling, self-perpetuating prophecy as the story creates the ideas, which then reinforce the story. The tragedy is the individual and collective potential that has been crushed by the power of a single story.

What is it that makes facing mistakes, weaknesses, or regrets so terrible that they must be completely and utterly denied? As long as the dominant culture holds fast to a story of white as right, the possibility of hearing other truths gets shut out, and the cycle continues: white folks experience people of color's versions of events as incongruent and therefore inadmissible. How then does the dominant narrative become one of many, so that American history becomes a collection of short stories, as opposed to an epic told by a single author?

Q Think of a historical event in American history, perhaps the signing of the Declaration of Independence, the arrival of the Statue of Liberty, or any one of the wars Americans have fought. Where have you learned what you know about this event? Whose perspective did you learn? If you went in search of a fuller story, whose viewpoint would you seek?

The snap judgments that fueled my racial anxiety.

MY PARENTS TRIED TO INSTILL in me the importance of replacing judgment with empathy. You couldn't grow up in my house without hearing my mother's refrain, "People who are mean are usually sad or angry." They also encouraged me to put myself in other people's shoes: "His mother's been ill, Deb. Put yourself in his shoes." Despite their efforts, I still developed a robust capacity to make snap judgments. As I'm learning how and why they got there, I'm also learning to let myself off the hook and work with the judgments, as opposed to letting them drive or shame me.

The monumental cognitive task of processing the millions of pieces of information that flood us daily requires that we sort and categorize. It's a natural human function. Information, which comes to us through all five senses, travels via our nerves to the brain, where it gets registered, sorted, and stored. Categorization is a necessary part of the memory-retrieval process, the cognitive equivalent of providing us with a well-labeled filing system versus a room full of unsorted papers. This level of efficiency is what would have allowed one of our ancestors, meeting up with a life-threatening enemy in the jungle, to assess the situation quickly and react accordingly. If we had to start from scratch, gauging each potential threat before us, we wouldn't have survived as a species. Like all animals, we have built-in survival skills; sorting is one of them.

One way people differ from animals, however, is the way we use symbols to make meaning of the world around us. This idea helped me understand why a little thing like a logo could sway me so quickly toward or away from a product. In his book *Language in Thought and Action*, Samuel Ichiye Hayakawa writes, "Animals struggle with each other for food or for leadership, but they do not, like human beings, struggle with each other for things that *stand* for food or leadership, such things as our paper symbols of wealth (money, bonds, titles), badges of rank to wear on our clothes, or low-number license plates." America's marketing machine capitalizes on this symbolic process. Show me the Nike, Apple, or Bank of America logo, and I'll fill pages about each brand with the stories I've attached to it. And businesses hope the story I have is one that works in their favor.

But what about when I turn an actual human being into a symbol, a logo, complete with a fully formed narrative? *People with multiple piercings must be angry.* Does this mean people without them are not? *People who drive certain kinds of cars are shallow.* Does this mean people who drive other types of cars are deep? *People who wear a lot of makeup are insecure.* Does this mean those who wear no makeup are confident? Where do I get my stories? Where does all my accumulated information come from? The gathering and sorting I've done all my life has happened largely subconsciously and often shocks me when a piece of previously unexamined information emerges, betraying the judgment with which I once filed it away.

In high school my friends and I used to play a game we called "Instant History." We'd sit on a park bench, pick someone in our view, and invent an imagined profile for the unsuspecting subject. Using their body language, physical attributes, and attire alone, we'd come up with long-winded biographies. One imagined truth led to a whole set of other imagined truths. Before long we'd spun a conceptualized version of the person that was put together as beautifully as a well-worn photo album—and likely couldn't have been further from the truth. It strikes me that even without a concerted effort to create an "Instant History" for a person, I still seem to do a version of it.

Sociologist Allan Johnson's writings helped me understand this habit. This particular reference stuck with me: "As the philosopher Susanne Langer put it, using symbols to construct reality lies at the heart of what makes us human: Only a small part of reality, for a human being, is what is actually going on; the greater part is what he imagines in connection with the sights and sounds of the moment." This phenomenon is front and center in the PBS documentary *People Like Us.* Individuals shown a single photograph of a person are asked to guess at what that person is like. Relying on lightning-quick visual cues such as clothing and hairstyle, participants guess at social class and associated character traits. At one point in the film the camera captures a high school student standing in a crowded school hallway. She's been asked by the filmmakers to describe the other students as they pass her. Without missing a beat she labels each student "geek," "emo," "jock," and so forth. Snap judgments about people are not always about race. White people make them about other white people. Black people make them about other black people. Turning people into logos, symbolic of a neatly wrapped story, is not race-specific.

Language, even just a single word, is a significant player in the symbolic process that facilitates logo making. Johnson says, "If there's a word for something, we're much more likely to 'see' it and treat it as real." We invent not only the words but also the stories that come with them. The word "race" itself is a perfect example. It's as if I have an imaginary file folder in my head for "race" into which all my race-related words and stories get tucked away. The file is then at the ready to reaffirm old beliefs by rejecting any that don't catalog neatly into the carefully constructed "race" folder.

At times, challenging the racialized language and images I've collected over my lifetime has made me question my entire sense of reality. Take the word "slave." My association with the word had always been limited to the dark-skinned African people enslaved to work on America's Southern plantations. I hear the word "slave," and—POW—an instantaneous image of a large black man emerges in my mind, just like a logo.

A misguided one in fact. The word "slave" likely originated as "Slav," the term used for captured white Slavonic people sold by other Europeans to Arabs as indentured servants during the eighth and ninth centuries. Throughout history societies around the world have forced those they have conquered to work lowly jobs without pay. Ethnicity and skin color sometimes had nothing to do with it. Even in America, the earliest "slaves" came in a variety of skin colors, from a variety of countries, and worked in the capacity of indentured servants. In the mix were white homeless children from London, poor white women, and white convicts, paying off their ocean voyage with three to seven years of hard labor. Unlike white European indentured servants, African people were imported against their will, kept here against their will, and defined and treated as a separate and subhuman species.

For the colonial ruling class, African slaves' easy-to-identify dark skin ultimately made them a more practical investment than their white-skinned and Native American counterparts. Enslaved indigenous people could too easily escape and blend in with the first Native American population they came across. Escaped white indentured servants could blend in even more easily. Limiting the slave population to just black-skinned people subsequently reduced white America's association of word and person to a single, skin-color-coded narrative. In an effort to weaken the logo effect of the word "slave," many racial justice educators and descendants of those enslaved have changed the language from "slave" to "enslaved African" to convey the label as an act done to others, not as an inherent identity. Words matter.

I find it easy to label people who aren't white—*he's Hispanic, she's black, they're Asian*—but until recently, I've not labeled white people. When I think of the way I label *African* Americans, *Asian* Americans, and *Native* Americans, I wonder why I never thought it strange not to also say *German* American, *Greek* American, or even a generic *European* American. Not having a label for white people reinforced for me the idea that white populations are the norm, raceless and ethnicity-less. No label is needed because it's a given. I realize that for years, when I spoke about an encounter with a white person, I would say something like, "I met the sweetest lady this morning" or "One of my students brought me a delicious brownie today." The term "white" was always assumed. On the other hand, for people of color, I was more likely to insert a label. "I met the funniest guy, a black guy, waiting for the bus today," or "Rosie, my Haitian student, made a beautiful bracelet for me today." People of color get labels, complete with narratives and stereotypes.

This is hugely problematic, given how skewed my perceptions were. Because of the way racial bias plays out in the media, I see the black guy on TV getting shoved into the cop car. Because of the way racial bias plays out in our real estate and lending systems, I don't have a black neighbor I can see going out at midnight to get his feverish daughter cough medicine. My personal interactions and real experiences with people of color are far outweighed by the negative images that have saturated my data field through the media. While I have a multidimensional and nuanced understanding of the range of white people in my life, I have a narrow definition that fits neatly in a file labeled for one race or another. No matter how much I try to stay open-minded and follow Dr. Martin Luther King's advice to "not judge people by the color of their skin but by the content of their character," I am fighting against the tide of stored negative data. When the word or image comes up, the story comes with it.

In my late twenties a back spasm led me to try a chiropractor for the first time. My white doctor recommended someone he and several of his patients had gone to with great success. When I got to the appointment, I was caught off guard to find a black chiropractor. Immediately, my subconscious began spewing forth feelings of being unsafe. As I began to question his credentials and abilities, my conscious mind was horrified. I tried to turn off the voice of prejudice in my head but couldn't. Every move made me wonder, *Did he do that right? What if that snap permanently injures me?* When he suggested I get some X-rays, a suspicion flashed into my mind that he was somehow in cahoots with the X-ray business and scamming me. Back in his office, as we recapped our first session and laid out a plan for the weeks ahead, I noticed the wall behind him slathered in framed diplomas and certificates from his extensive education at white institutions. Suddenly I relaxed. While the symbol of his skin color triggered negative thoughts, the symbols of the white-dominated institutions triggered positive thoughts. Both of these responses made me feel confused and ashamed. Where was my commitment to judge people by the content of their character? Each incident like this only fueled an inexplicable anxiety that would carry over to the next interaction with a person of color.

Though today I am still taken aback by intrusive racialized thoughts, it's happening less often, and I no longer find them bewildering or judge myself for them. How could I live in a racially organized society and not have filed away racial stereotypes? Though I may never get beyond my mind's tendency to lump and label, at least now I'm aware enough to say to my overloaded subconscious, "Thanks for sharing—buh-bye."

A favorite read of mine, Claude Steele's *Whistling Vivaldi*, takes its title from an anecdote by *New York Times* columnist Brent Staples. As a black college student he noticed that, upon seeing him walking down the street, white people would react, reaching for the hand of the person beside them or even stepping off the sidewalk to cross the street. In his words, "I'd been walking the streets grinning good evening at people who were frightened to death of me. I did violence to them just by being." When he started whistling a Vivaldi tune, a symbol from the white European American culture, the atmosphere would change—bodies would relax; a few even smiled. Staples used one symbol to counteract another.

Though I've gone through most of my life not identifying myself as white, I've learned that people of color do in fact see me as white. I'm as much of a logo to them as they are to me. I am as much at risk of being judged by the color of my skin and not my character. In a racially ordered world, I too am, at least to people of color, in a lump, a group. I have a label. Being lumped and labeled puts me in a box I don't want to be in. I want people to take the time to know me the person, not sum me up with a four-hundred-year narrative I want nothing to do with. How could I have avoided labeling the white population, when I seemed to do it so naturally to every other cultural group? Easy: I had no language and therefore no file folder in which to collect stories and stereotypes for the white race, the invisible race.

Q What have you filed away? Create a column that contains these labels: African Americans, Asian Americans, Native Americans, Jews, Latinos, Muslims, Whites. Next to each, quickly write at least five stereotypes that come to mind for each. Do not pause, censor, or correct; rather, let emerge what will. Now look at what you've written. Does it surprise you? If you are white, do you have any stereotypes for whites? Why do you think this is?

RETHINKING KEY CONCEPTS

Not everything that is faced can be changed,
but nothing can be changed until it is faced.

—James Baldwin

*How it was possible that I was both
a "good person" and utterly clueless.*

WAKING UP FELT LIKE STEPPING OUT OF A DREAM, a fantasy world I'd been living in since birth. In fact, in her book *The History of White People*, Nell Irvin Painter uses the term "cultural fantasy" to characterize the system of racism that's evolved around skin color interpretations. Leaving behind the bubble of white ideology and stepping into a new shockwave-laced reality came with a strange mix of alarm and wonder. I couldn't shake the feeling there must be more I didn't know. What other errors and omissions might I stumble on?

Every fiber of my being had once believed that the rule makers and system operators in America were good people, leaders who looked out for everyone, who would never make selfish decisions. Wasn't that why people like Richard Nixon stood out? Wasn't his selfish greed an aberration? People were good. My family was good. I was good, right? After all, I'd been taught never to reach across the plate to grab the biggest cookie. That would be selfish. Part of growing up, I thought, was learning to be polite and honest and do things for others because that's what grown-ups did.

Learning about how racism works didn't challenge me just because it was new information. It was *completely contradictory* information, a 180-degree paradigm reversal, flying in the face of everything I'd been taught as a child and had believed up to this moment. America's use of racial categories seemed fraught with unfairness, cruelty, and dishonesty. Yet my parents', grandparents', and entire extended family's life philosophy, as I understood it, had revolved around fairness, compassion, and honor. This was my legacy, the one I took the most pride in passing on to my children. Discovering I'd been complicit in perpetuating a system that was so very terribly bad flew in the face of all I'd understood about myself.

I thought hard about where my own attachment to being a good person had come from. I remembered the way my parents encouraged me to be empathetic. I recalled my mother's own capacity for compassion and kindness, how when her divorced friend Louise felt shunned and excluded from dinner parties, my mother organized one and sat Louise beside my father with strict instructions to him to "make sure she's being included in the conversations." I thought of how when I came home from high school one day saying a classmate had been beaten and then kicked out of her home, my mother said, "Bring her here. She can live with us." Which she did.

Then there was my father. If he wanted one thing from his children, it was for us to be honest. While my mother might say little things like, "Did you just cheat on that Parcheesi move, Deb? You want to win or lose honestly—otherwise it won't mean anything. Take that turn over," my father made a sweeping, explicit demand that being honest at all times was non-negotiable in our family. And believe me, I put him to the test.

One evening, when I was about eight, I appeared at the dinner table with a copy of Heidi.

I proudly plopped it on the table. "Look what I got today," I said, flipping through the hardcover book full of spectacular full-color illustrations.

"Where'd you get that?" asked my mother.

"The Sheffields have boxes of books like this in their garage. I took this, and Cathy [my friend] took Black Beauty."

My parents glanced at each other. "Do the Sheffields know you took them?"

"No, but they have tons of them. They'll never know."

We finished dinner quickly. My mother called Cathy's parents, while my father explained to me that we were taking the book back to the Sheffields. I wished I'd kept it secret. When we got to the Sheffields' house, panic set in as we bypassed the garage and headed for the front door. With a hand on my shoulder, my father rang the bell.

"What a nice surprise, Bob and Debby!" Mrs. Sheffield said, still in her apron. I hugged the book close to me and stared at the porch floorboards.

"Well, actually, we're here to return something." My father went on to explain that I'd taken a book from their garage. "We've spoken about how this is stealing. Debby understands now that going into your garage is wrong and that taking anything that doesn't belong to her is wrong. It won't happen again." He gestured for me to hand over the book.

"Well, that's perfectly understandable," Mrs. Sheffield said.

I burst into tears.

"I think you still owe Mrs. Sheffield an apology, Deb," my father said, patting me on the back.

"S-s-sorry," I blubbered.

We walked home slowly, my father's silence allowing me ample time to feel my regret. I would never steal again. Or so I thought.

A few years later, when my friend Mary invited me to go to Woolworth's with her to shove candy into our oversized raincoat pockets, we got caught. The store manager called our parents. My father brought me to the store the next day, toured me up and down the aisles, and explained about the vast chain of people who'd created, transported, and organized the store's contents. Each was a good person doing their job, he told me. Each expected the items to be bought, not stolen, in the final step of the consumer process. People all around the world, I learned, were counting on me to pay for the merchandise they'd worked so hard to get to me. In comparison to my father, so wise and good, I felt like a total loser. I had failed him, failed the Woolworth's people and all the people around the world who'd worked together to make and deliver the cool stuff I loved. At the end of the tour he brought me up front and motioned for me to apologize to the manager. I crumpled over in a heap of sobs. My father and the manager waited for me to pull it together, which I couldn't muster. Eventually my father said, "I think we can all agree Debby regrets what she did." The long, silent ride home left me, once again, to reflect on the responsibility I had to be an honest and upright citizen. And how awful it felt to be anything less.

My childhood takeaway was that learning to be good, fair, and honest was as much a part of becoming an adult as growing taller. Sure, there were some bad eggs out there—Richard Nixon, Charles Manson, the kid who lived across the street from us who put our sprinkler behind our car's back tire so we'd run it over and ruin it while backing out of the driveway—but most people the world over were good. And my family? We were definitely good. Our parents impressed the importance of it on us all the time.

Not only was my family good, but our extended family was good, our friends from Winchester were good, and my parents' college friends, work friends, and ski and golf friends were good. I remember in my teenage years, when one of my parents' couple friends stopped being a part of the dinner party crowd, I asked my mother, "Why don't the Littles come over anymore?" In a low voice she told me, "Daddy and I are very disappointed in something he learned about Mr. Little." I pressed her. "It had something to do with a less-than-honest business dealing," she told me. I felt disappointed in my old pal Mr. Little, but very proud of my parents for drawing the line. We associated only with good people.

Which is why, when I learned about the discriminatory policies and practices in lending, housing, and higher education during the GI Bill era, they did not align with my view of leadership. I knew executives, real estate moguls, media guys, and politicians—people who ran stuff. I loved these men. They were family, friends, and neighbors. I never questioned that the white guys in charge were good people, bringing compassion, fairness, and honor to every part of their life. Didn't they live by the Golden Rule and treat others the way they themselves would want to be treated?

And what about the bankers I knew? My father explained to me at a young age, when he took me to open a savings account, that the bank would take my money, lend it out to someone who needed it, charge the borrower a little bit, and share that little bit with me, the saver. Banking felt darn near like a good deed. I never questioned who was doing the borrowing or for what. I certainly never entertained the idea that borrowing rules and procedures might differ according to skin color.

I wondered how much my parents' generation and the ones before it had thought about their part in the racism scheme. If I didn't get it, and the majority of the white people I'd been speaking to didn't get it, could it be possible that the system was being in part perpetuated by white people who also thought of themselves as good people without any connection to racism?

About this time I came across Edmund Burke's quote "All that is necessary for evil to triumph is for good men to do nothing." *That's me*, I thought. *I've been doing nothing*. I hadn't been doing nothing because I didn't care or lacked the courage. I did nothing, at least nothing with any real impact, because I didn't understand how racism worked. If you can't see a problem for what it is, how can you step in and be a part of its solution, no matter how good a person you are?

For years, as I contemplated the plight of those "less fortunate," of all colors, I had pangs of guilt. As I became older and increasingly aware that others had so little, it felt less comfortable to have so much. Learning the ways in which racial categories had been used to elevate the status of whites in relation to all other humans, however, mitigated my sense of passive guilt. Guilt got crushed by culpability. Seeing myself in a system with people

as opposed to a sympathetic observer on the sidelines changed my relationship to the problem. I understood then that it was possible to be both a
good person and complicit in a corrupt system.

Once I saw myself as part of the system, I recognized myself as part of
the problem. If that didn't sting enough, I also faced the dawning realization
that I was now raising my own children to continue the pattern. I'd encouraged them to feel compassion for the "less fortunate" and be grateful for
all they had without helping them to see the bigger picture, the system that
connected their good fortune to the "less fortunate" they experienced as
separate from themselves. I was passing along what I'd been taught, teaching them to be benevolent do-gooders, not critical social thinkers and problem solvers. What I would give to have started my life as a parent with the
racial awareness I'm now developing.

Q How would you complete this sentence? I never thought I could
perpetuate racism because I am_____,
and I believe_____.

Why saying "I don't see race" is as racist as it gets.

UNTIL I TOOK THE WHEELOCK COURSE, racism had remained an undiscussed topic among my closest circle of white friends and family. It's not that we made a pact never to talk about it; it just never came up. In the same way cancer might not come up if you didn't know anyone experiencing it, we didn't understand that we *were* experiencing it. Racism simply was not on our radar. Moreover, I think I'd concluded early in life that racism was an unseemly topic of conversation. After all, if you didn't have something nice to say, you didn't say it at all. Did I on some level know how "not nice" conversations about race and racism might get?

In an early Wheelock class, we'd been asked to fill out a survey. One of the questions went something like this:

How often do you talk about race with your family and friends?
a) daily
b) once a week
c) once a month
d) a couple times a year
e) never

I went back and forth between "once a month" and "a couple times a year," thinking, *Who talks about race daily?*

All of the students of color answered "daily." I couldn't believe it. I couldn't even fathom what there would be to talk about every day. I didn't yet understand that not talking about race was a privilege available only to white people. I was months away from learning that parents of color had no choice but to teach their children about race and racism. In the film *White Privilege 101: Getting In on the Conversation*, which explores different racial groups' understanding of white privilege, I watched a mirror image of my talking-about-race epiphany: a young black woman explained, "I couldn't believe it when I found out white people don't talk about race every day. I thought everybody talked about race every day. Not talk about it? How can you not talk about it?"

While most people of color struggle daily to brace themselves for and make sense of our racialized world, navigating its hurdles and setbacks and reaffirming their own right to exist, I'd been gliding through life unaware race was factoring into my life. In his article "The Right Hand of Privilege," Dr. Steven Jones explores invisible privilege by reminding readers of the myriad ways our society is set up for right-handed people. He asks readers, "How many of you, who are right-handed, wake up in the morning thinking 'My people rule'?" It got me thinking: how often do I come home and say, "Whew, not followed by a single cop or store manager all day!" Or, "Man, I just love the equity I've got in this house thanks to hundreds of years of racial advantage!" Invisible privileges are exceptionally easy to ignore.

For me, one by-product of a worldview devoid of race was the absence of overt bigotry. When I say my childhood was all white, I'm actually exaggerating. I had two Asian American friends over the course of my childhood. When one of them came over, my parents likely would have said something positive like, "Isn't that Danny a fun friend for you," or "Anna is so tall and beautiful." I sized up both of these friends pretty much the way I'd size up any friend. Were they fun to be with? My elementary school friend Danny loved to laugh and told great jokes. I adored him. My junior high school friend Anna liked to eat candy and smoke cigarettes. She shared both and taught me how to blow smoke rings—the perfect teen companion. I never spoke about their heritage with them. They never spoke to me about feeling different. If they spoke about race or cultural difference regularly with their families, I knew nothing of it.

One sleepless night this year, as I tossed and turned, thinking about my previously unrecognized white privilege, I imagined what my life would have been like if just one parent had been in a historically undervalued racial group. What if my father had been black? I had heard that to effectively compare skin color difference, one should hold constant other variables such as socioeconomic status, education, health, and so forth. So I imagined my father, still a lawyer, still making a good income, still healthy and robust. Yet despite all these, I realized we could not have lived comfortably in Winchester in the 1960s and '70s, even if the realtors, lenders, and residents had allowed our family into the town. To borrow an anthropology term, my life would have followed the "hypo-descent rule," in which the "inferior" race in my mix would have become my racial assignment.

We would not have been accepted into the Winchester Country Club, the place where my family spent hours swimming, golfing, playing tennis, and making friendships that would become lifelong personal and professional connections. As a biracial child in Winchester I would have been a visual standout. During my teenage years, when I most longed to be like everyone else, I wouldn't have stood a chance. Instead of nourishing my sense of belonging, my daily life would have planted seeds of insecurity and resentment about my tentative place in a white world. My family's annual summer excursions to our grandparents' hometown in northern Maine would have been no more comfortable. My extended white family would not have looked like versions of me, but reminders that even among my own lineage I didn't fit in. Could my black father have even safely traveled to an isolated town in northern Maine? Chances are a significant portion of our income would have gone to support my father's black parents, who—without a lifetime of access to good education, jobs, and housing followed by a pension and/or Social Security–funded retirement—would have needed our financial assistance. Perhaps they would have moved in with us. When my paternal grandparents died, more than likely there would have been little if any inheritance to pass along to future generations. Just about nothing in my white life could have happened as it did were I anyone but the child of two white parents.

Though it once felt polite to ignore a person of color's race and just see all people as individuals, my former color-blind approach was actually allowing me to ignore my own part in the system of racism. Color-blindness, a philosophy that denies the way lives play out differently along racial lines, actually maintains the very cycle of silence, ignorance, and denial that needs to be broken for racism to be dismantled.

Q If both of your parents are white, imagine just one of them being a person of color. Rethink your life from birth to the present. How would your race have influenced your experiences and your outcomes?

How I perpetuated racism by taking advantage of my "good luck."

AFTER FOUR YEARS at the almost exclusively white Kenyon College in Ohio, and study abroad at an all-white program in Vienna, I returned to the Boston area in 1984 with my childhood ideas about a level playing field, a world teeming with opportunity, and myself as a good person fully intact. As a student I'd worked for Kenyon's professional summer theater and discovered a knack for arts administration, so this, I decided, would be my career path. My father suggested I call one of his pals, who was involved in the Boston arts world. I think no matter what profession I had chosen, my father would have had someone for me to call. My parents' educational, professional, and social circles connected us to Boston's leadership across nearly every industry and discipline.

One of those circles revolved around our ski club. The club formed just after World War II, when a group of Harvard buddies sought to maintain their wartime bonds. After renting a small cabin in the New Hampshire woods, they'd eventually chipped in and bought an old ramshackle hotel to accommodate their growing families. On Friday nights my family of seven would load up the station wagon, piled high with ski equipment and sleeping bags, and drive three and a half hours north to the White Mountains. I'm not sure what I loved more—the long, cold days on the ski slopes or the evenings around the fire. Back in those days, the women did all the cooking. As they toiled in the kitchen, the men would linger by the fire, while the kids listened to loud music and played Ping-Pong. I preferred hanging out with the men, and, interestingly, no one ever redirected me. Listening to their business chatter, smelling smoke and whiskey on their breath, and talking about the day's athletic events felt familiar and grounding. When I think of "my good people," I think not only of my family and neighbors but of these men. From all I could see, and all I still know, they were good fathers and husbands and friends. They were my heroes and role models. They also held positions of power.

The friend my father suggested I call, one of these men, presided over WGBH, Boston's public television station. "Give him a call, Deb. I'm sure he'll have some ideas for you." So I did. He seemed genuinely happy to hear from me and suggested I come in and start volunteering. "You know, just get a sense of the place," he offered. "Let people get to know you. You never know who you'll meet here and what opportunities might present themselves." I started the next day, unaware that volunteering was a privilege reserved for those who could afford it.

On my first day, Herb, a preppy-looking, super-friendly black guy from Fundraising, introduced himself. I explained that I'd just started as a volunteer as a first step in finding a career in arts and entertainment. Slightly older than I was, and a two-year veteran at the station, Herb took me under his wing, inviting me to lunch regularly and stopping by my cubicle daily. He asked for my résumé so he could personally hand it to anyone he came across who was hiring. Herb became my first close colleague and first black friend. He changed my life in two ways. First of all, knowing Herb made it impossible for me ever again to buy into the idea that black people are lazy, less intelligent, dangerous, or any other sweeping malignment. Herb was as much a scholar, friend, and "good person" as anyone I'd ever met. In fact, in contrast to a lot of the white guys I'd known, he was much more real and fun to be with.

Second, Herb found me the job that would set me on my career path.

"Manage! But I've never *managed* anything." I remember whispering loudly to him in the hallway. He'd just suggested I apply for a job as managing director of a local dance company for which he served as a board member.

"Hold on," he laughed. Putting his hand on my arm, he leaned closer to whisper, "Well, here's the thing. They don't have a very big budget, so they can only pay $12,000 a year. They need someone willing to learn because they can't afford someone with experience." He stood back and looked at me with a "gotcha" kind of look. "They'll *train* you," he urged. "You'd be great." After one interview I was offered and accepted the job.

How could I afford to live on $12,000 a year, you ask? Easy. A family friend from Winchester owned three rent-controlled apartment buildings in Cambridge, a small city just outside of Boston. For $143 a month, I was able to live in a two-room apartment one block outside Harvard Square. With no college loans and a car paid for by a small inheritance from a childless uncle, my expenses were minimal. I also lived with the constant comfort that my parents would always be there for me financially if I needed help. Among other things, socioeconomic privilege affords the freedom to explore, take risks, and find work you truly love—the kind that brings out your best.

Within a mere six months of returning to the Boston area, I had my own digs and an awesome job. I was high on having put my adult life together so quickly. I remember feeling lucky and grateful for the family connections that had provided everything for me. But I remember something else. I remember silently and fleetingly questioning the morality of Boston's elite filling rent-controlled apartments. Apparently I didn't think too hard about it. Somehow I must have justified my entitlement to access all the privilege I had without really questioning who wasn't living in the apartment I'd just moved into, or who wasn't getting the job I'd just gotten. Dismissing the plight of others comes easiest when you don't actually know them.

How ironic that a white, old-boy connection led me to a new, young black friend, who then connected me to the career that would ultimately lead me to this journey.

Q Have you ever benefited from family connections and/or family funds to further your career? Get into a school? Attain housing? From which racial group were those family connections?

The audacity of thinking I knew what was good for "others."

MY FIRST PROJECT at the dance company was to increase corporate and foundation support so that the choreographers, dancers, and musicians could spend more time creating and performing work, as opposed to balancing multiple nondance jobs to make ends meet. Two board members and I arranged a meeting with the Boston Globe Foundation.

That meeting was the first of many with local corporations and foundations in which we were told, "You know, we're trying to focus on programs that serve Boston's inner-city youth. If you could develop a vision that includes that population, we'd be more interested in supporting you."

I felt a charge of excitement. Not only could I help my organization raise money and create more dance and music; I could help "inner-city kids," who, from the sound of it, needed help. I phoned and wrote my social network thick with Boston's decision-making elite and raised the money within a few weeks.

Knowing nothing of nationwide redlining, failed urban-renewal promises, or white flight in the 1940s and 1950s, and little of Boston's busing crisis in the 1970s, I had no context for why these neighborhoods needed help. No one explained to me the way these neighborhoods had been wronged and wronged again and that now, twenty years later, reparation funds had been created in an attempt to compensate. I wouldn't have known what the term "reparation" meant or why it mattered. All I thought about was how I could help the needy. I would have told you at the time I was doing it for them, but as I think about it now, I wonder how much of what I was doing contributed to my ability to justify all my new acquisitions and achievements. Did I imagine it virtuous to live off my riches and give to the poor? Or to involve friends and family so they too could feel upright and honorable? It's a noble idea, but without greater context or racial awareness, a precarious one.

I now understand that what I was doing is called "dysfunctional rescuing," helping people in ways that actually disempower them. As always, one can find analogies outside of racism to help understand these warped human dynamics. Here is mine. When I was at overnight camp in the sixth grade, I fell and scraped my knee. Blood was running down my shin, a little flap of skin was hanging off, and the kids around me were screaming, "Ewwwwww!" but I wasn't fazed. A self-sufficient outdoor girl from way back, I was completely prepared to wash it off and apply the disinfectant, gauze, and tape that I, not my mother, had packed. Instead, a frantic counselor rushed over, picked me up in her arms, and carried me to the infirmary. I was mortified. They scoured the scrape and put on iodine, which felt like hot oil. They put on a series of Band-Aids that ended up coming off with my sweat about an hour later. My tap water, painless Tincture of Zepherin, and gauze and tape solution would have been 500 percent better. They disempowered me and "fixed" my problem in a way that aggravated my wound and infantilized me.

In my efforts to help the "inner-city youth," I spoke to funders and other arts organizations about what life in the inner city was like. What did these kids need? What were their schedules like? What programs already existed? Never once did I visit the actual neighborhoods. Never once did I sit down with a group of these kids, their families, or their teachers and ask, "What is it my organization could do for you?" Nor did I ask, "What role would you like to play in shaping this program?" And entirely off my radar was the question, "Do you even want me here?" Instead, I decided that what they needed was to come to a majestic downtown theater and be a part of the world I knew and valued.

In one of my first efforts, I got a grant to bus five hundred inner-city children to a sixty-minute daytime dance performance at the Boston Shakespeare Theater, located on the tony residential St. Botolph Street. We filled the theater with students and teachers. I remember standing outside the theater, watching eight big yellow school buses crawl down the street, feeling as if I were Robin Hood. My connections and efforts would give hundreds of kids a chance to get out of their neighborhoods to downtown Boston and see live theater. I had loved the theater as a kid. Certain that many of them would be so taken they'd go on to become regular theatergoers, I also felt my efforts were good for business. It was a win-win. My puffed-up, good-person feeling swelled.

When the kids started pouring off the buses, I couldn't believe how many were black. They just kept pouring off the buses and streaming into the theater. I had never seen so many black faces in one place in my life. I felt complete shock that "inner-city" seemed to equate with "black." Without an understanding of systemic racism, I couldn't understand why, after all the years since slavery had ended, these kids' families hadn't made it out to the suburbs or into workplaces like my father's. I concluded these inner-city black folks just needed more chances to see what opportunities existed. I felt sure my efforts to bring kids downtown was a good place to start.

Over the next ten years, I ended up managing three different arts organizations. At each, while my primary job was to run the business end of things, bringing inner-city kids to downtown theaters remained my passion. I assumed the kids and teachers felt as I did: these were exciting and inspirational opportunities. I rarely went to inner-city neighborhoods, fearful of their reputations for violence and unfamiliar with the lay of the land. Not once did it occur to me that the reverse might hold true for the people who called those neighborhoods home and mine unfamiliar. The idea that my world might feel uncomfortable or even dangerous to someone else would have been inconceivable to me. Had someone tried to point out to me that I was part of a national pattern of white people deciding what people of color needed, and white people holding the purse strings, I'm guessing I would have silently smiled while thinking, How ungrateful.

From 1990 to 1994 I served as general manager of First Night, a New Year's Eve "citywide" arts festival held in downtown Boston. Each December 31, one million people came to view ice sculptures, see indoor and outdoor performances, make art, watch an elaborate parade, and celebrate at midnight with fireworks over Boston Harbor. In 1993 a funder challenged me: "You know, you call yourselves a citywide festival, but I see a lot of city neighborhoods not taking part." By now I knew exactly which neighborhoods he meant. "Also, if you want more support from us, we'd like to see you find a way to extend your activity beyond just one day."

The board and artistic director and I contemplated his ideas and proposed a plan to partner artists with "inner-city" after-school programs to work through the fall to create artworks for the festival. We came up with the name "The First Night Neighborhood Network" and set out to find support for it. The money rolled in, with everyone excited to have artwork from a variety of ages and neighborhoods and eager to see if the students who came downtown with their artwork would bring family and neighbors with them.

Not long after hatching this plan and raising the funds to implement it, I became pregnant with my first child. Because Bruce's job required long-term travel assignments, we decided this would be my last First Night celebration so we could keep our young family together. I was determined to leave my pre-parenting career on a high note. The First Night Neighborhood Network seemed the perfect ending, a legacy of sorts, perhaps even something of a gift to the city of Boston.

We hired an outreach coordinator—Nan, a black woman—to identify and work with participating after-school programs and community centers. I never went to any of these organizations myself. I delegated that to Nan, who by virtue of her skin color, I figured, could do the work better than I. Though that's probably true, the fact that I kept such distance disturbs me. Nan did an outstanding job, and the program continues to this day. Yet I've had to ask myself, Why was I so willing to be uninvolved? Why didn't I think it important to have Nan take me to these neighborhoods to teach me about what she was learning? Why didn't I initiate conversations with Nan about why she was so much better equipped to be in these neighborhoods? I would have told you my plate was full with raising money, managing finances, coordinating staff and board, and hiring my replacement. But now I wonder if a part of me couldn't go there, literally or figuratively. As general manager of the organization I thought I would have been remiss to put myself in a conversation or location where I didn't feel comfortable and in control. Unprepared for any potentially challenging conversation about racism, my comfort zone extended only as far as the general concept of "diversity." I was decades away from grappling with its deeper components: invisible privilege, the Zap factor, missing narratives, and horribly misguided stereotypes.

The Robin Hood in me surged with the unveiling of the First Night Neighborhood Network. New Year's Eve rolled around, and sure enough, inner-city neighbors and friends came to the celebration for the first time. I was asked to be Grand Marshal of the parade that year and marched at the front, very pregnant, in a white Tyvek suit waving a giant banner. I felt high as a kite seeing black families lining the parade route. I remember thinking, *Wow, those funders were right—this really was an all-white crowd.* I felt foolish that it had taken funders to point this out to me. In my imagination not only were the kids and their families having a great experience, but now that they'd seen all that downtown Boston had to offer, surely they'd come back more often. Mission accomplished.

In hopes of repeating the program in years to come, we'd planned to debrief with artists, students, and families in early January. On a cold, dark evening, an assortment of twenty people gathered in the First Night board-room, located in the heart of downtown Boston. I think I expected an out-pouring of gratitude from the kids and their families. Instead, an awkward silence filled the room. The artistic director started off by thanking everyone for being part of our pilot program and speaking about how impressed she was with their artwork. Then I explained that we wanted to get feedback so that each year we could get better and better at working together.

Silence.

"So we'd love to hear about the experience from your perspective," I said.

Never having facilitated a cross-cultural conversation like this, I was confused by the deafening silence.

"Let's start with the actual night of the festival. Was it fun for you?" I asked enthusiastically.

Silence.

Finally, a black teenage boy broke the silence. "Man, it was freaky. I've never seen so many white people in my life! I was scared!"

Some combination of nervous laughter on the part of the neighbor-hood groups and shock for the First Night staff gradually subsided enough for us to continue. I couldn't believe it. The boy and I had had exact opposite perceptions of the evening. All I could see were the unfamiliar black faces; all he could see were the unfamiliar white ones. Where he felt the fear of an outsider, I felt the comfort of being an insider. In a flood of memories, I recalled the busloads of inner-city kids pouring onto unfamiliar sidewalks to go into dark, unfamiliar theaters. Had those children been fearful too?

Though the program was tweaked and improved by my successors over the years, this was my last meeting at First Night. I remember feeling some relief to be leaving and not having to deal with this unexpected, imperfect ending to my final initiative. It made me tired to think of what other con-versations I would have had to have and the ways the program might have needed to be adjusted. Having to roll up my sleeves and really learn to work across cultural differences was easy for me to avoid at that time.

Though my new status as a full-time parent allowed me to retreat back into my white world of family and friends, recurring images of that last meeting haunted me. I never could shake the sense that perhaps I'd done more harm than good. I tried, from my white cocoon, to imagine how I could have worked differently to make the experience less jolting for the individuals journeying out of their comfort zones, across the city's color line, and into mine—an experience I had initiated.

My Robin Hood era had ended with the sound of a deflating balloon, not the accolades and gratitude I'd anticipated. I felt demoralized, saddened that the ending hadn't turned out as I envisioned. I'm discovering now that neat and tidy endings, especially happy ones, are yet another luxury of the entitled.

Q If you were to be given $100,000 and told to give it to one charity, which one would you pick? What are the races of the organization's three top executives? What race is the chair of the board?

TWENTY-FIVE YEARS
OF TOSSING AND TURNING

Children have taught me to confront unvarnished truth
and unpleasant facts I'd often like to avoid.

—Marian Wright Edelman

Winchester me, Cambridge me,
and the man who helped me find the real me.

AFTER TEN YEARS OF LIVING IN CAMBRIDGE, retreating into my white cocoon came less easily than I'd hoped. I'd spent hours with friends and colleagues—including gay folks, immigrants, artists, and community activists—from a range of backgrounds. I admired them for their passions, which weren't related to wealth and status, but silently cringed at their frequent mocking of Boston's upper crust. Having my new friends ridicule my old world confused me. I felt that my family, and people like them, worked hard and deserved respect. Yet I'd also developed a diminished appetite for the suburban, country club world that I'd once called home. I couldn't figure out where I belonged and had a pressing sense I needed to pick one or the other. But I couldn't. I would never reject my family. I loved them and needed them. But I also couldn't reject my new friends. I craved the fire they lit in me.

So I'd spend time with my family, luxuriating in the old familiar jokes and ribbing, the status and security, and the deep love I felt. Then I'd go to dinner at the country club and get a sick feeling as I realized that many of my friends would never be accepted as members, nor would they feel comfortable even sitting in the room. I'd feel torn in two as I listened to conversations about vacations, home renovations, and golf scores. I imagined how my new friends would mock my family. When I'd return to my urban life, I'd feel myself come alive with the depth of conversation and the lack of restraint. But before long, the feeling of being free would become tainted by the fear that I was somehow betraying my family by hanging out with people who mocked their type. I never dared speak to either group about my feelings. I was too conflicted to know what to say. So I lived with a foot in each world, needing both, never mixing the two, and often playing down the world I'd come from, the whole while feeling like a hypocrite.

I'm still fascinated by the way different cultures spark different parts of me. For as long as can I remember I've been drawn to other cultures, as evidenced by my early Native American fantasies. When I learned about igloos, I spent an entire winter trying to fashion igloos out of snow cubes I made by packing snow in an old shoebox. When I read the book Heidi, I longed for a life on a Swiss mountain and put a poster of the Swiss Alps on the wall by my pillow so I could imagine it as the view from my bedside window. I wanted to wear bright clothes like the Mexican dolls I saw. I wanted to eat food as delicious as what I'd tasted when a friend's family took me out to a Chinese restaurant. I longed for difference, signs of life from other ways of being. They awakened in me something I couldn't name.

My work in the arts both satisfied and fueled this longing. At the second arts organization I worked for, Dance Umbrella, we brought in dance companies from all over the world, matching our audience outreach efforts to each show. When we presented Japanese Butoh dancers, for instance, we reached out to Boston's Japanese community. When we brought the National Dance Company of Senegal to Boston, not only did we promote the shows heavily to Boston's black community in general and Senegalese community in particular, but we staged the show in the Strand Theater, located in a predominantly African American neighborhood.

I loved being surrounded by people of different cultures at the very moment they were celebrating their own heritage. Because I'd organized these events, I felt no sense of being an intruder—I felt like an enthusiastic participant, craving new rhythms. Vibrant, colorful, flowing, and gyrating bodies and costumes had the power to move people in a way I'd never seen before. Often, as I'd feel the theater come to life with the sights and sounds of a culture unfamiliar to me, I'd ask myself, "What is American culture? If we were to showcase our dance in another country, what would it be? Ballet? Modern? Jazz? Contra dance? What defines us?" I didn't come up with answers; rather, I stayed stuck, feeling undefined amid other cultures that seemed so succinct, aligned, and alive. Never once did it occur to me to ask myself, "What is white American culture? And why is it so different from other American cultures?"

During this uncertainty about who I really was and where I belonged, I met Bruce, the man who (as by now you know) would become my husband. Bruce is kind of a cultural hybrid. A white guy from Darien, Connecticut, Bruce looks every bit the part of a WASPy guy, but acts and thinks like no one I'd ever met. Though Bruce had grown up in a town very much like Winchester, his childhood was nothing like mine. His parents had stretched themselves financially to buy a small house on the edge of affluent Darien so their kids could get a top-notch education. Bruce's family was of modest means and had faced hardship in ways mine had not. His father's career was full of layoff-related stops and starts that created financial and emotional instability. Bruce's older brother suffered from a degenerative cerebral palsy that ultimately killed him at age eleven. Bruce himself developed Type 1 diabetes at age seven. He grew up feeling like an outsider, watching the lives of rich, healthy white families like mine living out all sorts of privilege without even knowing it. His identity as a belonger never a sure thing, Bruce took the liberty of developing his own style in the world, one in which his natural exuberance knew no bounds and he didn't give a damn about fitting into this box or that.

Meeting Bruce was love at first sight for me. His warm brown eyes, good looks, alarming honesty, and edgy sense of humor enraptured me. Without either of us understanding it at the time, Bruce offered me an invitation, which I accepted, to step into his no-baloney world of authenticity and adventure. Unlike me, Bruce felt no conflict as he traveled among and between social groups. Unlike me, he made no effort to adjust his language or behavior according to the company around him. I marveled at his ability to go against what I considered decorum and still win respect and affection. Time and again I watched him push the envelope and get people to rise to his challenge with unexpected animation and depth. His questions and prompts drew out of my own family and longtime friends information and sentiment I never knew. Whether on the subway, in a grocery store, or at a social event, Bruce engaged people in ways I wouldn't dream of.

Once, when we stopped to ask two nuns for directions on a hot day, he said, "Those robes look hot," and then immediately feigned horror and said, "Oh gosh, I didn't mean it that way." I hadn't even thought of taking it that way. I was horrified. Making sexual innuendos with nuns? The nuns started giggling and posing, joking with him about the various ways their habits made them sexy. Nuns! The nuns went on to tell us all about the history of the habit, how they varied according to religious order and nun's rank. Engaging and educational conversation drove Bruce's every social interaction. As we walked away, Bruce shook their hands, thanked them for the directions, and said, "It's been great chatting, but let's not make a habit of it." I could still hear our nun friends giggling a block away.

Bruce, who has little tolerance for "light" conversation, the kind I'd been raised on, pushed the envelope on the home front as well. While life with him has been fun and adventurous from the start, he also brought a communication style that stressed and challenged me. For me, family life meant being nice and polite so everyone could get along. For Bruce, getting to the heart of the matter was what counted, no matter how messy it got along the way. When a conversation got tense, Bruce would dig deeper. My training told me tension was my cue to change topics.

I told Bruce about the teenage boy's unexpected comment at the First Night recap: "'Man, it was freaky. I've never seen so many white people in my life! I was scared!'" Bruce responded, "Yeah, go on—then what? What did you find out?"

"What do you mean? I just told you. He said it is was scary for him." I rolled my eyes, irritated by Bruce's pushiness.

"Yeah, but then what? What about other people in the room? What did other people say about how it was for them?"

I had to admit I didn't know; I hadn't thought to ask. I had quickly changed to safer subjects, such as how their partner artists had worked out and would they like to be assigned the same partnerships the following year. What a lost opportunity to learn more about one another's expectations and realities, all because I couldn't risk making myself vulnerable. I wanted to be seen as a good person. I wanted my good intentions lifted up and applauded. Maybe I just wanted a pat on the back that night, not the hard work of seeing where I had room to grow. What I didn't understand yet was that by signing on to a life with Bruce, there'd be no more avoiding discomfort, no more retreating into a cocoon of denial. Growing through discomfort would become my new normal.

Q Think of different groups of people in your life—your family, your friends, your coworkers, and so on. For each of these groups or contexts, think about whether you feel like an insider or outsider and how that status affects your desire to spend time with the group.

WHY DO I ALWAYS END UP WITH WHITE PEOPLE?

*I moved to Cambridge for the diversity
but ended up surrounded by white people.*

LONG AFTER THAT WRAP-UP SESSION in the First Night board-room, the teenage boy's comment buzzed like a fly around my conscious mind, unable to find a route into my preexisting belief system. In retrospect, I think hearing him say that seeing so many white folks at once felt scary marks the moment it hit me just how messed up it was that a city could isolate people in segregated neighborhoods, making it uncomfortable for any of us to step outside of our assigned territory. Though I knew neither the historical depths of segregation nor its re-creation through more recent housing and lending schemes, I did know that the concept of people living in color-coded pockets gave me a sick, gut-punched feeling. Every time I thought of the boy's comment, this same feeling bubbled up. And vice versa: every time I felt that feeling, his comment sprung to mind.

In the year after our first daughter was born, Bruce and I considered moving to the suburbs, where our children could ride bikes to friends' houses and be educated in great public schools. Because we mistakenly thought these things impossible in Cambridge, we started looking in the nearby suburb of Lexington. As the realtor drove us around, gushing about the town's attributes while showing us one single-family home after the next, I became overwhelmed with anxiety I couldn't explain. Three hours of dizziness, a racing heart, and sweaty palms left me with a splitting headache by the time we got home.

"I am *not* moving to the suburbs," I announced angrily, marching into the house and grabbing an ice pack from the freezer. I crawled into bed and put the ice pack over my throbbing eyes. "I don't know what it is, but I can't do it." I had no words and certainly no framework in which to understand my reaction, but the gut-punch feeling was screaming at me, *Something's really wrong here. I don't get it, and it hurts my brain trying to figure out something I just can't get*. Now I wonder what towns and neighborhoods the realtor would have shown us if even one of us were black.

Though Bruce didn't have quite the allergic reaction to suburbia I'd had, he admitted it didn't feel right to him either. We reflected on what had drawn us to Cambridge in the first place. We concluded that its lack of uniformity had played a role. There seemed to be little sense of normal to constrain us. From religion practiced to country of origin to languages spoken, people were all over the place. Single people, retired people, married with no children, two-mom families, two-dad families, single moms, single dads, mom-and-dad families, you name it, people and their lifestyles came in all varieties, and all seemed acceptable. Absent the pressure to conform, I felt freed from the kind of homogeneous, dominant culture I'd known in Winchester. In Cambridge I felt released from the constraints of a narrowly defined normal, and the city's culture played a huge role as I sought to define myself on my own terms.

I'd been introduced to the city in 1972, when I was twelve and my aunt moved there. In fact, she moved into the exact same rent-controlled apartment complex I would move into twelve years later, the one owned by family friends. Located near Harvard Square, the neighborhood bustled with students in animated conversation and buses roaring by. My mother, my aunt, and I used to make an afternoon of strolling through Harvard Square, soaking up the aromas of unfamiliar foods and spices and the sounds of live music, foreign dialects, and Hare Krishna chants. My eyes bugged out at the sight of hippies with waist-length hair and tie-dyed shirts, and storefronts with wild fabrics, stacks of books, and packaged foods from around the world. Far from Winchester's all-American feel, I devoured Harvard Square, letting the city transport me.

A few years after my aunt's move, my mother enrolled at Radcliffe Extension School, located in Cambridge, to earn a degree in landscape design. She regularly brought home new outfits purchased on her lunch hour at Design Research, a hip new store renowned for importing cutting-edge Scandinavian textiles, furniture, and home wares. She swapped out her winter wool plaid slacks and summer Lily Pulitzer clothes for bright, colorful, flowing dresses for all seasons. She even followed the saleslady's suggestion and went braless under the loose-fitting frocks. These dresses brought my proper, preppy mother to life with new joy and exuberance. I adored this side of her. I suppose I came to equate Cambridge with personal liberation.

I now understand that deep in my consciousness was a desire for Cambridge to do for me what those flowing dresses had done for my mother. Eventually it did.

When I first moved to Cambridge, I'd hoped to meet people from all over the world. In my naïve and romantic way, I'd envisioned dinner parties with a variety of people sharing tales of their home cultures and swapping exotic recipes. It would be like traveling without having to travel. I wanted variety. I wanted life in all its color. The strange thing was, however, that here in this multicultural city I began to surround myself with friends who were a lot like me—white, American, thirty-something, middle-class to upper-middle-class, mostly of northern European heritage. Where was the variety I sought? Why did I keep attracting and being attracted to clones of myself? How, in the end, was this any different from signing up for a life in a white suburb? Cognizant of this disturbing trend, I set out to make friends with people less like me. Because much of my life at this point was spent at playgrounds, they seemed the logical place to start.

I began noticing how two distinct groups of mothers formed at the playground, both white. My group, the private-college-educated women who'd grown up in a variety of US suburbs, was one. The other consisted of women who had grown up in Cambridge, had gone to state colleges, and were now working part-time or odd-shift jobs. My group's husbands worked all over the world in white-collar jobs. Most of the other groups' husbands worked for the city of Cambridge or in blue-collar jobs. The two contingents positioned themselves in separate areas of the park, group members intersecting only when one needed a spare diaper or extra snack from the other. Though we were all white, the division was unmistakable. So were the attitudes and behaviors attached to each.

Eager to stretch myself beyond my own type, I decided to make a special effort to get to know the women in the other group. I was fascinated by the way they could pack up their strollers with supplies and paraphernalia for the entire day and do errands while their kids napped in their strollers. My group was more likely to get our kids home and in their own beds according to schedule. Overwhelmed by errands when we had small children in tow, we saved them for times when a sitter or spouse could cover child care. While my friends and I treated our kids like precious gems, I noticed a no-nonsense style among the group across the playground.

One day, while I was borrowing a diaper from one of the no-nonsense moms, her son came up holding a coin he'd found buried beneath the woodchips by the swing set.

"Oh my God, Matthew!" she barked. "*What* do you have in your hand?" She squinted. "Is that a nickel, for Christ's sake?"

He looked up, half smiling, anticipating her next move.

She took it from him, shook her head, and said, "What are you doing picking stuff up off the ground? That's disgusting!" He smiled and lifted his hands in an "Oh well, I tried" kind of way.

One of the mom's friends standing about twenty feet away hollered over to see what was going on. "He picked up a nickel!" the mom yelled back, still glaring at Matthew. She gave him a playful swat on the head. "How many times have I told him not to pick stuff up off the ground, for God's sake?" she bellowed to her pals. The moms had a good laugh, and Matthew went off to play, utterly unfazed by the incident or the fact that a group of grown-ups was talking about him in the third person and laughing at him. I couldn't believe what a good sport her kid was. It made me question my own group's super-gentle, Mr. Rogers–like parenting style. Had one of our kids found the nickel, the scene would've played out something like this:

"A nickel? Oh sweetie, come show it to me. Wow, what's this here? Can you tell me what kind of animal this is?" "Ooooo, it does look like a dog. That's a buffalo, honey. Can you say 'buffalo'?" Likely, upon arriving home, we'd spend an hour crafting a tiny bed out of a ring box for the nickel to live in.

I wanted my daughter to have some of the resilience I saw in Matthew. It occurred to me that for every cultural group there might be other parenting lessons to be learned. I started going around the city to other playgrounds, hoping to meet mothers and children from different cultures who could expand my understanding of parenting approaches. Yet playground after playground offered up the same basic demographic: predominantly white, divided into the white-collar group and the blue-collar group.

Where were all the black moms and children? Three blocks from my house sat Rindge Towers, three enormous subsidized apartment buildings full of families of color. Why weren't we going to the same playground? Were they, like the First Night boy, uncomfortable around crowds of white people? Were my friends off-putting to them? Was I? How could I be scary to anyone? Not yet in touch with the fact that I harbored my own subconscious feelings of discomfort and avoidance, I could only focus on the shocking notion that a person of color could find me, or white people in general, "scary" or "freaky." Little did I know that my lack of self-awareness fueled the Zap factor, making any hope of building close relationships across racial lines a pipedream.

There was a black teenage boy who walked down the middle of my street most afternoons, just about the time my daughter and I would be strolling off to the playground. We passed each other day after day, and each time I tried to meet his gaze. I wanted an opportunity to connect. But he always stared straight ahead, jaw shut tight, as if I didn't exist. One day I decided to say something.

"Hi there," I offered. "Isn't this a beautiful spring day?"

The sound of my voice just hung there, unanswered. It was as if I hadn't said a word. My first response was embarrassment. Had anyone else seen my unrequited gesture? Then I felt pissed at being ignored. *I'll bet he wrote me off just because I'm white*, I thought. It didn't take long for the irony to sink in. *Is this what it feels like to be stereotyped?* I wondered.

Though I can't be certain of the sentiment behind his behavior, I couldn't help imagining myself through his eyes as a cheery, white-skinned, Suzy Creamcheese character. It felt horrible to think I might be on the receiving end of prejudice. Though I had no knowledge of the deep and traumatic history of black men being tortured or killed for speaking to a white woman, I knew I couldn't stand to be unable to communicate comfortably with a fellow human being in such close proximity. I felt more certain than ever that sticking to our own was a setup for more of the same. Yet my desire to connect and my ability to do so were still years from meeting up.

Q Have you tried to form relationships across racial lines? How have they worked out? If they didn't get very far, how did you explain that to yourself?

The harder I tried, the worse it got.

IN THE FALL OF 1996 I missed a golden opportunity to expand beyond my social circle of white friends. The time had come to choose a preschool for my daughter. Instead of researching which schools had developed racial diversity among staff and families, and which among them had integrated cultural competency into their work with children and families, I simply chose the school that my mom friends were sending their kids to. I was pregnant with child number 2 and sick as a dog. I was in survival mode, retching around the clock. I made the easy choice, the path of least resistance.

By the fourth month of preschool, my morning sickness lifted. As I came to, I realized I'd just signed myself up for a repeat of the playground: more white grown-ups, more white children. Yet my daughter had quickly fallen in love with the school, and I hadn't the heart to tear her away from it. The preschool, I observed, included a few white European families and one Korean family but was hardly reflective of Cambridge's multiracial population. I wondered if I would ever be able to break the habit of surrounding myself with white people. The private cooperative preschool I'd chosen required parents to pay about $5,000 a year and also to volunteer in the classroom one day every three weeks. Had I done my research I would have understood that these two factors would make the school an unlikely choice for single parents or families with two full-time jobs, especially when the city offered free or far less expensive options with no time demands on parents. The school was a custom-made option created by and for upper-middle-class white parents.

A year or two into what would ultimately be a six-year run at this school, a new director came on board. A white South African woman, she had racial diversity on her mind too. The two of us formed a diversity committee and hired a professional to run a workshop for parents. Our goal was to learn how to create an environment capable of attracting and maintaining families of color. A white man showed up. *Hmmmm, diversity being taught by a white guy?* I was surprised and a little disappointed. I wondered what he could teach us.

"Exploring our own issues with race is an important part of this work," he started off. "If we can't be comfortable with it, our children will pick up on it." He then posed this question to the group: "How would you handle it if you were in a grocery store and your child pointed to a black man and said loudly, 'Why is that man's skin dirty?'"

The room filled with the sound of air sucking through teeth as we twisted and grimaced at the idea.

"That would be awful," someone said. "I'd just try to get to another aisle as quickly as possible."

"I'd say, 'Shhh,' to my child. Then later I'd explain that we don't talk about people that way," another offered.

"Those are the kinds of things most people say," he said gently, "but if you send your child the message that skin color, or race, is a taboo topic, you risk a few things. First, you're suggesting there's something wrong with the black man, so wrong it can't be mentioned. Second, you teach your child that curiosity can get you in trouble. And third, you miss a chance to explain that dark skin isn't dirty—it's just a different color. What we really want is to use moments like these to make talking and teaching about race natural. Kids notice difference without judgment, if we let them."

"Ahhhhh." The group let out a collective breath of recognition that of course we didn't want to plant race as a source of anxiety in our kids' minds. What a simple paradigm shift. *Honesty is the best policy*, I thought.

We batted around some words and phrases we might use to answer our child's question. "Remember," he said, "you want to keep the topic open for discussion. See how you might keep it going."

One woman volunteered a different approach. "What if you said, 'Skin color comes in lots of shades of brown—even your skin is brown, just lighter.' Maybe I'd try to make eye contact with the man and smile, like 'I'm trying.'"

Someone else imagined she might say, "Just like eye color and hair color can be different, so can skin color." She said she'd want to keep it simple.

The facilitator encouraged us to add in something like, "That was a good question," to let our children know we valued their curiosity.

Before this workshop, I would have thought a quiet "Shhhh" followed up by a "We don't speak about people that way" would've been the way to go. It excited me to know that there were professionals in the world, "diversity trainers," who could help people like me navigate the complex world of cross-race relations. If this white guy could learn how to navigate multiracial groups, maybe I could too.

Though I had made a shift from wanting to help and fix people of color to wanting to develop my own "diversity" skills, I didn't get how problematic my approach still was. Far from the important work of understanding systemic racism and its impact on my life outcomes and perspective, my new aim was to understand some magical set of cross-racial manners. What drove my pursuit was a desire to learn how not to screw up and embarrass myself so I could preserve my good-person image. Still trapped in my white-dominated belief system, I didn't know what I didn't know. Topping the list was the unknown truth about just how much humility would be required to become an effective agent of change.

So, desperate to be a good white person and not say something embarrassing, I started seeking out diversity workshops. I hoped to gather more tips like the "Don't say 'Shhhh'" one that seemed so helpful. Yet every workshop I went to left me feeling increasingly aware of how easy it was to say something offensive, ironically serving only to ramp up my fears of putting my foot in my mouth and humiliating myself. For the next eleven years I found myself caught in a cycle of seeking wisdom only to become increasingly anxious. The more I became aware of the ways in which I might say the wrong thing and of how fed up many people of color were with white ignorance, the more I sought wisdom.

In January 2008 I attended a diversity workshop at my daughters' middle school. The parent organizers had hired Boston Improv, a theater group, to act out typical scenes in which white people make an unintentional racialized remark, leaving the person of color reeling. Boston Improv encouraged the racially mixed audience of about sixty parents and staff to raise their hands and come up on stage to replace any one of the characters so as to change the course of the scene. The group would then analyze the interactions and replay it using a higher level of racial consciousness.

Sitting in the back of the room, I watched a scene up on stage in which a black teenage boy (an actor) was touring a school to which he was considering applying. The football coach had exchanged one or two words with him as he checked out the gym, and then the boy's mother approached. The coach thrust his hand out enthusiastically to greet the mother and launched in to tell her how great her son was. He repeated several times, "He's so *articulate*; I think he'd do just *great* here. We could really use someone like him on the team." On about the third or fourth "articulate," a black parent seated just behind me shot her hand in the air and stood, her chair toppling over behind her. Though composed on the outside, the force of her energy sent a shockwave through me. *What just happened?* I wondered frantically. *What did she see that I didn't?* She wove her way through the sea of chairs and marched up onto the stage. She took the place of the boy's mother. "I'll take it from here," she said.

"What do you mean my son is articulate?" she demanded of the coach. "You barely spoke two words to him. How would you know whether or not he's articulate?" Then she added, "And what do you know about his football skills? Have you ever watched him play? Have you spoken to his coach?"

They played it out for a bit, the mother finally educating the coach that his job was to evaluate her son based on his athletic merits, not to make assumptions about how his skin color made him a good athlete. She also drove home the stupidity of praising a person for being articulate when you've barely spoken to them.

I was stunned. I hadn't caught either point on my own.

It turns out the word "articulate" is one of those words white people tend to use to describe a person of color who is able to string a sentence together, the implication being that this is a rare thing, an exception. For a racial group that has had to prove its intelligence over and over again, setting the bar this low is insulting.

I drove home that night thinking, *"Articulate"? Are you kidding me? I use that word all the time. I'm not sure if I've ever used it to describe a person of color, but I call my white husband articulate. What if I slip and use that word around a black person?* My anxiety was through the roof. If that word could cause such rage, what else might I say that would enrage someone? My fear about saying the wrong thing reached an all-time high.

I had never been socialized to say what I thought or felt. Instead I'd been trained to say what I imagined the other person wanted to hear. At the age of eight I'd had a particularly humiliating experience because of saying the "wrong" thing. My mother had driven me to my friend Mary's house to get a sleeping bag I'd left there. My mother parked the car at the curb, and I ran up to the house on my own. When Mary's young, beautiful mother, whom I adored, answered the door with my sleeping bag, she asked, "How are you?" A few nights earlier, my father had picked me up from Mary's house at three a.m., when I'd developed a stomach bug. I gave Mary's mother all the dirty details of how many times I'd thrown up, what color it was, and how I had now progressed to a diet of Saltines and ginger ale. She shook her head with compassion and told me how glad she was that I was better, for goodness' sake. It seemed to me like a typical good chat with Mary's mom.

When I got back to the car, my mother asked, "What on earth were you talking about for so long?"

I told her about our conversation.

"Why did you tell her all that?"

"She asked how I was."

"Oh my goodness, Debby, don't you know? When someone asks you how you are, they don't want to hear how you *really* are. The proper response to 'How are you?' is 'Fine, thank you.'"

I was mortified. There I'd been yammering on, and maybe all she'd wanted was a "Fine, thank you." I felt exposed and foolish. I remember blushing for one of the few times in my life. My face burned, and my stomach felt bouncy.

The feelings I experienced following the Boston Improv workshop reminded me of this "Fine, thank you" moment with my mother. I felt exposed, vulnerable, and terrified of potential humiliation. I got home that night and wrote an email to the parent, a black man, who'd led the effort to organize the forum and had closed the session by inviting people to contact him with feedback or questions. I poured my heart out in the email, totally dumping all my race-related baggage on this poor man. I confessed to a mounting stew of confusing and upsetting feelings around race. I listed about twenty emotions I was wrestling with, including guilt, despair, fear, hopelessness, confusion, and anxiety. I told him that I didn't feel I was getting any closer to understanding cross-race relations and I didn't know how to proceed. "Do you have any advice for me?" I wrote in closing. I was years from learning just how weary people of color are of being in the position of having to educate white people. I hadn't made the connection that this is one reason why white people becoming racially aware and coaching other white people to do the same is so important. I still thought race was something that belonged only to people of color, and I wanted the rule book.

I got an email back the next day in which he reassured me this stuff was tricky but to try to remove the guilt piece—it would only interfere with progress—and to please stick with it. I liked being encouraged not to feel guilty, but I still felt red-hot, prickly apprehension about saying something stupid and hurtful along the way. And I still had no idea why I kept feeling as if I were banging my head against a wall.

Because my main objective was to learn how not to screw up around people of color, my mind was trained away from what I really needed to learn. Had I understood racism as a social system, or explored the way race had shaped my identity, my perspective, my values, and my achievements, I would have made more progress sooner. Instead, I made the mistake of overlaying my cultural values, such as "Say the right thing" and "Be a good person," on a new, markedly different social situation. I now understand that fear of doing or saying something offensive perpetuated my cultural incompetence.

As I look back now, I can see why our efforts at Agassiz Preschool were lackluster. We put photographs of kids from around the world up on the walls. We attracted a family or two of color, none of whom completed their children's full three years there. When I found out recently that Louis Agassiz, the school's namesake, had devoted much of his nineteenth-century scientific career to proving racial classification and white superiority, I wondered if we'd looked as ill equipped for racial integration as we were. And once again, I had to ask myself if I'd done more harm than good.

Q Think about five rules from the "rule book" of social interaction that you grew up with. For each rule, can you imagine how it interferes with honest cross-cultural dialogue, given what you've learned in this book or from other sources?

The power of inclusion.

IN 1999, when the time came for my oldest daughter to go to kinder-garten, we entered the Cambridge Public Schools' Controlled Choice lottery. About twenty years earlier, the Controlled Choice program had emerged as a method to desegregate schools by untethering one's residential location from one's school assignment. The goal was for each classroom population to reflect the city's racial diversity. Though this meant we had no guarantee our daughter would end up at our neighborhood school, I liked knowing an intentional diversification strategy existed. It ensured the kind of racial mix I'd come to Cambridge to be a part of.

Fortunately for us, our kids did get into our neighborhood school, the Haggerty School. On the first day of kindergarten, I felt my prayers had finally been answered: the room was full of joyful children, with a variety of skin colors, playing side by side. *At last, I thought, my children will grow up in a racially diverse world and be imbued with the kind of cross-cultural interaction and competence I long for.*

The school's motto, "Everyone Is Different; Everyone Belongs," owes its origins to its longtime principal Joe Petner, an entrepreneurial white educator who placed at the core of his educational philosophy the inclusion of children with special needs in regular classrooms. Dr. Petner had masterfully cobbled together grant money, volunteers, and interns to build classrooms with two or three assistants able to support lead teachers as they strove to meet the widely differing needs of every child in their room. Dr. Petner believed that including and supporting students labeled by the educational system as cognitively impaired, emotionally disturbed, or physically disabled would empower all the children by offering a range of teaching and support strategies. "No one is really a 'typical' learner," Dr. Petner would say. "We all have unique learning styles." People's academic, physical, and social abilities are variable, he stressed, as opposed to "normal" or "abnormal," better or worse. This fundamental understanding, he argued, would make for more cohesive and productive communities both in the classroom and beyond it.

The power of this inclusive approach became especially potent for me in my oldest daughter's third grade year. One of her classmates since kindergarten, Richard, had substantial physical and learning challenges. Though his speech was particularly difficult for me to understand, my daughter and her classmates not only understood him but found it surprising that many of us parents didn't. Richard's language had become part of their "normal," his gentle kindness fully a part of their classroom culture. My daughter's friendship with Richard made me ashamed of the way my friends and I had treated the one deaf boy with whom I'd gone to grade school. The potential realized by simply encouraging children to take care of one another—as opposed to having them compete for attention, grades, and social status—amazed me.

Under teacher Chris Colbath-Hess's deft direction, the class had put together a performance about the American Revolution, showcasing the individuals whose acts of courage had helped colonial New Englanders defeat the British. The students worked together to design every aspect of the show. Everyone participated, Richard included. During the performance, a light would shine on one student, in character, as he or she spoke about his or her role in the Revolution. Every once in a while, the barely visible unlit actors, would repeat in unison something the lit-up actor had just said. So the group might say, "Did I hear you right? Did you say you were a tanner?" to which the individual would repeat, "That's right—I am a tanner." This was an interesting theatrical twist. For one, if a student forgot their line, the rest of the group used this method to prompt them. As a parent, the format made me feel comfortable, knowing those awkward moments when kids forget their lines would be seamlessly resolved.

The real beauty of the approach became apparent when it was Richard's turn. As he stood and spoke his well-rehearsed lines in speech I still struggled to decipher, the whole group echoed him by asking, "Did I hear you right? Did you say you were a blacksmith?" to which Richard would repeat, "That's right—I am a blacksmith." With the support of his class, Richard's every word came across. The entire play had been constructed to set up the students, the teachers, and the parent audience members for success. It was the first time I'd seen a school play free of stops and starts and gratuitous moments where the kid with special needs has some fluff role. I remember feeling overcome by this approach's humane contrast to the "Can't keep up? Tough luck!" attitude or the "We'll see what we can do to fit you in" mindset.

My daughter Emily thrived in this setting, where one of the cultural norms was to figure out how to meet all individuals' needs in each group activity. Students took enormous pride in their ability to tackle this challenge, becoming eager problem solvers attuned to the needs of various class members and conscious of the way excluding even one individual can compromise the entire group.

Yet even in this school, with its ample staffing and fervent intention to meet all children's needs, something alarming happened before my eyes. Kindergarteners who'd learned side by side became first graders who were split into different reading and math groups, uncannily along skin color lines. While the white students became increasingly jazzed by school and their rapid progress, the students of color slowly began to look disheartened. By second grade the social and academic divide was unmistakable, and by third grade the gap was so stark as to cause me to question my memories of kindergarten solidarity. As I witnessed once fully engaged black and brown children lose their spark, my agitation at not understanding the forces behind the phenomenon grew. My hopes of my children forming close cross-racial friendships dwindled as I observed what I could neither explain nor ignore.

Though there were exceptions, the trend was clearly visible. In her third grade year, Emily sidled up to me at the kitchen sink and gingerly asked me, "Mom? Why is it that the black kids are all in the lower reading groups?" Her tone let me know that it had taken a lot for her to ask a question she wasn't sure was okay to ask. It crushed me not to have an answer. "Emily, I don't get it. It makes no sense to me either. And it really bothers me." Finally, I'd gotten my child into the kind of environment I thought would result in racial equality, and all it seemed to be doing was reinforcing racial stereotypes.

By the fourth grade, the white kids dominated the student body, taking on leadership roles, creating clubs, and forming bonds over books such as the Harry Potter series. What I could not yet see was that as the white kids went about deepening friendships through white-affiliated roles and subjects, they dominated the classroom and school culture. I can see now how effortlessly the cycle of white domination can creep into young lives, generation after generation.

Of everything I saw that marked the pattern of white achievement alongside black and brown withdrawal, none disturbed me more than the sight of black boys sitting on the bench in the principal's office, a near daily occurrence. The boys' expressions, ranging from rage to detachment, are seared in my memory. Though I recall a faint urge to blame the boys and their parents for not taking school more seriously and not proving black stereotypes wrong, on some level I must have known that there was more to the story, because what kept surfacing for me was not a judgment, but a question. *Why*, I wondered, *did black boys spend a disproportionate amount of time sitting on the bench in the principal's office?*

Eventually, in 2005, my passion for the "Everyone Is Different; Everyone Belongs" philosophy and my desire to understand why it wasn't reaching the students of color led me to apply for an assistant teacher position. Over the next four years, I moved from kindergarten, to first, to second grade, tracking the trend I'd been observing up close and personal. Still, I couldn't explain it. Without yet understanding that a system was in play, I looked to individuals for answers. Teachers were mostly kind and supportive. White children were mostly kind and supportive. There was no overt racism that I could detect.

One day, as I watched a group of black fourth grade boys get left behind while their classmates headed off on a field trip, I wondered, *Would that have happened to four rowdy white boys?* I can't remember their offense, but likely they'd disrupted the classroom or done something on the playground that had gotten them in trouble. I put the question to a colleague, a white woman.

"What is going on?" I asked. "I just can't imagine seeing that happen to four white kids."

"Absolutely it would," she said forcefully. "It's all about holding everyone to the same standard."

Then why is it so often black boys are the ones on that damn bench in the principal's office? I asked myself. I could just imagine the parents of four white boys who missed a field trip storming the principal's office in protest and flooding the parent Listserv with angry missives about the injustice.

Though my curiosity wouldn't quit, I never considered asking one of the school's few staff of color for their perspective on the trend. Because I so feared saying something stupid or embarrassing around people of color,

I stuck to white adults, which I now see was a huge part of why it took me so long to find answers that would make sense. When I'd ask white teachers how they explained the divergent outcomes according to skin color, some would just raise their eyebrows and not say much. My interpretation of this was that they saw the gap as proof positive that black kids were inherently less able and willing—or perhaps just poorly raised. This theory never made sense to me. What I saw was profound disengagement that worsened with each grade. I knew to my core nobody wants this for their child. No child wants this for themselves. Staff members who were willing to talk about it would say things like, "Look at their home lives. What are they eating? Are they sleeping enough? Can their parents help them with their homework? How can these poor kids keep up?" I felt like a two-year-old because I just kept wanting to ask "Why?" "I can see all those things too," I wanted to say, "but why are their lifestyles so different? Why does it get worse with every grade? Why can't someone figure out how to give families the support they need to get out of this cycle?"

Without knowing it, I was witnessing the manifestation of cradle-to-grave headwinds and tailwinds that touch nearly every aspect of Americans' lives, creating divergent outcomes that ultimately get misinterpreted as an ability to achieve or a lack of ability. In schools, the pattern is referred to as the "achievement gap." The countrywide phenomenon in which black and Latino students exhibit lower standardized test scores, lower grade point averages, and higher dropout rates than their white and Asian peers is explained by socioeconomic factors, including poor nutrition and limited access to health care, as well as cultural barriers involving language, early exposure to books, and parental involvement. In recognition of the connection between opportunity and achievement, some people have begun using the term "opportunity gap" instead of "achievement gap." Either way, it's a pervasive issue with which American educators are grappling.

I found it easy enough to imagine how nutrition, health care, and language challenges would hinder one's ability to learn. I could also see how being exposed to books early and often would help a young mind start to recognize letters and sentences as well as develop an appreciation for the art of a well-told story. But again, I kept wondering, *Why? Why? Why? Why all these patterns together, at once? Why is an entire population experiencing lower socioeconomic standards? Why aren't black and Latino parents as involved as white parents?*

I was years from learning that the answer lay not just in looking at those who were not achieving but in examining the experiences of children like mine, the white kids who thrive. Now it seems obvious to me, but for most of my life I couldn't see how much easier life is for most white people in America, and how that ease includes a level of comfort in taking one's place as a leader—be it in a classroom or a boardroom. I couldn't yet see how books and curricula that focused on the accomplishments of my race made me feel included and inspired. Nor could I see how as white people assume leadership roles, their voices and actions can squeeze out those of their peers and colleagues of color, reestablishing a pattern in which white people appear more able. Like so much about racism, the cycle is self-perpetuating.

I now understand that the inclusive approach at the Haggerty School was no match for the long history of white dominance, no matter how unintended. I believe that until all teachers are given thorough and ongoing training about the manifestation and impact of racialized bias, parents and children will enter school communities and, without meaning to, assume their historical roles. Despite symptom-management programs and services, without awareness and intention, the gap will persist. I also believe more than ever in Dr. Petner's "Everyone Is Different; Everyone Belongs" philosophy. Now, however, I see that to reach its full potential, its believers must take into account not just variable abilities, but variable realities—realities that are very different according to racial identity.

Q Make a list of all the factors that you believe contributed to your own achievement as a student. How do you think being a white person or a person of color influenced each of those factors?

How my sense of belonging also allowed me to feel entitled.

IN A PERFECT EXAMPLE of how racialized assumptions and attitudes can ooze into every crevice of organizations, a typical school's parent body manifests an achievement gap of its own, an "involvement gap" one might say. From day 1 as a Cambridge public school parent, I noticed that a majority of kids of color came to and from school by bus, while many white kids were dropped off and picked up by parents, grandparents, or caregivers. I wondered why the parents of color didn't come to school as often. Eventually I settled on this self-congratulatory sentiment: *If they're too busy to be here, I'm glad parents like me can be so there's a parent presence at the school.* Once again, I saw my role as a helpful one. And once again I was wrong.

All across America, white parents, disproportionately able to drop off and pick up their children, gain an edge in the community-bonding department. Socializing in the halls and on the playgrounds, white parents like me form a close-knit adult community. We arrange play dates and carpools for our white children. We sign up to be committee members and room parents. Without thinking about the repercussions of our actions, we deepen white bonds and strengthen the voice of the white parents. I imagined my efforts good and helpful. Unaware of the social forces in play, I assumed the low involvement of families of color a result of parents working long hours. I had no idea that the more white parents like me—already comfortable in America's public spaces—bonded and took over, the more uncomfortable the school culture became for families of color.

One of the most resounding patterns that has echoed through my conversations in recent years is the way that white people, in general, grew up with a sense of belonging in America, while people of color did not. From large-scale policies like the GI Bill to small Zap-filled interpersonal moments, people of color are too often reminded that they are not valued or understood by many white Americans. White people who cross the street when they see a black man walking toward them send a message: "I don't like seeing you here." People who ask, "Where are you from?" of an Asian American whose family immigrated here two hundred years ago send a message: "You'll never look like you belong." A government that isolates Native Americans on remote reservations sends a message: "You are not wanted." Saturating our culture is the ultimate message: "Belonging to Club America is primarily for white folks." Already on guard in America's public spaces, and especially in schools, where chances of painful childhood associations are high, parents of color often need to take a deep breath and brace themselves before stepping through a school's front door.

I never questioned whether I belonged in America and its institutions. I grew up believing that the government existed to provide services— schools, highways, law enforcement—to its citizens, me included. I grew up believing the police were there to protect me. "If you get lost or feel worried, just look for a policeman," my mother would say when I headed out to the annual town fair. I've now learned that just five miles away black mothers in Boston were teaching their children not to play hide-and-seek outside lest it appear they were sneaking around and up to no good. "If you get stopped by the police," black mothers routinely tell their kids, "keep your hands in plain sight so they don't think you have a gun." Could there be two more different relationships with the police? What must it feel like when providers of life's most basic goods and services aren't seen as there for you? Or even worse, are seen as against you?

In the same way I learned at an early age that police were there to serve and protect me, I learned that our schools were also there to serve. My parents weren't overtly demanding people by any stretch of the imagination, but they had high expectations for public institutions. They also felt a strong sense of engagement with these institutions by helping out at school events, serving on boards and committees, and working at the annual fundraiser for our local hospital. The institutions and my parents belonged to the community, and the community belonged to them. Even aside from exclusive clubs, a sense of belonging, it turns out, is a luxury not conveyed to all.

Growing up feeling like a belonger is a key ingredient in my perceptions and belief system. For me to say to a black person, "The police aren't there to judge or suspect your kid! What's wrong with you to think that? They're there to help. That's what we pay them for," would be to use my white perspective to explain their reality. Though race may not be based in biology, as a lived experience it is all too real, and drastically different for white people compared to everyone else.

In her book *The Education of a White Parent*, former Boston School Committee member Susan Naimark, a white woman, uses the term "entitlement gap" to describe the way white parents bring a host of assumptions and attitudes to a school community. If you'd asked me a few years ago what the word "entitlement" meant, I think I would have offered up Thurston Howell, the blatantly superior-acting *Gilligan's Island* character, as a prime example. Yet as I read in Naimark's book about the "entitled" behaviors of white parents that can feel oppressive to families of color, I saw myself smack in the middle of her description.

Each spring, for instance, many white parents think nothing of contacting their school principal and requesting (or even demanding) their child be placed in so-and-so's class next year. They specify the teachers and peers they want as well as the teachers and peers they don't want. It's a common white practice in America's public schools. I did it every year when my children were in elementary school, clueless that this seemingly benign act in fact fueled the achievement gap. How? My white children ended up in the stronger cohort with the stronger teacher. Children of parents who felt less entitled ended up with the leftover teacher and the leftover students. Headwinds and tailwinds.

In an article, Naimark tells the story of a parent meeting she and others organized to discuss this seemingly innocuous practice. After all, everyone has the right to advocate for their own kids, right? But when the parents of color heard about what white parents were doing, they were shocked. They never even considered it an option. Parents of color explained that often the trauma left by their own educations in white institutions made them bristle at the idea of coming into school, let alone talking to teachers or administrators. Telling the principal what to do? Unthinkable.

Toward the end of my time at the Haggerty School I served on a newly created committee called Family Connections, specifically organized to reach out to and include our growing population of Ethiopian, Somalian, and Haitian families. Our primary concern at one particular meeting was a rift arising over one of the school's longtime traditions, the annual Halloween parade. For years students, staff, and several camera-wielding parents (myself included) had been dressing in elaborate costumes for the event. The gym teacher banged a marching drum; the receptionist played a glockenspiel; the principal, wearing a festive head-to-toe costume himself, led the school community around the block. My photo albums display years of the parade, a testament to the important role it played in my life.

Everyone loved the Halloween parade. That is, everyone who celebrated Halloween. What went underappreciated for years was the growing number of children and families for whom the parade presented deep conflict. Through these meetings, I learned that in some cultures Halloween is experienced as an offensive and potentially spiritually harmful celebration of the dead. As the school population shifted to an increasing number of families whose cultures found Halloween troublesome, more children came to school saying they could not participate in the parade. The school created a form to send home, asking parents to give or withhold permission to participate. I remember receiving the form and thinking, *Who on earth would say no to having their child participate in a simple parade? It's so much fun! It's school tradition! C'mon folks—lighten up!* For a few years each classroom's one or two kids who couldn't participate would stay in the classroom, watching their peers help one another put on costumes and makeup and then gleefully march out of the room. The nonparticipants were left behind with a staff person, possibly resentful to be missing the parade. They'd be entertained in some alternate way until the paraders, high on their experience, returned for a sugar-filled celebration to cap off the event.

As the years went on and the number of nonparticipants increased, an alternative event was held in the school library on the building's top floor. The school's longtime assistant principal did her best to make this an enjoyable alternative but reported each year that the kids, distracted and distraught, flocked to the windows to catch a glimpse of their peers in the colorful and noisy parade below. We learned that some parents were taking time off work to pick their children up mid-morning and bring them home.

At the first Family Connections meeting, the principal asked those who did not allow their children to participate in the parade to help the rest of us understand the experience from their perspective.

"Ahhhh," one woman shook her head and looked at the ceiling. "It's so complicated."

Other parents nodded in support, one by one explaining that for them, Halloween represented a celebration of the dead, an act tantamount to a satanic ritual. There was no way they could support it. Yet their children came home begging to participate. One mother told about the one year she'd acquiesced—after all, they were in America now, and she was trying to negotiate life as an American. She tried to encourage her kids to use materials from home to make costumes. They rebuffed her, saying all the American kids bought costumes. In an effort to help them feel like belongers, she took them to Target, where, to her horror, she watched them sort through costumes with fake blood and daggers. In the end, she was able to steer them away from the ghoulish costumes and toward Disney and cartoon alternatives. She spent her week's grocery money on costumes that were worn only once. On parade day her kids came home sick from the amount of sugar they'd eaten. Needless to say, the experience left her more conflicted than ever.

At this point I had started the Wheelock course and learned enough to know that listening to "outsider" feedback would be key to dismantling any "insider" behaviors, including traditions, that were creating cross-cultural conflict. As the meeting progressed, it became clear that the school population had changed since the tradition's inception and that in contrast to being a school-wide, feel-good, spirit-building event, it had become, in this new context, a divisive event, undermining the efforts of people trying their best to become productive Americans. By the meeting's end, a majority vote ended the once-beloved parade's eighteen-year run.

Not only did the Halloween parade move toward a swift end, but the school used the situation to teach the children about cultural sensitivity and the need to be responsive to change. Once on board with the need to create a more inclusive tradition, students were asked for suggestions. Engaging them in the process ended up re-creating the feel-good, spirit-building vibe that the parade had once delivered. In the end, the community of students and staff chose a new parade tradition in celebration of Read Across America Day. With the controversial celebration of the dead gone, all the school's children are now able to noisily, colorfully, and equitably march around the block dressed as favorite book characters.

Though the parade discussion was enough to rock my world for one day, the meeting was only halfway done. The second item on the agenda was increasing parent participation beyond the current all-white body of parent volunteers.

Again, the principal posed a simple question. "We're wondering how we might attract more families from your communities for the room parent and other volunteer jobs. We'd love to see more diversity in our parent volunteers."

The room was quiet for a while, until someone asked, "How do you get one of those jobs? I assumed you had to be elected." A lot of white palms smacked against white foreheads. Once again, a simple cultural difference had put white American parents in charge without meaning to exclude others, but effectively had done just that.

Every year as a parent, with all the enthusiasm and good-person volunteer spirit one could imagine, I'd marched into my kids' classrooms and said, "Hey, I'd love to be your room parent!" I assumed I was filling a role no one else wanted. I thought I was stepping up and doing a good thing. The fact is, I had enough of a sense of belonging—in that classroom, in that school, in my city, in my country—that I felt entitled to jump in, roll up my sleeves, and make myself even more of a belonger.

Studies have shown that parent involvement in their children's schools improves student achievement. But where does this leave parents who lack trust in America's institutions, have traumatic memories from their own days as students, and lack the sense of belonging that would lead them through the door to ask in a perky voice, "Hey, can I volunteer?" How can parents, already tentative, gain a foothold in a community laden with people like me, eager and ready to take the lead?

As I sat at lunch one day with organizational behavior educator Dr. Stacy Blake-Beard, I mentioned my thoughts about the power of belonging. She pointed out how much of it is about context. "Everybody has a context— groups, neighborhoods, and organizations—in which they feel empowered, and everyone has a context where they feel 'otherized,'" she said. "And it's not just about race. In India I'm an other because I'm an American. At Simmons [the all-women institution where she teaches MBA students] I feel a sense of belonging because I'm a professor *and* I'm a female. Depending on where you are, you can feel more or less empowered."

Her insights helped me understand how important context is to American racism. Though people of color have vibrant communities in which they feel comfortable and empowered, white-dominated American schools, workplaces, and other institutions are not among them. Yet this is where they must spend hours and hours of their lives if they are to access adequate education, work, medical care, and financing. Understanding that the context, or environment, in mainstream America can feel simultaneously threatening to one racial group and empowering to another is a key to appreciating racial inequity.

Q   Did you or your parents ever ask for specific teachers or classroom placement? Did you or your parents ever volunteer for a school role, such as room parent or committee chair? How might you navigate those situations differently now? List three specific ways for a white parent both to be involved and to be inclusive of parents of color.

The psychic costs of racism.

I'VE HAD PLENTY OF MOMENTS where I've felt underappreciated, invisible, or misunderstood. I can't imagine feeling that way most of the time at school, at work, on the train, on the street, at the doctor's office, at the bank. Feeling that I don't belong, that I am invisible, or that I am not wanted puts me in survival mode. My humor, creativity, compassion, and ability to connect seize up, and I become a smaller, weaker version of myself. How would I fare if I had to face this every day?

It turns out that a spontaneous experiment in 1968 provides some answers to that question. Jane Elliott, a white third grade teacher in Iowa, devised a controversial and powerful experiment to expose her white students to the experience of harsh judgment and inferior treatment. The day after Dr. Martin Luther King's assassination, she watched her students arrive upset and confused. Why, they wondered, would anyone murder a man they considered a hero? Ms. Elliott decided there would be no better way for her classroom of all-white students to understand the discrimination that Dr. King sought to extinguish than to experience it firsthand. She asked her students if they'd like to participate in an experiment. Though they all began with an enthusiastic "Yes!" classroom tensions soon divided the group. In the experiment she divided the students into two groups based on eye color. On the first day, the blue-eyed kids were treated as superior, getting extra recess time, extra food at lunch, and an overall lack of harassment, which she was inflicting on the brown-eyed kids.

On day 1 Ms. Elliott had the brown-eyed kids wear collars so they could be easily identified. As she went about her day, she laced her lessons with derogatory remarks about the brown-eyed kids—things like, "Forgot your glasses today? Well, that's typical." Within hours, the brown-eyed kids looked demoralized through-and-through. More shocking to me was the way the blue-eyed kids totally bought into their superior status, taunting the brown-eyed kids, piling on when Ms. Elliott said something judgmental and unkind, and puffing up as if they actually were better people. The divide manifested itself both socially and academically, the blue-eyed students performing above average on the day's work while the brown-eyed kids performed below average. The next day she reversed the experiment so that the brown-eyed students were treated as the superior group.

After the initial two days, the students spoke together about what it had felt like to be on either side of the inferior/superior equation. They talked about the confusion, alienation, and frustration at the unfairness and powerlessness when in the oppressed group. They spoke of their inability to concentrate on schoolwork. One boy said, "The way they treated you, you felt like you didn't even want to try to do anything." Fights broke out as kids of the superior eye color taunted those with other-colored eyes. The superior kids noted how their own cruel behavior left them feeling lousy. "I watched cooperative, wonderful, thoughtful children turn into nasty, vicious, discriminating children," Ms. Elliott observed.

Jane Elliott has spent the rest of her life repeating this experiment not only for young students but for adults in workshops at GE, Exxon, AT&T, the FBI, the IRS, and the US Navy, among others. Adults attending her workshops show up thinking they're coming to learn about working better in teams. To simulate the pervasive experience of discrimination, the differentiation begins the minute they show up for their workshop. Ms. Elliott greets the brown-eyed folks with a matter-of-fact tone and the blue-eyed with a suspicious and gruff tone. The blue-eyed folks are given dorky Pilgrim-like collars to wear and are put in a small, windowless room with no seats, food, water, or bathroom access. For an hour or so, the blue-eyed conference attendees endure their crummy quarters with a surly security person checking in and brusquely reminding them not to complain or act up. Meanwhile, the brown-eyed folks are given a comfortable room with food, coffee, water, and bathroom access. During this hour, Ms. Elliott briefs the brown-eyed group on the intention of the workshop and asks that they join her by accepting their superior status and not standing up for the inferior group, whom Ms. Elliott is about to demean.

When the blue-eyed group is let into the room, Ms. Elliott tells them to sit on the floor in neat rows. Seated around them in a horseshoe configuration are their brown-eyed colleagues. As Ms. Elliott proceeds to chastise and ridicule the blue-eyed folks on the floor while they perform tasks like writing answers to simple questions, the brown-eyed folks look on silently or subtly scorn their blue-eyed colleagues. She takes any opportunity—talking out of turn, looking smug, just about anything—to put the blue-eyed people on edge, badgering them with humiliating questions and demanding compliance. By using tactics such as changing the rules and making no-win situations, Ms. Elliott continually reinforces her position of power while keeping the oppressed group in what she calls their "child ego state." Imitating the dynamics of racism and other forms of oppression, she punishes them for acting like the children she forces them to be. In debriefing after the experiment she explains, "We keep people down by lowering our expectations of them and then forcing them to live down to them." Another phrase I've heard her use repeatedly is "Go along to get along," describing the kind of forced compliance that comes with oppression.

A video documenting the experiment both in an elementary classroom and in a corporate workshop shows how consistently the experiment reduces the discriminated group—children or adults—to tears, hand wringing, fury, and the urge to fight back or leave. Powerlessness creates a state of fear, which puts people in survival mode. Who can be anything close to their best in this state? It's what Andrea Stuart describes in her book about slavery's effects over generations as "psychological disfigurement."

Ms. Elliott's mission is to demonstrate the fact that people aren't born inferior or superior; they just respond to the environment in which they're placed. Despite the fact that the vast majority of the 450 elementary school students who endured the experiment remain grateful for the unforgettable experience of being put in the shoes of the discriminated, many of the white adults in her town reacted negatively at the time. Not only did Ms. Elliott receive death threats, but her parents lost their business when locals boycotted it because of their daughter's controversial work. Though I do think it's tricky to justify putting children through this kind of pain and humiliation, I wonder why that same outrage against her experiment, which ostracized white children for one day, doesn't carry over to how white people respond to the way people of color, especially black men, women, and children, have been treated for hundreds of years.

Q   Think about a time when you were treated unfairly. What do you recall of your emotions (e.g., anger, resentment, anxiety) and your physical state (e.g., elevated heart rate, stomach clenching, sweating)? How did you respond to the unfair treatment?

Witnessing the impact of racial legacy.

WHEN I WAS A SECOND GRADE TEACHER, I felt a sense of desperation. The feeling of losing children to the march of time left me anxious for answers. Jared, a black boy in my class, particularly concerned me. He'd had a rough time at another Cambridge school, and his parents had sent him to our school for a fresh start. Barely getting by academically and suffering from the isolation of feeling unable to catch up and keep up, the light in his eyes came and went with his successes and failures over the course of each day. I wanted to grab him and pull him up before it was too late. I went into overdrive wondering what I could do to keep that spark alive. How could I help him succeed?

Our three-person teaching team decided that at the start of each day one of us would check in with Jared, let him know the day's plan, and see if he had any concerns about the schedule. We thought he could use a reminder that we were there for him and wanted him to have a good day. In teacher-speak, we ramped up our efforts to set him up for success.

Yet his struggles persisted. While we were doing math one day, Jared became overwhelmed by a particular problem and threw down his pencil, screaming, "AAAARRGGGHHHH!!!" He got up and ran to a carpeted, pillow-strewn "calming corner" of the room we had set up for moments just like these.

I went to check on him. Squatting beside him and putting my hand on his back, I asked, "What was that about?"

"I'm stupid. I'm so stupid I can't do anything," he sobbed.

"It sounds like that was a hard math problem for you, Jared, but it doesn't mean you're stupid," I tried to reassure him.

"Stop telling me I can do this! Every day you tell me I can learn this stuff, but I can't!" He was bawling.

I decided to let him get it out. I sat quietly with him.

"Anyway, what's the point?" he said. "I'm going to jail when I grow up anyway."

This I was not prepared for.

After a long pause, I asked, "Jail? Why do you think you're going to jail?

He went on to tell me about this and that cousin, this and that friend—all men—who'd gone to jail.

"When I'm eighteen, that's when I'm going," he added at the end.

It struck me that the pattern of behavior he saw included black kids going to the principal's office and black family and friends going to jail. It would make all the sense in the world to see himself on a similar trajectory. Not yet aware of the mass incarceration system plaguing his community, I tried to reassure him that crime was a choice, not a predestined path. Unprepared, confused, and upset, I felt ill equipped and lost for any other words of wisdom or support.

I was no stranger to looking at patterns of behavior around me and imaging myself on a similar trajectory. I thought about how when I was Jared's age, I already assumed I'd be going to college like my siblings and cousins, the same as my parents and their siblings had done. I never questioned whether I'd be able to be a good enough student. It was a given. Did that same sense of inevitability shape Jared's thoughts about his future? The sense of perpetual predestination according to skin color made me feel hopeless.

I decided to do an experiment with the kids the next day. I brought in a little footstool from home and taped under it a piece of orange construction paper with the words "The Year 2027" written on it. That was the year these students would turn twenty-five. As they sat on the floor in a circle, I told the kids I had a "magic" (wink wink, we all knew it wasn't really magic) step. Once they stood on it, they'd be twenty-five years old. A reporter (me) was there to write an article about them and needed to interview them. "You don't have to do this, guys—only if you want to," I explained, mostly with Jared in mind. The class included black- and brown-skinned children from Ethiopia, Somalia, and Pakistan, all recent immigrants. They and their families, new to America, had not endured the generations of American-style discrimination Jared and his family, longtime Americans, had. Their hopes and dreams were still intact. I wanted Jared to see some of his other black and brown classmates imagining a more positive future.

I asked for a volunteer to be the first to step up. Every hand shot up. Kid after kid stood on that stool, lit up like a firecracker and just dying to tell the group about who they were and what they were doing. As interviewer I asked them questions like, "What do you like to do in your free time?" "What do you like most about being a grown-up?" "What do you do for work?"

"I live in Florida and go to the beach every day!" one said.

"I'm a scientist and get to do cool experiments in a huge lab!" raved another.

"I'm a doctor. I operate on people. I live in New York near my brother," explained yet another.

When I called on Jared, he sprung up out of his cross-legged position on the floor, ran across the rug, and leapt up onto the stool. All puffed up and clearly in character, he barked at me, "Hurry up, I don't have much time. I gotta lotta people wantin' to interview me."

The whole class cracked up, including me.

"I'm sorry," I said. "My boss sent me here, and I'm afraid I don't even know what you do."

"You don't know *me*?" he said, dramatically pointing at his own chest. Egged on by the class, he said it a few more times.

We learned he was a famous football player and listened as he described some of his more memorable plays. We learned his two childhood cats, Purity and Faith, were now living with him. No one pointed out that they'd be ancient or dead by then. We all bought into each other's fantasy lives—no challenging, no teasing.

For the rest of the day, Jared had a little spring in his step, and that special light in his eyes sparkled. But at dismissal time, full of vim and vigor, he bumped into a girl, knocking her over. She started crying. Another kid yelled, "Jared! Look what you did!" The light in his eyes went out, his rage filled the room, and he stormed out. Another teacher intercepted him and put him on the principal's bench. I went in and sat beside him. "That was a bad end to a good day," I tried, reaching out to put a hand on his shoulder. He whacked my hand away. "I told you I couldn't do anything right." He glared straight ahead. He clamped his folded arms tightly to his chest and through clenched teeth muttered, "Leave me alone."

I felt completely at sea. Though I didn't yet understand the centuries of history that had put Jared and me on our respective paths, sitting on either side of an invisible barrier, I felt its presence more than ever. I was pretty sure we both wanted the same thing—for Jared to feel engaged and hopeful—yet our different cultures made working together toward our common goal elusive. Who was I to console him or give him a little Suzy Creamcheese pep talk? Our worlds barely resembled one another. Mine made me believe I belonged to a country where I could do anything I set my mind to; his reminded him every day that achieving in white-dominated institutions was for people who didn't look like him. What did I know about his world? Why should he believe me? Did my attempts to build up his sense of self-worth just set him up for a fall and deepen his belief in his own inferiority? I felt utterly unable to help him cope with what I was learning were two cultures on a collision course. With my growing consciousness of the way Jared and I had each developed our sense of worth and place in the world, I felt discouraged by racism's intractability.

Q Can you recall your childhood expectations of how you'd fare in school? How did you imagine your adult life would be? Where did you get these ideas? Think about lifestyle, family, and work. How close is your life to those of your parents and other adults you knew? How much do you think race influenced your life vision and outcome? How much do you think class influenced your life vision and outcome?

Finally realizing what I'd missed all along—and feeling like a fool.

I WONDER HOW I might have navigated the Halloween parade conflict had I not already embarked on the Wheelock course and the process of waking up. Would I have thought, *You're in America now, people; you need to do things our way,* or something like it? Would I have become tight-lipped and not engaged in the conversation? Would I have silently blamed the outside folks for rocking "our" boat and not just going with the program? I think this is exactly what I would have done. Because being a part of American organizations, institutions, and traditions came so easily to me, I couldn't imagine what could be so tough about adjusting to them.

By 2009, the year the Wheelock course finally broke me open, I had spent twenty-four years trying to "help" and "fix" others so that they could "fit in" without once considering my role in perpetuating the dominant culture that was shutting them out. That disconnect created a gulf of ignorance from which all the confusing and upsetting feelings about race sprang—the nagging feeling that there was something I wasn't getting, the anxiety about saying something offensive, the wall I could feel but couldn't explain. I knew there was an elephant in the room. I just didn't know it was me.

Breaking through the invisible veil of privilege left me feeling as if I'd just unfairly won a two-contestant running race. I imagined myself panting and high-fiving people at the finish line without knowing that the woman I'd just beaten by two seconds had had a ten-minute start delay and worn a twenty-pound vest. I could see myself tossing her a line like, "Hey there, good race. Better luck next time." Then I put myself in her shoes and imagined how infuriating it would be, when her achievement had actually surpassed mine, to have me all puffed up and self-congratulatory. What an ass (or an elephant) I'd be, strutting around as if the playing field were level.

As I reexamined my life from an awakening perspective, the whole Robin Hood role felt particularly humiliating. The idea that my career in the arts had revolved around trying to help those I'd been taught to see as less fortunate felt twisted. Understanding their misfortune as directly related to my good fortune made me feel as if I'd offered a hand to a drowning person, who was drowning because moments earlier I'd burned their ship out from under them. And worst of all, I had been giving myself a pat on the back for offering them a hand.

There was no shortage of real-life memories for me to replay. In each I emerged as the elephant. I thought about a conversation I'd had with my friend Kathy, a black woman, in 2008. Kathy and I had met when our daughters were in kindergarten together. A native of Trinidad, Kathy had immigrated to Florida with her mother and two sisters when she was a teenager. Despite the fact that she was fifteen years my junior, and from a world utterly unlike the one I'd grown up in, we each felt an instant connection neither of us could explain.

I loved getting together for coffee with Kathy and talking about parenting, friends, and romance—girlfriend stuff. I cherished stories about her childhood in Trinidad, how her life changed when she came to America, and how it had changed again when Harvard Law School offered her a scholarship and thrust her into the white world of corporate law. In turn, Kathy showed curiosity about my American childhood in my all-white New England suburb with my corporate lawyer father and uncles. At one point we even toyed with the idea of writing a piece called "How Do I Know You?" exploring our connection across racial and cultural differences. We spoke often and openly about race, except for one thing: we never discussed the side of the race equation that remained invisible to me—the white side.

One day, peering at me through the steam coming out of the coffee mug pressed between her hands, she said, "You know, most white people don't even think of themselves as having a race." She looked directly at me.

I went blank. Then I remember thinking quickly, *Well we don't*, before I thought, *But wait, we must*. I did, after all, check off "white" on the census form. We didn't have much of a conversation about it that day because my mind went fuzzy. Since I was not yet aware of whiteness, white privilege, or the language needed to engage in such a conversation, her words sat there much like the First Night teenage boy's had. Her observation neither sunk in nor went away; it just hovered, like a pesky fly buzzing around me. So when the veil came down, a lifetime of comments and conversations, like the one with Kathy, came crashing in on me.

I thought about the time my husband's college friend, an upper-middle-class black guy and the best-dressed man I knew, was visiting us from out of town. On Saturday morning, as he headed off on a day of errands, I teased him for wearing his best Brooks Brothers casual for such a mundane day. Lightheartedly, at least on the outside, he explained to me that this is what it took to avoid being followed or stopped while he shopped. I remember thinking, *I go around in torn sweats all the time. Thank God I don't have to deal with that.* For years his words, like Kathy's and the First Night boy's, rattled around, neither sinking in nor evaporating.

I thought about Sara, a black friend I'd recruited for the First Night board, and how she'd looked disheartened one day as we left a downtown lunch meeting. In an effort to raise money for the First Night Neighborhood Network, we'd gone to a luncheon hosted by corporate donors, mostly white people—maybe even entirely white people. On the walk back to the office, she sighed and confessed to me how exhausting and humiliating it was to be the only black woman in the room.

"Really? What do you mean?" I asked.

"Oh, it's just sitting down at a table of white people, knowing they're wondering, *How'd she beat the odds? Where'd she go to school? What are her credentials to be here?* I'm like a novelty, and I can just feel people checking me out."

I remembered wondering if that were actually going on in people's minds or if it were just a fear of Sara's. Twenty years later, with the veil down, I realized how I'd judged her experience from my vantage point, as opposed to trying to be with her in hers. In full elephant mode I'd said, "You had every right to be there. Just ignore those ignorant people." Unaware of what a persistent and uncomfortable story this is for people of color, I ignored not only her pain but the fact that it was I who had put her in the situation.

I adored Sara. She had all the qualities I look for in a good girlfriend, and I would have told you our relationship was full of mutual affection and respect. But recruiting her for the First Night board, without really understanding the intricacies of racism or having the skills to talk about it, was irresponsible. First of all, I put her in the uncomfortable position of being the only black board member. When I consider how we ended up at the luncheon that day, I have to ask why Sara was my board member of choice. Wasn't it to show the fundraising world that First Night—that I—was hip to the diversity thing? Doesn't that mean I outright used her? Tokenized her?

Did she connect my actions to the hurt she felt that day? (Good Lord, this is painful to write about and take responsibility for.)

I cringe now to think I tried to comfort her by telling her that what she experienced wasn't important enough for her to worry about. I doubt the impact of my minimalizing her sentiments was comforting in any way. The effect would more likely have been a message along the lines of "Your experience doesn't count" or maybe "It's all in your head." I've had people dismiss my concerns; it's shaming and alienating.

My inadequate frame of reference allowed Sara's comments, and the unspoken epic story behind them, to fall away like a bird hitting a window. My lack of understanding of the different worlds we lived in made our cross-racial relationship fraught, as both of us danced around the Zap factor. I certainly gave myself away that day as having very low racial awareness. Did Sara realize at that point my limitations as a friend and colleague? People of color were right to guard themselves against the chance that I would judge their painful experiences as imagined or as the result of some personal weakness, and not as an indication of an unfair system. The system was still invisible to me.

I wonder now how it would have played out had I been more racially aware and able to ask Sara how she felt about going to such a luncheon. I wonder what might have happened if I had had the wherewithal to stay in a conversation with her about the way she felt scrutinized and sized up. What if I had been in touch with my own ethnocentric perspective and could have admitted to myself that what she felt from the white luncheon folks likely was real—that I often found those same questions floating through my head, distracting me from the individual before me? I might have learned a thing or two. She might have felt seen and heard in a way that would have allowed her to open up to tell me more. What if I could have had the courage to take responsibility for my part in what had just happened and had apologized?

How can racism possibly be dismantled until white people, lots and lots of white people, understand it as an unfair system, get in touch with the subtle stories and stereotypes that play in their heads, and see themselves not as good or bad but as players in the system? Until white people embrace the problem, the elephant in the room—and all the nasty tension and mistrust that goes with it—will endure. And the feedback efforts of people of color will fall on ignorant ears at best, or be misconstrued as too whiney or too angry at worst.

At one workshop I attended, a young white teacher from a school with a 96 percent African American student body shared her story of an upsetting back-to-school night she'd experienced a few months earlier. As she'd been organizing her materials for the evening, two black mothers walked in and took their seats. She heard one say to the other, "Uh-huh, she's white. Looks like it's gonna be another bad year."

"Wow, so what did you do?" asked the workshop leader.

"I kept looking down, looking busy. I had to pull it together to make my presentation. I had to keep it together."

"Did you ever address their concern with them?"

The young teacher, and many of us in the room, looked somewhere between perplexed and shocked. *What could she possibly have said?* I remember thinking.

"So, any parents of school kids in the room?" the workshop leader asked. Half of us raised our hands. She called on a white woman. "What do you want from the person who teaches your kid?"

"Um, to know they'll take him seriously, watch out for him, let me know if he's having trouble, make sure he's working hard and doing well. Make sure he has a good year and is ready for the next grade, I guess."

Then she asked, "So, you think that's along the lines of what most parents want?"

We all nodded.

"So how about if you approached those mothers after the presentation, or said it to the whole group, or called parents individually by phone, and said something like, 'I just want you to know I'm working hard on understanding how my being white can get in the way of my being the best teacher for your son. I really want him to have a great year, and I hope you and I can work together to make that happen. Please email me, call me, or come in to talk to me anytime, and I'm open to any feedback you can give me about how I could be doing a better job teaching your son.'"

The idea of trading in my need to be seen as having it all together for being totally honest about how inept I can feel when it comes to racism feels somewhere between liberating and terrifying. Little did I know when I began the awakening process the degree to which I'd need to leave behind my culture of bravado, comfort, and polite conversation to open up and grow.

Q Can you recall a time when you knew there was an elephant in the room and you only discovered what it was later? Once you've recalled that time, make a list of the feelings you experienced. How did you feel once you got the full story and the elephant was exposed?

LEAVING MY COMFORT ZONE

Faith is taking the first step even when
you don't see the whole staircase.

—Martin Luther King Jr.

Just because I didn't mean it to hurt doesn't mean it didn't.

LEAVING THE COMFORT OF MY WHITE WORLD of clear-cut rules so I could learn to navigate multicultural waters was something of a sink-or-swim endeavor. It felt like being tossed from a small, safe swimming pool into an open, at times choppy ocean, all the while being called to from the shore, "Oh, by the way, you can't use any of the strokes you already know." The swimming pool sounds easier, I know, but it came with the promise that all I'd ever reach was the same old concrete edge. And for me, that concrete edge had become soul sapping.

Another motivator to leave my white comfort zone was a growing understanding that people of color swam in unfamiliar and often unfriendly waters every day. They've done so for centuries, disproportionately shouldering the burden of racism's discomfort. The choice to me felt like cop out or dive in. So I dove. Mostly my efforts to learn the new waters of multicultural engagement involved small moments of discomfort and small moments of growth amid an overall feeling of warm connection to new people and ideas. One four-day period, however, stands out for its extreme pain and colossal gain in my quest to understand racism and my place in it.

The phrase "intent versus impact" had been stressed at nearly every conference and conversation about racism I'd been a part of. Race need not be a factor for intent-versus-impact moments to erupt. Everyone can cite examples of times when their intentions have been misunderstood or they've misunderstood another's. Recently I asked my husband the simple question, "Did you empty the dishwasher yet?" My intention was to find out if my favorite coffee cup was clean. Bruce, however, felt as if I were monitoring him. Regardless of my intent, the impact was that he felt nagged and pissed off. The way I meant it, and the way he heard it, were miles apart. Race adds an especially challenging layer. Cultural difference combined with pent-up emotions can lead to complex and charged intent-versus-impact upsets. It didn't take long for me to find myself smack in the middle of one.

On the advice of a racial justice colleague, I'd traveled to California to attend a conference by and for professionals of color. "I know you'll get a lot out of the talks and workshops, but I think the real learning will be the experience of being in the minority," he'd said. I remember thinking, *How different could it be? I have no problem being around people of color. In fact, I really like being around people of color.* Of course, my naïve thinking stemmed in part from the fact that I couldn't imagine what it would feel like because I had never put myself in such a position. There are some things in life you simply can't fathom without personal experience.

The first unexpected sensation was my reaction when walking from the hotel to the gargantuan conference center on day 1. With 2,500 people attending, the street was full of people making the four-block walk from hotel to conference. Most everyone was a person of color. It struck me how unusual it was to see so many confident, well-dressed, black- and brown-skinned people in one place at one time. It also struck me how rare it was to be in a slick downtown area and see predominantly black and brown faces. On the surface I thought, *Great, this is what I'm here for,* but from a deeper part of my consciousness arose a feeling of fear and anxiety. All these people of color looked so professional and composed and joyful. I, in contrast, felt apprehensive, like an imposer and a faker. After all, I had no job and was writing about a subject I was just beginning to learn about when I wasn't even an experienced writer. I felt vulnerable and exposed. I had a rush of fear that came with the thought, *What if this is the future? What if people of color take over the world, and I get reduced to an unappreciated, resented, has-been minority?* As quickly as that thought emerged, a sense of shock and shame overcame me for having had it. *Wow, this is going to be intense,* I thought with a sigh.

Stepping into the crowded, cavernous conference center only increased my uneasiness. I felt an unsettling combination of sticking out like a sore thumb and being invisible. Sticking out because my damn white skin made it impossible for me to blend in. Invisible because most people looked right through me as they made their way to warmly and enthusiastically greet old friends and colleagues. I looked forward to the conference sessions where I hoped I could lie low, be an observer, and fly under the radar.

On the first day I chose to go to a documentary made by professionals of color about the kinds of racial discrimination and discomfort they face from white clients and coworkers. I arrived early and took a seat midway back so as to "blend in." Next to me was a young black woman who put out her hand and introduced herself. She shared with me the work she was doing and listened as I explained my journey and writing project. Grateful for her warmth, I began to relax.

As the workshop began, the filmmakers explained their hope that this documentary would be a powerful and insightful teaching tool for white managers and employees. They noted that they hadn't been able to get the film to its final form in time for the conference, so we'd be viewing a rough cut. *Rough cut?* I perked up. Bruce, who'd been the producer of the TV show *This Old House* for most of our years together, regularly brought home rough cuts. I'd watched hundreds of rough cuts late at night, pencil and paper in hand. My task was to watch and see what the show might need to add or change simply because the production team was too close to the subject. Not knowing a whole lot about home renovation, I was an ideal focus group of one as I watched it with the eyes of an average viewer and pointed out anything that felt unclear. The term "rough cut" allowed me all too easily to slip back into the familiar role of advisor. I watched, taking notes for "helpful" feedback.

When the lights came up and the Q&A began, a black woman stood up and said something like, "Whether this is good or not, I want to know why we're making the same damn film we made ten years ago. Why are we still dealing with the same old issues?" Her frustration moved me. I raised my hand and stood up to share my observations.

"The anecdotes in the film aren't as clear to me as I wish," I said. "I feel like, as a white person, I need more detail to really get what you're saying." I gave an example of one anecdote that did hit me hard, because of the level of detail in it.

A woman in the front row turned around and said in a tone that let me know I'd said something wrong, "What *details* do *you* need to know about *our* stories?"

I tried to elaborate, but sensing I had said something wrong, and being clueless as to what it might be, I began to fumble. Another woman stood up and strongly suggested I "study my whiteness." A third stood to tell me I was "just the kind of person" who would send one of her community members to her office devastated by hurtful racist behavior. I listened, crushed by the degree to which I felt misunderstood and falsely accused. I wanted to defend myself and started to stand. The young woman beside me put her hand on my leg and whispered, "Don't—there's a lot of history in this room." I sat, feeling the eyes of all 150 people on me.

That I slipped into an old rough-cut-watching role was certainly a part of what happened to me in that room that day. That's the easy explanation. The harder thing to understand and acknowledge is how readily I slipped into a comfortable old role of the white person who feels entitled to express her opinion and offer advice. When I'd heard the black woman's frustration, I also slipped right into my old white role of being a fixer and a comforter. Though this is what comes naturally in my white world, I had no idea how misplaced my efforts were in this one. Why was it so hard for me to allow the people in that room to feel and process their own emotions and ideas? Where might the conversation have gone had I not interrupted? Why on earth did I think I had the answers—or even the questions? I robbed from the workshop organizers and attendees a chance to do their own important work. Robin Hood strikes again. For this I have deep regret.

When the workshop ended, five men and women of color and one white man approached me with looks of distress and empathy on their faces. For the first five or so minutes, all I wanted to do was explain my intent or, more accurately, hide behind my intent in an effort to protect myself from my own sense of regret, humiliation, and vulnerability.

After patiently listening to me and generously acknowledging my good intent, the group encouraged me not to take it personally but to shift my focus from my intent to the impact I'd had. They helped me to see that just by standing and speaking, I'd reminded some people in the room just how sick and tired they were of white people thinking they have the answers. It had not been my intent, but it definitely was the impact, at least for some. Another thing I learned that day was never to ask a person of color for more detail in their stories of discrimination, at least not without careful consideration of the context and the person or people involved. My words, so innocuous to me, had, at least for the three women who spoke up, been heard as "I don't believe you" or "Those stories aren't good enough; give me details that show me some real pain."

The people who had approached me stayed with me for a full hour, missing their own next sessions, which in a way made me feel even more shame. Now I'd messed up a whole workshop *and* six people's chances to go the workshops they'd probably carefully circled in their programs. Though I don't know what moved the five people of color to stay with me that day, I am forever indebted to them for the lessons they offered me. Facing up to the unintended impact I could unleash on people through sheer ignorance was painful. It humbled me and motivated me to become more of a learner and less of a knower. It taught me that efforts to defend my intent in the name of my "good person" status had no place in this world or in my efforts to learn and grow.

Even though for me it felt like a personal attack, I now understand that for most if not all of the people of color in the room that day, I triggered an unleashing of years of stored and recycled pain, whether they stood to tell me about it or not. After all the centuries of hurt and oppression white people have inflicted on people of color, I can see how my actions, and my very presence, could stir up feelings of rage, especially at a conference in which people of color are supposed to be having the rare experience of letting down their guard, safe among racial peers.

Unfortunately I had none of this perspective while at the conference. It took months for me to fully internalize the lessons I learned that day and transform them from painful memories into critical wisdom. At first I just felt bullied and misunderstood. "I feel like I should leave this conference," I whimpered to the group standing near me. I felt as if all eyes would be on me as I walked the halls and attended other sessions. White me sticking out like a sore thumb. White me shuffling around the conference reminding people of a truly awful moment. "What if just seeing me reinjures people?" I asked the group. I wanted to hop on a plane and go home to my white family, who knew and loved me.

"Are you kidding? What you said was nothing compared to what those people have lived through," one guy said.

"I promise you we're all going to learn a lot from this. Don't go. Stay, stay for me," another guy pleaded.

"You'll be suffering over this long after they will. They're probably already done with this one. No one's as in this as you," a woman added.

I realized in this moment that thinking about or dealing with the emotionally fraught subject of racism is a choice for me. I could walk away. I could retreat to my white world, where racism would be off my radar. But five of the people standing around me, and any person of color who has ever lived in America, must think about and deal with racism on a daily basis. For me to have walked away in this intensely uncomfortable moment would have been invoking my white privilege. Though I wanted more than anything to leave, I stayed.

I stayed and had the most powerful experience I would have throughout this entire process. To say my feelings were raw would be an understatement. Every once in a while I'd feel a tickle on my cheek, only to find my fingers wet with tears when I went to scratch it. Of the many feelings I experienced in the following days, one must have been grief. I grieved for the mess we were all in and for the life of blissful ignorance I'd compromised in choosing to dive into it. I grieved for the hurt I'd inflicted on others. I grieved for the breakdown of my own naiveté.

I couldn't shake the standing-out-like-a-sore-thumb feeling. I became acutely aware of how I might be perceived. I worked myself into an anxious state of second-guessing my words and actions. I felt as if I'd not only disappointed myself and others at the workshop but dealt a blow to the generations of white people who'd been working to dismantle racism for years. I'd shamed not just myself but my entire race. I felt pressure to be either invisible or perfect, yet I'd just discovered how impossible it would be for me to be either outside of my white world.

Unlike my home culture, in which I could sniff my way through social cues effortlessly, this one had me feeling like a fish out of water, guessing at how to behave, when to speak and when not to, what to say and what not to. I wondered how much of this sore-thumb, fish-out-of-water feeling translated to the experiences of people of color, so often in the minority at schools and workplaces. Imagining the ways I might be sticking out, screwing up, or disgracing my race put me in survival mode, a mere shadow of my best self. I thought of the phrase "lonely only" that one of my black friends used to describe times he'd been the only person of color in a meeting. Sticking out feels awful. The pressure of representing my entire race was more than I wanted to bear. Not being seen as an individual demoralized me. Being judged as a brand that packed a four-hundred-year-old punch made me feel invisible and worthless.

I longed for my family, for people who knew me. If this were at all representative of the experience of a minority in a white person's world, I concluded, I'd have been a tragic person of color. I don't believe I could have weathered such stress with anything close to grace. More likely I'd have ended up feeling either very small and depressed or very big and angry.

Think of a time when you hurt someone's feelings without intending to. Was your impulse to defend yourself? If so, why do you think that urge to defend your intention felt so important? If you eventually shifted from focusing on your intent to focusing on the impact of your words or actions, what inspired you to do so? What was ultimately required to heal the rift?

Freeing myself from the conflict-free world of WASP etiquette.

ONE OF MY FIRST CHALLENGES in the hours and days following the workshop upset was to stay at the conference and just let the feelings come. Avoiding negative emotions was a remnant of my upbringing that still fit like an old glove. The process of socialization I underwent in my early years to adjust my naturally emotional self to the more constrained customs and expectations of my culture left me with some less than helpful coping skills. Rather than face feelings like anger, embarrassment, or guilt head-on, my first reaction usually involved an urge to run, defend myself, blame someone, or have a stiff drink. Over time, however, I'd learned to listen to my grown-up self and remember that if I didn't deal with unwanted feelings, they'd catch up with me sooner or later.

As much as I wanted to escape the conference, I understood that staying and using the discomfort to learn and grow would be the wiser choice. One of the things that kept me going was the indebtedness I felt to the rough-cut group who had supported me in my worst moment. Rarely in my life had people engaged with me so authentically during a time of distress. In my culture, we would have pretended everything was fine, that it wasn't a big deal. I too once thought avoiding painful topics the best tonic for one who's hurting. Had a family member or friend from my home culture seen what happened in the rough-cut workshop, I'm guessing they'd have called home and, with the best of intentions, forewarned others in a hushed tone, "Don't ask Debby about the workshop. It didn't go so well." I would have pretended to be fine around this person and then distracted myself with one of my aforementioned avoidance tactics. This was my first experience of having a group of people—strangers, at that—help me hold my pain and encourage me to stick with the discomfort to learn from it. In a strange sense, I felt more cared for and understood by my workshop allies than by many people I'd known for years. I felt broken yet connected, in pain but acknowledged, a welcome contrast to what I'd known for much of my life.

My parents—warm, funny, kind, and smart, so competent in so many ways—were utterly unprepared for one thing in life: navigating emotional conflict. Typical of their era, race, and class, they believed unpleasantries belonged under the rug, where, the hope must've been, the magic winds of time would blow them away. Bucking up and soldiering on without complaint—this is how successful people got on. Our ancestors did it, and so should we.

I'm guessing more than a few people reading this will say, "Wait a minute—my family's white, and we yelled and screamed at each other all the time." Not every white family buys into the culture of niceness and shuts off their feelings. In fact, I'm guessing my brother, who married a French woman, may have this very response. When he first met his wife's family, he couldn't believe the way they'd erupt with anger, hear each other out, and be done with it, moving on with the conversation or day's activities as if nothing out of the ordinary had just happened. It's true: not all white families adopt the dominant WASP culture as thoroughly as mine did. However, for centuries, people have learned that in America's classrooms, boardrooms, and public places, those who most often succeed are those who conform to the dominant culture prototype, which demands emotional restraint.

In my home, expressing "troublesome" feelings not only was not rewarded but was met with punishment in the form of silence or being exiled to my room. Complaints brought a quick "You'll be fine," perhaps intended to reassure me but having the impact of making me think I shouldn't feel the way I did. The message I took from it was that negative feelings were wrong, and something was wrong with me for having them. I learned to keep my unseemly emotions to myself until, over time, I learned not to feel them at all. The admonition "If you don't have anything nice to say, don't say anything at all" served as a cultural signpost as I developed an acute sense of what not to say and what not to feel in order to remain valued.

One of my earliest memories of trying to resist the culture of niceness into which I was being indoctrinated has to do, coincidentally, with a race-related family upset. My oldest sister, Diane, was nineteen, and I was five. The year was 1965. One day at breakfast, Diane was crying—something I'd never seen her do before.

"What's going on? Why are you crying, Diane?" I asked. Her vulnerability made me uneasy. Her sadness made my heart heavy. She didn't answer.

Eventually another sister, Emily, eleven at the time, leaned over and whispered, "Mom and Dad won't let her go to *A Patch of Blue*." *A Patch of Blue*, Emily explained, was a movie in which a "Negro" kissed a white girl. Diane's boyfriend had invited her to go see it with him. I couldn't grasp the problem. I had no idea what a "Negro" was—a cookie, maybe? Furthermore, I couldn't remember my parents ever saying no to a movie.

I started in again. "Why can't she go? I don't get it."

I couldn't stand Diane's crying and my siblings' awkward silence. I got up from the table and tracked down my mother. I found her in the sewing room.

"I think it's stupid Diane can't go to that movie," I said defiantly. "I think you should let her go."

My mother, working on a sewing project, ignored me. To my right sat a McCall's dress pattern piece she had laid out, its delicate brown translucent paper ready for tracing the fabric beneath it. I reached up, crumpled it, and whipped it at her like a snowball. Now I had her attention. She glared at me, hands on hips, her lower jaw thrusting forward. We stared at each other. We stared and we stared, until she turned away from me and leaned onto the sewing machine table, her clenched fists now open, holding her up, as she began to weep. She had been trained over a lifetime not to raise her voice or to engage in conflict, so her anger and confusion must have turned to tears because she felt completely unprepared to navigate the confrontation I presented. "Go to your room," she whispered weakly.

So through the house I wound, to my room, none of my questions answered, feeling an anxiety-provoking mix of guilt and anger and concluding that raising objections and questions made me less loveable. I learned nothing that day about what the word "Negro" meant or how my family felt about dark-skinned people. I learned nothing of the civil rights movement and its activists, who had risked lives to make a black man kissing a white woman legal. All I learned was not to come out of my room until I had made myself right. Sociologists would say this is an example of how a culture uses rewards and punishments to enforce its cultural norms. This one—emotional restraint and its partner denial—sunk its claws into me, leaving scars that would take years to heal.

I internalized this "Nice is good" norm so thoroughly that I came to loathe conflict and judge harshly those uncivilized enough to stir it. I bristled when anyone—even my own husband—raised unpleasant subjects, created conflict, or expressed anger. *Poorly raised*, I'd conclude. Though I don't think my parents ever actually used the term "poorly raised," the number of times they referred to someone who'd been "well raised" made it clear to me what "poorly raised" would look like.

Internalizing all that optimism at the expense of dealing with negative feelings ultimately cut me off from being able to hear people in distress, even when that person was me. As a young adult, I discovered the fallacy of imagining it possible to selectively turn off some emotions. What I discovered about myself was that my range of emotions could shrink or grow, depending on how much discomfort I was willing to tolerate. The more I could tolerate anger, fear, and grief, the more I could feel joy, love, and serenity. It's the old "No pain, no gain" philosophy. The culture of niceness did nothing short of program me away from my humanity and into a socially scripted role with diminished capacity to feel my way through situations.

Like so many of the behaviors I adopted in childhood, silence and avoidance became subconscious habits. My parents didn't silence me because they didn't care about my ideas. They silenced me because their own childhood socializations engrained in them a subconscious habit of steering away from conflict and authenticity and toward the more socially accepted culture of niceness. They were passing onto me a survival skill, one that bought a place in the high-class world of comfort and gentility, even if that meant diminishing one's capacity to plug into the circuitry of feelings, cutting oneself off from one's own heart and soul.

I adored my parents and the many other fun-loving adults in my life, the very adults whose approval I sought and around whom I learned to douse my emotions and buck up. But did I connect to them deeply? Did I really know what was in their hearts and souls? Did I know their fears or shames in a way that would allow me to be supportive, a way that would allow me to feel less fearful or repulsed by my own? In all honesty I have to say no. I did not know my parents or my aunts and uncles or any of my parents' friends in this way. Our relationships were not the kind in which unfettered conversation leads to greater common understanding and deep personal connection.

In 1994, at the age of seventy-one, my mother suffered a massive brain hemorrhage. She never fully recovered, largely because she was in the early stages of Alzheimer's when it struck. Though her body would survive another twelve years, I will always feel that 1994 was when I lost her. I was thirty-four years old with a five-week-old baby, just beginning to gather questions to ask my own mother now that I had become one myself. Her loss all but shattered me.

As she lay in the hospital following brain surgery, I wandered around her room at home looking for clues as to what her last days and hours had been like. On her bedside table I noticed the book *Too Good for Her Own Good*. A bookmark sat wedged in a page about three-fourths of the way through the book. *My God, when and why did she get this?* I wondered. I turned it over and read the back cover. My heart pounded as I read the words "work so hard to be so good—and end up feeling so hopelessly inadequate." I fell to my knees, clutched the book to my chest, and wept. I wanted her back to ask her why she went out and bought this book. In what ways did she feel inadequate? Was the book helping her? Was she talking to Dad about it? We'd never dug this deep together, and now, just as I was losing her, it seemed she was willing to do the kind of self-examination that would have brought us closer. Never having had the opportunity to sit with her and hear about all her thoughts and feelings, the good and the bad, the humiliating and the heroic, still haunts me.

Whom exactly does the culture of niceness serve? I suppose it serves the people for whom life is going well, the people in power. But where does this leave less empowered individuals and populations with legitimate complaints? Speaking truth to power too often results in feelings of judgment and anger at the complainer. The way my mother ignored and silenced me when I tried to advocate for my sister's desire to see *A Patch of Blue* is not so far off from the way people in power have long ignored and silenced entire populations who voice injustice. It's hard work to engage in conflict, and even harder to have to change your mind. People in power have the privilege of avoiding both. The culture of niceness provides a tidy cover, creating a social norm that says conflict is bad, discomfort should be avoided, and those who create them mark themselves as people who lack the kind of emotional restraint necessary to hold positions of power. Another vicious cycle. What a predicament for people of color, and what a debilitating deficit for those who buy into it. Ignoring feelings and trying to smooth them over with pleasant chitchat only promises to hold people back from allowing their hearts to join their minds in recognizing injustice when it's right in front of them, or even inside them.

Despite its potential to create healthier individuals, households, organizations, and communities, embracing the discomfort of conflict in the name of resolution eludes most people raised in the culture of niceness. As long as feedback from unhappy people puts the blame on the complainer, the status quo will be maintained. Change requires tolerating the kind of emotions that arise when the constraints of nice conversations are lifted. I've long felt the term "tolerance," as related to racial and cultural difference, isn't quite right. I've understood it to mean that I'm supposed to tolerate people who aren't like me. Is tolerating someone really the best I can do? Tolerance was what I mustered up when my toddler was having a tantrum and I knew I simply had to endure it.

If there's a place for tolerance in racial healing, perhaps it has to do with tolerating my own feelings of discomfort that arise when a person, of any color, expresses an emotion not welcome in the culture of niceness. It also has to do with tolerating my own feelings of shame, humiliation, regret, anger, and fear so I can engage, not run. For me, tolerance is not about others; it's about accepting my own uncomfortable emotions as I adjust to a changing view of myself as imperfect and vulnerable. As human.

Q What lessons were you taught about crying? Do you feel differently if you see a man, woman, or child crying? For whom do you tend to feel empathy? For whom do you tend to feel judgment? Why?

Learning to listen and speak across difference.

THE COMFORTABLE, POLITE WORLD OF MY YOUTH not only made me fearful about saying something wrong but left me empty-handed in terms of having the skills to navigate an upset should one occur. Much of the work happening in diversity and antiracism addresses this dominant culture limitation by creating conversational ground rules to guide the group through potentially volatile conversations. A typical list might look like this:

- share airtime
- speak or pass as you like
- speak honestly from your own perspective; use "I" statements
- notice when you judge others
- respect confidentiality
- welcome discomfort—this can be where growth happens

Guidelines like these reflect the value placed on the kind of honesty required to build enduring understanding and trust. I appreciate the settings in which I am freed from having to make nice, where comments are considered no matter how partially formed or controversial they may be. The risk may be a blowout like the rough-cut workshop, but the reward of being in the mess together, where we increase the chances of healing the divide together, seems well worth it.

At one such workshop, the topic was "invisible differences." As opposed to visible differences such as race, gender, and physical ability, people can hide or disguise invisible differences such as class, sexual orientation, religion, and mental illness—engaging in what is called "covering." Success at covering, however, often comes at a terrible cost, one the school hosting the workshop wanted to explore. The organizers decided to expand the definition of "invisible differences" to include any way in which one feels inadequate or ashamed. Participants were asked to write down on an index card something that weighed on them daily but that they would not feel comfortable sharing publicly within the school community. The hope was to better understand how the school's culture might be alienating people by sending the signal that unpleasant subjects are taboo. The cards were collected, tossed in a basket, and passed around, one to each participant. Each person then read from the card they'd picked, none of us able to link the sentiment to its author. As the cards were read, the room grew heavy. People had written phrases like "I worry every day about money," "I don't know what I'd do if my child told me he was gay," "I feel too old to change careers and am unhappy with the one I'm in," "I struggle with an eating disorder."

One white woman began to weep. "I have no idea why I'm crying," she said. "I'm sorry." She looked embarrassed by her tears.

A few of us white people offered up explanations.

"People never talk about this stuff."

"It feels like a weight gets lifted when we do."

"Maybe they're tears of relief."

A friend of mine who also attended the workshop and is black chuckled, shook his head, and said something like, "It's kind of shocking for me to hear you say you don't talk about this kind of stuff. This feels like normal to me. In my family, and with my friends, and in my church, we talk about this stuff all the time. This is everyday conversation." Then he shook his head again and asked, "What *do* you talk about?"

"The weather," a white man said sheepishly. Nervous laughter filled the room.

As we walked back to our cars, I turned to my friend and said, "You know, there I was growing up in Winchester with all the material comforts a kid could want, and what I wanted more than anything was the kind of honest conversation and connection you and your family had in Harlem."

I don't believe anyone really benefits from having to hide who they are and what they feel. For people who fit the cultural norm—white, Christian, heterosexual, and so forth—the culture of niceness might be more palatable. But how are people who do not fit the narrow norm supposed to cope if just speaking one's truth can result in further marginalization?

As a teenager in the 1960s and '70s, I remember thinking the feminist movement was full of poorly raised women. *Stop complaining,* I silently judged and scorned. *It makes you look foolish. Just make yourself likeable, and then maybe you'll get what you want.* My youth and my upbringing had shielded me from understanding what it meant to be overlooked for a promotion or to make less money than a man for the same job. I failed to appreciate the impact of being excluded from all-male clubs and sports, where essential professional ties were formed and strengthened. All I heard was a whiny "What about me?" that my upbringing had taught me deserved condemnation. Today I bow to these women for having had the courage to make their voices heard and paving the way for a world in which my daughters and I have increased respect and rights.

I've come to feel that the straightforward airing of experiences and beliefs is a necessary, albeit uncomfortable, pathway to interpersonal and intercultural understanding and healing. Intimate human connection and enduring trust are the rewards of courageous conversation. The trick for me has been learning to stay in the conversation long enough to get to the other side, where niceness gives way to authenticity, understanding, and trust, the ingredients necessary for social stability. The futility of sweeping grievances under the rug rests in the reality that they don't disappear, they can still be felt, and worst of all, they fester and create more discord. These days I find the tension of avoiding fraught topics far more uncomfortable than a head-on courageous conversation.

In retrospect, thinking I could control or deny negative feelings sounds ludicrous. Thinking I shouldn't feel this way or that way is like thinking I shouldn't be thirsty. I can't not feel thirsty if I am. I can't not feel angry if I am. I can do something about both, but only if I first acknowledge the sensation. If my words or behaviors are hurting someone, I want to know so I can do something about it. I much prefer a room of outwardly angry people than a room of polite, silently seething ones because I'd rather know what I'm dealing with than try to guess at it. No problem can be appropriately addressed without an honest assessment of its form, warts and all.

I think of how I stifled my feelings as a child, how I pressed them down. Then I turned around and did it to other people. Isn't this what "oppression" is? Pressing down and invalidating feelings and pressing down and invalidating people? The great irony is that while denying negative emotion and feedback might be an attempt to maintain individual or group control, it actually fuels anxiety and social unrest, states of being that then require more efforts to control. It's the psychological equivalent of "Penny wise, pound foolish."

Though some may worry that opening ourselves individually or collectively to negative feelings or to angry people will result in all hell breaking loose, I would suggest that the state of racism in America is a brewing, toxic stew. Allowing anger and mistrust to fester between groups of people promises a cycle of division in which each group can reaffirm its narrative about the other, keeping us in a self-destructive holding pattern. Not wanting to live in a state of unresolved conflict motivates me to learn to dive into it with enough skill so that the other side—resolution—might be reached.

I think about the angry-black-man stereotype and my old thought, *If only they weren't so angry!* What an ignorant and inhumane mindset that was. People aren't born angry. People don't choose arbitrarily to be angry. People become angry for a reason, and they deserve to be heard. I know that when I'm angry, nothing makes me madder than to air my frustration only to be ignored or judged. In contrast, nothing diffuses it faster than someone showing a sincere desire to understand what's agitating me. Were I to choose to ignore people of color's complaints about unfair living, working, lending, health care, education, and law enforcement conditions, I'd basically be saying, "Don't rain on my parade." I'd be telling them, "Quit your complaining because it's stressing me out." I would be declaring that my right to feel good and comfortable is more important than theirs. To judge their complaints as illegitimate would be like saying, "I know your world better than you do, and I'm telling you that you have nothing to complain about. Just buck up and soldier on." I might use the logic, "It worked for me, see?" I might even be thinking, "You're less of a person for having complained about it in the first place." I'd be using my white life experience to explain theirs.

Ignoring and invalidating dissatisfaction and anger is tantamount to throwing gasoline on a fire. White people must learn how to listen to the experiences of people of color for racial healing and justice to happen. I've heard it said that conversations are the way human beings think together. That helps me as I embolden myself to take part in listening to truths I wish did not exist.

Q Make a deal with someone you trust in order to practice giving and getting honest feedback. Set your own guidelines, such as: If I ask your opinion, you will give me an honest answer, even if you know it might hurt, or, Feel free to gently point out to me [name one of your flaws] when I do it, so that I can increase my awareness of when and where I do it. Keep in mind the words of pastor Warren Wiersbe, "Truth without love is brutality and love without truth is hypocrisy."

The liberation of letting go of my self-image.

IF THE IDEA of being in the midst of a courageous conversation is making you break out in hives, let me give you another way to think about it. One of the motivations for me to get into and stay in the conversation is knowing that in our racialized social scheme, white people have been given not only better access to America's goods and services but disproportionate amounts of comfort, safety, and choice, including the ultimate choice—whether or not to deal with racism.

Choosing to engage in the effort to dismantle racism promises to bring with it discomfort, yet how can I compare my discomfort to what people of color endure? If someone had told me, prior to this journey, that I would attend a workshop where I would be called out by three enraged black women in front of 150 onlookers, mostly people of color, I would have cringed and said, "No thanks, I don't want to go down that road." When I think about the fear of saying something wrong that held me back for so long, I think I was a whole lot less afraid of hurting a person of color, actually, than I was of saying something that would expose my ignorance and make me look bad. I was working overtime to protect my self-image and my ego. As my friend Vernā Myers likes to say, "Get over yourself!"

How silly, really, that when confronting a four-hundred-year-old problem that includes millions of people, I should put my own self-image front and center. Where did this fervent desire to protect some imagined self-image come from, anyway? In a culture that espouses belief in the rugged individual, placing myself as a solo player at the center of my universe isn't all that surprising. After all, if the belief is that success and failure ride on individual merit, it puts a lot of pressure on individuals to be damn near perfect. The sense of freedom that came when I let go of worrying about "how good I am" at courageous conversations, or antiracist work, or life in general has sent new currents of energy through my body. Embracing humility has opened up my heart and mind and made way for vital relationships with people of all colors.

For so much of my life, wanting to be perceived as flawless caused me not only to avoid tricky conversations but to feel horrible about myself if I wasn't measuring up to some cultural standard. This came to a head when I had my first child. I had a husband with a good job, a tidy little condo in a family-friendly neighborhood, a healthy baby, and the extraordinary luxury of being a stay-at-home parent. But there was a hitch—an invisible, secret hitch. Though I didn't yet know what was happening to me, I was trapped in a severe case of postpartum depression. I hid from everyone but my husband just how out-of-sorts I was feeling. The shame was suffocating.

Never having experienced depression before, I had no idea what had hit me. All I knew was that as my friends happily plopped their kids in their snugglies and headed off on excursions, I could barely get out of the house because of exhaustion and anxiety. Unlike the kind of postpartum depression in which women have no interest in their babies, or want to hurt them, I lived in fear of dying and abandoning my baby. I dropped into a hole of hypochondria that twisted my head and body into something unrecognizable. Every ache, pain, and twitch sent my mind into a flurry of possible diseases and an irrational fear of leaving my baby motherless. The anxiety flooded my body with unfamiliar sensations. I didn't understand what was happening to me, and the cycle of anxiety worsened.

I didn't dare tell anyone about it for fear it would damage my image as a rugged individual capable of bucking up, soldiering on, and never complaining. So I kept it to myself—which only made it worse. Finally, after about five months, when I was so wracked with anxiety I could barely sleep, I told my doctor. Once I learned I had postpartum depression and that many people experienced it, it quickly subsided. I marveled at how just naming it and talking openly about it took away its power and allowed the healing process to begin.

As I began to feel like myself again, I started telling close family and friends about the experience. The more open I became about a condition I thought might make me a social pariah, the more common I found it was and the more the idea of it normalized. It stunned me to have close friends and family lean closer and tell me for the first time, "Oh my God, Debby, I have panic attacks all the time," or "My sister had postpartum depression too." These were people I'd known for years. Why were we all hiding from one another? In my experience, vulnerability, the opposite of bravado, is where humanity reconnects and recharges its circuitry. It is the hardware of the life force that sustains us.

Getting over myself in the racism department has been similar. All that effort I put into maintaining my self-image served only to strengthen racism's invisible hold on me. Talking about how I experience racism, even when it's unpleasant, even when it betrays my own level of ignorance or stored racialized thoughts, is like taking the top off a boiling pot.

My heart has been touched many times in these past few years, each time I see the curiosity and hope in the eyes of people of color when I admit I didn't understand racism until I was nearly fifty years old. When I describe my efforts to understand how being white shaped my views and allowed me to perpetuate racism without knowing it, I see shoulders relax, and often a smile. Sometimes I even hear words to the effect of "Good for you." Ironic, isn't it, that admitting my ignorance and missteps is what is considered "good" in the eyes of those not attached to the idea of perfection but to the idea of truth?

Q How do you want people to see you? List five adjectives you'd hope people would use. What behaviors do you employ to convey this image? How would admitting ignorance or wrongdoing, no matter how unintentional, challenge your desired image?

The first time I saw myself as white—and scary.

LEAVING MY COMFORT ZONE didn't just create uncomfortable moments in the public realm; it unraveled me in a way that produced moments of private terror. Undoing the construct that had held my self-image intact for forty-eight years could be compared to having a cast removed. I've had a few casts, and each time they came off, I have wanted to cradle my limb and protect it; it felt exposed and weak. Reconstructing my racial identity, in comparison, involved not a limb but my entire being, inside and out.

If the rough-cut workshop was my worst public moment, the day I freaked out at my own white skin was the worst private moment. It happened one cold winter morning about a year into my waking-up process. In the weeks prior I'd been reading accounts of people of color's views on white people's physical attributes. I'd learned that the sight of white men by Native Americans incited shock: white men were "monstrous, hairy and pale skinned" with "eyes the color of the sea and hair the color of the sun." I learned that in some African American novels whites were described as having skin "the color of dead fish," "lank" hair, "clammy" hands, and boringly flat rear ends. "Thin-lipped," I learned, was a common way of describing white people. I found out that in some parts of the world white people are referred to as *gwailos*, a word stemming from the Cantonese term *gwai lo*, meaning "ghost man." In China, many refer to white people as "pink" people.

As I delved into this perception reversal, I became hyperaware of people's physical attributes. I couldn't look at a person without studying their face and skin tone. I noticed how different we all are, including within racial groups, and became acutely aware of my lifelong habit of measuring people of color's features against the prototypical white face, which happened to look a lot like mine. Why would one person's nose be considered big and not mine small? What is normal? Is there even such a thing? I listened to the news and wondered who ever chose that American newscaster accent to be the standard? Which part of the country is that accent from? I began to lose all sense of normal. Everything seemed to become fodder for examination.

In addition to my intellectual world eroding, now my physical world was starting to morph. As much as I understood the importance of leaving my comfort zone, I had not anticipated such extreme disorientation. Just a year after that first Wheelock class, little in my life felt the same anymore. I woke up every day feeling lost and afraid. I experienced bouts of dizziness and waves of nausea that could be stopped only by sitting and hanging my head between my knees. I kept a bottle of ginger ale with me at all times to quell the nausea.

One cold, dark winter morning, as I moved through my predawn routine, I stumbled downstairs, put on the teakettle, and went into the bathroom near the kitchen. Only half awake, I flicked on the light and caught sight of myself in the mirror. I jumped back in horror. There in the mirror were two bright blue eyes set against dead-fish white skin and unkempt hair the color of the sun. As quickly as the bathroom light had hit my eyes, a narrative of imposing white power had knocked the wind out of me. A montage of scary white faces streamed in opaquely over my own. First Hitler, then Yul Brynner in *Westworld*, and then a stream of white men in business suits whose images had filled my youth; all scrolled past my eyes, on the mirror, like a hallucination. I flicked off the light and bolted to the living room, where I dove for the couch and buried myself in a blanket. Suddenly I could see how a white person could engender not only the fear of "otherness" but the fear of an "other" with power—the power to choose my fate.

Perception, I realized, is a completely mutable thing. At times in my life the sight of a black man could spark fear in me. Now the sight of my own white face and blue eyes had aroused the same feeling, maybe worse. My own coloring had suddenly become a logo for the horrors I was learning white people had inflicted on people of color over the centuries. Though my own face is probably the most familiar thing to me on the planet, seeing white people through the eyes of people of color was what was unfamiliar. For the first time I saw myself as the "other."

Part of the terror I felt in the following hours was the fear that maybe I'd undone something and would never be able to put it back together again. I wondered if psyches had ever imploded while in the process of racial reconstruction. I called my fellow WASP friend and colleague Barbara Beckwith, who was not only older and wiser but ten years ahead of me on this journey. I told her what had happened to me, and she laughed and said, "Oh that's fantastic! Write that down! Write that down! That's amazing." (Barbara is a writer.)

"But what if I can never again look at myself without freaking out?" I asked. "Did you go through this?"

"Oh, you'll get through it. I never had that happen. It's different for everyone." She paused before plunging back into her mentor role. "Write! Write about it while it's fresh!"

She was right: the sense of terror and the spells of dizziness and nausea soon faded away. What remains to this day, however, is a sense of the symbolism that comes with white faces, white skin. Especially when I see photographs of white men in power—gathered around a boardroom or signing legislation—I feel a shiver of dissonance as I simultaneously feel my before and after responses. The very same image that once evoked comforting thoughts like, Look at those good, important men doing that good work, now also stirs the uncomfortable thought, This imbalance of power is so messed up.

I think about the 2008 election of President Obama. The warmth and unity many felt on election night and Inauguration Day quickly gave way to expressions of fear by white people behaving as if an invader had just taken over the White House. President Obama's black skin allowed his opponents to stray from political disagreement to racialized bullying. I watched in horror as anti-Obama actions sought to redraw the lines around the category "black man." Tragic pieces of white American history resurfaced, reigniting racial tensions. A New York tabloid cartoon portrayed the president as a monkey. The mayor of Los Alamitos, California, broadcast an email titled "No Easter Egg Hunt This Year," showing the White House lawn covered in watermelons. As this "otherization" through mockery incited white anxiety across the country, ammunition stores found themselves barely able to keep up with demand. Fear begets fear. Instead of uniting the people of the United States into a "more perfect union," the election of President Barack Obama served as a reminder of how deep in our waters the fear of the other runs.

There's nothing like fear to distort perception. During the 2008 presidential campaign, I listened to an NPR-hosted roundtable conversation with fifteen people from York, Pennsylvania. Representing an array of backgrounds, the group discussed the impact of a black candidate and potential president. A white woman, whose honesty I admire, admitted this: "I don't want to sound racist, and I'm not racist, but I feel if we put Obama in the White House, there will be chaos. I feel a lot of black people are going to feel it's payback time. . . . You know, at one time the black man had to step off the sidewalk when a white person came down the sidewalk. . . . And I feel it's going to be somewhat reversed. I really feel it's going to get somewhat nasty." A black male participant responded to her by acknowledging her fear, guessing it was in part a general fear of change, but ultimately reassuring her that what he'd anticipate would be cheering and dancing in the streets. He envisioned high fives all around, an atmosphere of liberation-induced exuberance, not oppression-produced rage. I imagine, though, that for white people who don't have regular conversations about race with close friends of color, there's plenty of suspicion that people of color want to re-create the current power system by reversing roles. Replacing oppression with equity is all I've heard people of color ask for.

One of the many gifts I've received by getting to know people of color who are working to dismantle racism has been learning about the rich and loving spirit of the dominant black culture. Dr. Martin Luther King's concept of the "Beloved Community," a vision of complete racial, class, and national integration and brotherhood, reflects a deep love of the human family and a desire for everyone to thrive. As I wrote this book, I periodically had white friends and family read it and offer feedback. "Beloved Community" more often than not evoked a "Yes! I want that too!" scrawled in the margins. I believe most white Americans want equity and believe in "Beloved Community." Why, then, is it so hard to make it a common goal?

Wanting is not enough. Intent and skill are our swords and shields in the war to dismantle a system with a life of its own. As People's Institute for Survival and Beyond trainer Suzanne Plihcik pointed out, "Just because I want my neighbor in the hospital to heal from cancer doesn't mean I get to go in there and operate on him." The same is true with racism. If we don't take on the task of educating ourselves about how to dismantle racism, both in ourselves and in our communities, we can do more harm than good.

Q Imagine a country inhabited by two groups of people. The groups can't stand each other. This is equal-opportunity prejudice. Now imagine that your group runs the bank, the government, the schools, the hospitals, and the media. Your group has the power to make your opinions the dominant ones while creating policies and practices that marginalize the other group. List the feelings and thoughts that might develop by being a part of the group in power. Then list the feelings and thoughts that might develop by being a part of the group not in power.

INNER WORK

Whenever a transition is called for,
view it as your soul knocking at the door of your life,
bearing more gifts for you to bring to the world.
Change is a call from your soul to grow.

—Sonia Choquette

Learning to navigate a complex world by using multiple approaches.

CREATING A RACIALLY JUST WORLD demands a reconsideration of the assimilation ("melting pot") model long enforced in America. By creating one dominant culture and multiple pissed-off, marginalized sub-cultures, the approach has wreaked havoc on America's economic and social systems. Though its intention may have been to create a united country, its impact has been to create social and economic divisions far from the ideals of most Americans. Continuing to pursue that path only promises more discord and wasted human potential.

The alternative, a multicultural approach, makes sense to me for many reasons. First and foremost, it's more humane, and more humane means more people able to strive and achieve. Second, collaboration creates benefits. Cross-cultural collaboration done well expands everyone's ability to innovate and solve problems. But there's a major catch: it's much harder than one might imagine because it starts with personal change. Just as I sought for twenty-five years to bridge the racial divide by "helping" others, many people hope that "helping" or "including" or "celebrating" people from nondominant racial or other cultures is the goal of multiculturalism—that it's all about the "other." In my experience, I could not begin to develop a multicultural sensibility until I first looked deep within myself to understand the ways in which the culture I'd lived in ended up living in me. Skipping over this critical step is what set me up to spend twenty-five years of my life futilely trying to help and fix people so they could align with my personal sense of normal, good, and right.

Just about the time I started thinking about how I'd internalized the cultural values around me, the *New York Times* published an article about how language, a primary cultural tool, shapes the mind. The writer explored the way words such as "left," "right," "above," and "behind" are "egocentric directions," putting the speaker at the center. In contrast, he pointed out, some languages use "geographical directions," using terms like "north" to describe where something is. A person from a geographical direction language sitting next to me on the couch might say, "Please move westward." Though I wouldn't know which way to move unless I had a compass or knew my location intimately enough to know where the sun set, I found it interesting to flip the script. If I said, "Please move to the left" to someone who spoke a geographic direction language, they'd be equally lost. Typical of cultural difference, neither is right or wrong.

Imagine if this person and I spent our lives trying to convince the other that our style of direction giving was the right one. What a waste of time. And how frustrating would that be? Unfortunately, this is what too often happens with cultural difference. Our way feels so right and easy to us that we can't imagine the other culture's approach holds any value for us. And yet it does.

There's no rule that says I have to reject my culture. But if I become aware of its beliefs, values, and practices, I can try to see it as one culture of many and expand my beliefs, values, and practices beyond it in the name of becoming a better global citizen. Learning to value other cultures' ways has demanded of me a kind of psychic stretching that taps into my human potential. As I let go of believing in "one right way," I'm discovering new ways to think about myself and the people and events around me. It allows me to be increasingly adaptable and nimble as I make my way through an increasingly complex world. One of the great ironies in my quest to understand racism is that the very populations I once sought to help and fix are the ones from whom I'm discovering I have so much to learn.

The real beauty of embracing a multicultural approach in America is that we have within one nation multiple cultures from which to learn and collaborate. Because in America people of different races have been segregated in terms of housing, education, and social roles, distinct cultures have developed around each. Unlike me, who grew up in a monocultural world with a household that looked a lot like my school that looked a lot like my workplace, Americans of color, by necessity, have operated across at least two cultures—the dominant culture and their own subculture—sometimes using different languages. Americans of color are already more likely to be multicultural as well as better equipped with strategies to cope with adversity. This is a 180-degree turnaround from the way I've thought about white people and people of color my entire life.

As the twenty-first century continues to bring demographic shifts, globalization, and fast-paced technological developments, change will be the new normal. Change requires flexibility, adaptability, open-mindedness, and resilience—qualities I'm stretching myself to develop but that many people of color already have embedded in their subcultures. Perhaps in the quest to create racial equity the idea of self as a place to start is what Mahatma Gandhi meant when he advised, "Be the change that you wish to see in the world."

Q   Think of a major change you've made in your life—a marriage, a divorce, a move, a new job, a lost job. List the strengths and skills you lost as a result of the change. List the strengths and skills you gained.

After years of wanting to help and fix others,
I learned I had my own work to do.

I FIND IT PARADOXICAL that so often in my life, when I've felt a relationship not working well, I've focused on the other person and how much I wanted *them* to change. Even though changing myself is the one thing I can actually do, it seems to be the thing I've been most resistant to doing. I spent the first ten years of my marriage, for example, ticked off at Bruce, wishing he would just settle down and go with my program. The way he related to time, order, and conflict drove me nuts. If he could just be more like me, I reasoned, we'd be free of these annoying misunderstandings.

"Why exactly do we need an agenda for the weekend, Deb?"

"Because we'll make the most of our time that way," I'd say, thinking, Duh, and expecting a thank-you.

"But what if I just want to hang out and let things happen?"

"We can schedule that in," I'd assure him.

After years of thinking Bruce deficient for not doing and seeing things my way, I had a revelation. One sunny Sunday afternoon, a friend who'd administered the Myers-Briggs personality test to Bruce and me showed up on our doorstep, the analysis tucked neatly under her arm. "This explains a lot," she said, patting the packet, raising her eyebrows, and tossing us a meaningful smile. I imagined the pat and smile indicated that Bruce was about to get straightened out, and we could finally get on with the fairytale marriage he'd been screwing up.

Perhaps you won't be surprised to learn that it was I who would have the epiphany that day. Bruce's answers came up all yin for my yang, driving home the point that he wasn't defective, just differently wired. For those of you who speak Myers-Briggs, we were an ENTP-INFP match made in heaven. While Bruce focused on the outer world, I lived in the realm of ideas. While he lived spontaneously and joyfully, I invested hours planning the specifics of our life. Though I never missed a detail, his freedom from them allowed him an ease I lacked. When I cheerily greeted him each day with a neatly printed to-do list, he felt the walls closing in. I felt unappreciated.

Once we understood that contrasting styles, not character flaws, were at the root of our irritation with one another, we explored the ways our divergent personalities shaped our habits. Increasingly we converted criticism into collaboration, using our complementary styles to be a better team. Our marriage and our parenting styles took on new energy and intelligence as we pursued a common path using our full complement of perspectives and skills. After all those frustrating years of trying to fix Bruce, to make him more like me, I finally found the mate I was looking for when I let him be himself.

Shifting from a superior/inferior paradigm to a strength-in-difference paradigm was kind of a good news/bad news situation. On the downside, I had to admit Bruce had been right to resist my Pygmalion makeover attempts. On the upside, I finally had someone I could work on: me. I noticed my tendency to micromanage him and made a conscious effort to let go. I practiced being a better listener. I kept my mouth shut and tried to put myself in his shoes before speaking. This approach, ironically, gave me the very control I had sought in making our marriage a more livable situation. This I could do, and with a lot less wear and tear. After years of hearing the old adage "You can only change yourself," I finally understood it.

About a year into my waking up white journey, I realized I'd been unknowingly caught in a similar dynamic in the racial arena. During all the years I'd tried to help and fix people of color, part of my subconscious expectation had been that people outside my culture should assimilate to my ways, see and do things the way I'd been taught was right and normal. Unlike in my marriage, however, where Bruce and I felt free to tell each other how frustrated we were, in cross-racial relationships such freedom of expression often does not exist. Because throughout history speaking up has cost people of color jobs, homes, and even lives, too often the choice is to stay silent. There's a long and painful American history of people of color, when in the presence of white people, conforming to survive. The cost is staggering. The silencing of feedback from people of color can create a deadlock dynamic in which white people remain ignorant about their impact, while people of color accumulate frustration.

Understanding and working toward breaking this dynamic is central to dismantling twenty-first-century racism. While slavery and Jim Crow laws provided white people tangible evidence of racism and clear-cut demands for its undoing, today's racism lives hidden beneath the surface, in individual hearts and minds. Today's work to dismantle racism begins in the personal realm. Until I began to examine how racism had shaped me, I had little to contribute to the movement of righting racial wrongs. My cultural markings, invisible to me, screamed "Caution!" to those outside my culture. It explains why, for so many years, my best efforts stagnated or backfired. Until I examined how racism shaped me, I had little hope that any person of color would want to engage with me around a problem I saw as theirs. Only when I began to explore and share my personal struggle to understand my racialized belief system did people of color start opening up to me, engaging with me in our common struggle.

I can never change the fact that I've spent my whole life soaking up the attitudes and behaviors of a single culture. As effortlessly as breathing, I can be fast, tough, competitive, goal oriented, and self-sufficient. When social tension stirs my gut, my first reaction can be silent judgment, distancing me from the discomfort I feel and squelching opportunities to connect, learn, and grow. Slowing down and making myself vulnerable to my own ignorance and to other cultures' ways of being and knowing requires intention and effort. As white racial justice educator Peggy McIntosh explained to me, "I see that I will never outgrow what I have come to think of as my hard-drive attitudes and assumptions, but when I install the alternative software, I discover that I have outgrown some of them or can talk to myself about figuring out how to outgrow them. The alternative software allows me to see or study them." Becoming culturally competent has required developing an intimate understanding of my culturally crafted hard drive.

Q Can you make a list of the ways in which America's dominant culture has left an imprint on you? I could not have created much of a list before this journey. If you have trouble making one, you're not alone!

Moving from not knowing what it was
to feeling it in every recess of my being.

THERE'S A PRACTICE I LEARNED about on Saint John, an island in the Caribbean, where local artisans tie thread around the young, hard-shelled fruit of the calabash tree. As the fruit grows, the threads force it to restrict itself here, expand itself there, shaping the gourd into a configuration far from its natural form. Its permanent guise forever bears the marks of its coercive strings. These contorted gourds remind me of the way cultural forces acted on me, shaping me as I developed, squelching certain impulses while cultivating others. I didn't concentrate on removing the constrictions; I focused on how to survive with them in place. Ultimately, cultivating an awareness of my cultural imprinting has meant identifying and teasing apart the threads that bound and shaped me—strings that until this journey I hadn't realized existed.

My cultural imprint bears all the hallmarks of the dominant white culture, a term I at first rejected. Much of the language used to discuss racism initially pushed my buttons so ferociously that I couldn't grasp the important ideas within them. The term "white culture" brought to mind the Klan and neo-Nazis. Imagining myself part of a "white culture" made me want to scream, "Don't lump me in with them!" What I've learned is that I need not embrace extremist white supremacist beliefs to be susceptible to internalizing a host of what are considered white traits, ones that serve to hold racism in place.

Since I've always viewed myself as an individual, succeeding or failing on my own merit, the idea of my white skin lumping me into a white culture felt foreign and offensive. I never felt white; I just felt like Debby. The only group associations I thought I had were as a Kittredge or a Pierce, a New Englander, a female, or an American. It's not that I had never felt a part of a group; I'd just never felt part of a *racial* group. Furthermore, though I could readily and proudly tell you what it meant to be each of those things, I could not have told you what it meant to be white. And I couldn't learn what being white meant in my life until I was ready to calm down long enough to tolerate the terminology.

What finally got me to come around to understanding the dominant white culture concept as it was being offered to me was the consistency of its description. From coast to coast, at conference after conference, ministers, social workers, educators, and psychologists working on the front lines of social issues described the same handful of mindsets and behaviors that hampered diversity initiatives. Harvard Business and Law School consultants reported how corporations and law firms across the country struggle to retain employees of color as a result of off-putting mindsets and behaviors from their otherwise well-intentioned white employees. Virtually anywhere you find a white-dominated organization you find the same set of issues hampering individuals' and institutions' well-intended attempts to diversify and be inclusive.

The list of dominant white culture behaviors that hold racial barriers in place is not endless; in fact, it's surprisingly short. As someone who at first was sure the term "white culture" was a bunch of baloney, I now confess that I have discovered in myself each and every one of the beliefs and behaviors listed below.

- Conflict avoidance
- Valuing formal education over life experience
- Right to comfort/entitlement
- Sense of urgency
- Competitiveness
- Emotional restraint
- Judgmentalness
- Either/or thinking
- Belief in one right way
- Defensiveness
- Being status oriented

The purpose of identifying and examining the dominant white culture is not to prove that white people are racist or that everything white people think and do is wrong. It's a way to provide feedback along the lines of "Here are some dominant white culture ways of thinking and acting that are holding back efforts to dismantle racism."

In bringing a product to the marketplace, for instance, time equals money, so efficiency and speed may well be the right tools for the job. In trying to examine human relations, however, trying to bring efficiency and speed to the process may actually backfire. Prior to this journey, I didn't think about having a relationship to time, let alone its impact on people around me. It turns out that I have one, adopted top to bottom from the dominant culture.

Time as linear, faster as better, a need to adhere to strict timelines, and a pervasive sense of urgency epitomize my embodiment of time. It's a construction that supports a society built around industry, capitalism, and wealth accumulation, and though it's one way to relate to time, it's not the only way, and not necessarily the best way for every situation.

The issue for me is that I have so fully absorbed the dominant culture's approach to time that I bring it with me everywhere I go, even when it's not helpful or healthy. I am schedule- and efficiency-driven. I live with a sense of urgency that ticks away inside me like a stopwatch, measuring my every movement against a to-do list or agenda. Slowing down requires intent and effort. My heart races when I'm five minutes late, even when it's just a casual lunch with a friend. My conscious mind understands it's not that big a deal, but deep down I am programmed to run "on time." Before I can reason with myself, my knee-jerk reaction is to judge people who aren't perfectly punctual as irresponsible or arrogant. I can seethe at them for wasting my time with the mismanagement of theirs. These days I wonder, *Is it even possible to "waste" time?*

Certainly my time management skills have a place in this world. I can be counted on to show up on time and complete tasks in a timely fashion. I can work backwards from a deadline, creating multiple schedules and overlapping timelines so that employees can work in sync with one another. I like outcomes, results, and knowing I haven't wasted a minute in getting from A to Z. There are significant benefits to me and any organization I work for to have these time management and goal-oriented skills. Yet in the world of racial healing and justice, my visceral sense of time and productivity can work against me. If I'm at a meeting at which staff are exploring racial tensions that have been creating organizational conflict, I can hurt the process by pushing people to go faster or forcing a predetermined agenda on the process. I can be impatient during extended silences, times I now understand can be critical learning pauses as people process complex and fraught ideas. Unlike a factory, human development—the heart and soul of racial healing—moves at a more organic pace.

My internalized dominant white culture traits are not limited to time considerations. I embody all of the attitudes and behaviors considered its hallmarks, each an asset in one context, a liability in another. Unexamined, each trait has the potential to impose growth-stunting attitudes on me and on others—be it in the silence of my head, in an interpersonal exchange, or in a policy I create. Understanding each is essential if I am to relate to people outside my own culture. The more conscious I become of my cultural adaptations, the more I'm able to choose when they are and are not appropriate.

It helped me to know that no one was saying *all* white people act this way *all* the time. Nor was anyone saying that *only* white people act this way. In fact, I learned that many of the qualities characterized as "white" have been internalized by people of all colors living in America's white-dominated society. Adjusting to cultural norms is a part of being human.

It also helped me to learn there's a general understanding that there's no single white culture any more than there is one Asian culture or one black culture. When racial justice educators refer to the white culture, they mean the *dominant* white culture, the one initially brought to America by English colonists and still based on Anglo values.

Over time I've experienced a shift from defensiveness to gratitude, as I recognize the vast wisdom in the racial justice movement. When I've listened to mixed-race panels discuss the white culture without shame or blame but with insight and humor, I've felt the "we're all in this together" spirit and understood the ways in which my own journey is not just entwined with racial justice advocates alive today, but built on the shoulders of those who've come before me. The feeling of being a part of a movement based on awareness, honesty, collaboration, and healing has brought with it the life-affirming sense of connectedness that had been missing all my life.

Q   Take a look at the continuums below. The qualities on the left are
often associated with the dominant white culture. Folks working to
break patterns that maintain racism notice that thinking and acting
in ways closer to the right side of the continuum can be useful
in addressing racial healing. Take a minute to place yourself along
each line. You may notice that you move more to the left or right
depending on your environment. What is it that causes you to
move one way or the other?

I don't like to rock the boat.	I'm comfortable giving/ getting honest feedback.
I mostly value intellect (data, facts).	I mostly value intuition (emotion, senses).
I choose comfort.	I tolerate or embrace discomfort as a way to grow.
I feel a sense of urgency and a need to fix things.	I like to slow down and see how conversations/ initiatives unfold.
I'm thick skinned and competitive.	I'm able to be vulnerable and cooperative.
I tend to judge people who feel differently.	I tend to be curious about other people's perspectives.
I prefer absolutes.	I'm comfortable with ambiguity.
I value outcomes and finished products.	I value process.
I tend to blame others when tension erupts.	I tend to reflect on my own role when tension erupts.
I care most about individual status.	I care most about group functionality.

Getting in touch with my either/or thinking habit.

THE NEXT FEW CHAPTERS examine some of my most stubborn, hard-drive assumptions born of the white culture. The first is my either/or mindset, the part of me that makes it so effortless to stereotype people as either this type or that, either this race or that. My either/or tendency interacts with a ranking habit, making people not just different but better or worse. I call these partners in judgment "boxes and ladders." Whether or not I want them to be, they're hard at work imposing on the world around me a misconstrued framework of what is and is not valuable. For a girl raised on the beliefs that people were either good or bad, ideas and behaviors either right or wrong, and I would go to heaven or hell depending on which side of each I fell on, thinking in both/and terms continues to be a stretch.

Without awareness, I'm less likely to listen to or take seriously the ideas of a person I've been taught to see as less-than. I'm struck by how easily I can dismiss a suggestion or opinion of someone who's black or whose grammar is less than perfect, race and language being two critical cues I've used in my life to place someone in a presumed social location. I'm not an active snob, just a well-programmed passive one. Whether I sort and rank by age, race, ethnicity, class, religion, or some other difference, the boxes and ladders mindset puts me in a mode of judgment that obstructs my ability to learn and connect.

When I think about where I got the idea that intelligence and insight correlated to a certain type of person, it comes back to what wasn't said. Though no one close to me bad-mouthed people outside of my culture, the constant praise for people, especially white men, within my culture made its mark.

I've had to be careful on this journey not to do a flip-flop and box and rank white men. Time and again as I've spoken to white men about my journey, I've found myself caught off guard by an eagerness to hear my story of racial ignorance and a willingness to make themselves vulnerable by sharing their own. It seems just as I ramp up my efforts to outgrow the habit of sorting and ranking, it shows up in a new way applied to a new group.

One white man from northern Maine shared this with me: "I hate stereotypes. I go to these national conferences, and when people hear where I'm from, I can just feel them sizing me up as that dumb white guy from the boonies." He took a deep breath and said, "You want to see who I really am?" He left his kitchen, where we were standing, and returned minutes later with the stack of books from his bedside table. The books, by authors like Malcolm Gladwell and Stephen Covey, struck me. *This guy's totally on a journey too*, I thought. Truth be told, though I may have put smart and capable in the "white man" box, I did not include emotionally intelligent, vulnerable, or seeking.

I've long prided myself on not trying to keep up with the Joneses in a material sense, but it's been disturbing to uncover my tendency to rank people according to all of these other attributes. Even among my own class and race, I sort and rank according to a range of criteria. Who's the better citizen? Who's the more authentic person? And my newest one—who's the better antiracist? These days I'm in a near-constant state of interrupting my hard-drive assumptions.

Falling into the habit of sorting and ranking people may well come from a triage-like, survival mechanism. Walking through the forest, I'd want to be able to quickly differentiate "wants to eat me" from "doesn't want to eat me." Boxing and ranking the mess of humanity also provides a kind of order. And I love order. My spices are alphabetized. My month is mapped out on my countertop calendar. I even had my own professional organizing business when my kids were young. Order rocks. But trying to cram the complexity of humanity into either/or and better/worse categories has robbed me time and again of connecting with and learning from fellow human beings.

The ingredient that takes the natural human inclination to sort, and adds to it the need to rank, is power. In the dominant culture, people are not just different but better or worse. "Better" means increased opportunities to climb the ladder. And the higher up the ladder one's situated, the more power one has to define the boxing and ranking parameters. It's a self-perpetuating, self-serving system—one that has a powerful role in holding in place racial and other social roles. People have lost friends, family, jobs, status, and lives by trying to speak up and take action for racial justice.

It's the boxes and ladders mindset that prevented me from engaging with racism sooner. Though I never feared for my safety, or that I'd lose status or friends, I did spend most my life thinking I had to make a choice between being either a polite person or an angry activist. I couldn't imagine myself as the latter, so I stuck with the former. Unexamined, these hard-drive habits kept me orbiting in my white world longer than I would have wanted, had I understood that between the two extremes existed a world of immense learning, compassion, and empowerment. Had I known sooner, perhaps I would have run toward, not stumbled on, the borderlands where people from different cultures come together to understand their connection to a shared social system.

Q   Pick a six-hour period in which you commit to noticing your tendency to box or rank a person or idea. Make a note about each incident, be it a person on the bus, a family member, a colleague, or a person in the media. At the end of your observation period, explore one incident in which you boxed and ranked a person with whom you were interacting. Does your conscious mind agree with your initial judgment? What, if anything, do you think you could have learned had you replaced judgment with curiosity in that situation?

Learning to value both independence and interdependence.

LIKE MANY CULTURAL MESSAGES, the idea that independence reflects strength while dependence results from weakness seeped into my psyche without anyone explicitly saying it. Somewhere along the line I'd picked up the idea that asking someone for help of any kind was tantamount to saying, "I can't do this alone. I'm desperate. I'm worthless." Depending on someone felt like a last resort for the destitute. "Let's not forget the needy," said at many Sunday suppers, confirmed my suspicion that needing help from others was for those less capable. My glorification of independence and individualism made me an easy target for the myth of meritocracy, and overshadowed what in my heart I knew to be true: the deep interconnectedness I longed for with family, friends, colleagues, and even strangers is core to human survival. Interdependence is our lifeblood.

Yet the urgency I felt in striving to be independent set in at a young age. In a home movie taken when I was six years old, there's a scene of my siblings and me paddling toward the dock at the family cabin in northern Maine. Next to my older siblings I am tiny, yet the look of determination on my face as I concentrate first on paddling, then on swiftly maneuvering out of the canoe, and finally on tying a seaworthy knot, reminds me of how intent I was on demonstrating my abilities and my independence. For me, showing that I could keep up without a lick of help from anyone meant not getting left behind. Though it motivated me to strive and achieve, it brought with it an unhealthy undercurrent of anxiety and condescension toward "the needy."

What I couldn't see until this journey was that my white family's lack of "need" in large part resulted from our dependence on large government systems that conveyed to us the right to citizenship, land ownership, subsidized housing, preferential education, medical care, and retirement benefits. Because I couldn't see that white-favored policies had assisted my family's climb up the socioeconomic ladder, I couldn't imagine the flip side: how the skin-color-based policies that favored white Americans could inhibit the hopes and dreams of Americans of color. Nor could I conceive of interdependence as a survival strategy in an under-resourced population. In my house we were taught to share cookies and toys. In communities of color sharing homes, child care, earnings, and grief is often the norm. As I heard over the years that this celebrity or that athlete of color bought a family member a house or a car, it struck me as odd, irresponsible even. I viewed it as throwing money at someone who'd failed. Why else would anyone need that help?

One night in my Wheelock class we were talking about the tension between the tradition in American education of expecting children to work quietly and independently and the growing evidence that peer learning is in fact a more effective strategy. Encouraging students to reason together and explain their thinking to one other, it turns out, results in higher levels of comprehension and proficiency. It piqued my curiosity to hear that while self-sufficiency and individual learning is a cornerstone in American schools, collaborative learning and interdependence have long been foundational in many other cultures. I discovered, for instance, that for children who come to the United States from Latin America, the idea of working independently goes against everything they're taught at home. Likewise, studies have shown that African American students perform better in collaborative learning settings. Both of these cultures revolve around a collective orientation as opposed to an individual one.

The next day in my second grade classroom, Rosie, a Haitian student, jumped up during math to go talk to a classmate across the room. This had been happening all year, multiple times a day, wearing me down. With each attempt to intercept her before she could interrupt a peer hard at work, Rosie and I became increasingly frustrated. No matter how many times I told her she needed to stay in her seat, the pattern repeated itself. My colleagues and I saw this as a serious self-control issue and had even put together a chart with stars to motivate Rosie to stay in her seat. Nothing seemed to work. Her response to my daily interceptions was to look devastated, return to her seat, and put her head on the desk, crushed to the point that she couldn't do her math. Both of us ended up feeling we weren't doing our jobs well.

That day, with the idea of collective-oriented cultures fresh in my mind, I resisted the urge to correct Rosie when she jumped up and skittered across the room to a classmate's desk. I watched to see if she was, in fact, trying to help someone. Without teacher interception, she was able to reach her destination. Rosie put her hand on her classmate's back and leaned in to help her with a math problem.

At lunch that day I squatted beside her.

"Rosie, I saw you get up and help Kendall today during math."

She gave me an "I know—whoops, sorry" look.

"It's okay," I said. "I'm starting to think you love helping people."

Rosie grinned at me, "Yup."

"I know a lot of times I've told you to sit when I notice you getting out of your chair."

With a roll of her eyes, she nodded.

"Do you think some of those times it's because you wanted to go help a classmate?"

She beamed at me, put down her fork, and hugged me.

"So tell me about helping Kendall this morning," I said. "How did you know she needed help?"

Rosie told me that from across the room that morning she'd heard her classmate mutter to herself, "I don't get this." Rosie's instinct was to help her.

I told her how sorry I was that for the entire year I hadn't understood that that was her intention. I told her how much I loved the way she cared so much about her friends and that I noticed how much everyone in the class loved this about her too. Then I explained that as great as that was, there were times when she really did need to stay in her seat because the teachers do want everyone to try to learn on their own as well as in groups. Later that afternoon the lead teacher, Rosie, and I went through each subject and talked about whether it was a work-alone class or a work-with-friends class. She got it.

Rosie and I were caught in a classic cross-cultural clash, one for which I was completely ill equipped. When confronted with cultural difference, my first reaction had long been to see what people didn't have that I did, not what they might have that I didn't. I saw Rosie's "inability" to work independently as a flaw, a deficit, not her exquisite ability to tune in to the needs of others as a strength and an asset. The Rosie incident washed over me like a downpour, wiping clean my mindset's muddy windshield, allowing me to see that every culture creates unique strengths. I will always see my experience with Rosie as the pivotal moment of my complete reversal in my approach to "others."

Until I understood Rosie's motive, and in particular her motive in *relation* to mine, the scene had played out day after day in a way that allowed each of us to feel misunderstood and undervalued. I had a story in my head about Rosie, one that said she couldn't follow instructions, couldn't sit still. Once I was able to see that I was asking her to conform to a value and behavioral style that contradicted hers, I could use the strengths from each of our cultures and try to make room for both. It allowed me to stop judging and instead guide her with intelligence and respect. I shudder to think how I, as an authority figure and an elder, had the capacity to diminish the way she felt about herself.

Rosie never lost the impulse to jump up and help, but now we had an understanding between us. I'd say "Pssst," and with a smile, mouth the word "helping?" She'd freeze, raise a finger as if to say, "Oh yeah," smile at me, turn around, sit back down, and get back to her work. Until I understood that my childhood of learning to value independence and Rosie's childhood of learning to value interdependence were cultural differences, not right or wrong, I couldn't have navigated this situation without judgment. By shifting from perceiving her behavior as a deficit to recognizing it as a strength, I freed Rosie from the oppression of feeling misunderstood and frustrated. To steal a line from *Avatar*, she felt seen. So did I.

As I reflected on Rosie's socialization toward interconnectedness, I wondered how I'd so thoroughly bought into the idea of independence as superior, when interdependence was also revered in my family. Part of my trust in the "one for all and all for one" philosophy comes from my experience in the Pierce family. Over the years, as my mother's generation has passed away, the old log cabin up in northern Maine transferred to my generation. At one point sixteen of us co-owned it. When I tell people I own a house with that many family members, the response is usually, "That sounds like a nightmare!" But it's not. It works because somewhere in the family fabric is the idea that the health of the whole family, and the cabin as its gathering place, trumps any one individual's wants or needs. When we meet annually to discuss the scheduling, repairs, and finances, I always walk away warmed by the way family members respect each other while working to create solutions that meet everyone's needs. Not every person gets their wish every time, but the commitment to group harmony gets articulated and reaffirmed by everyone at least once a year.

When my father spoke to my siblings and me about the process of dividing assets upon his eventual death, he stressed this: "Don't ever put money before each other." He went so far as to advise us to sell any artwork, furniture, or jewelry that threatened to pit family members against each other. When the time came to go, item by item, through every plate, fork, spoon, clock, rug, and painting, this guiding principle worked. We didn't have to sell anything to avoid a family feud, but when things did get tense, we worked together to figure out how to proceed in a way that all five of us felt comfortable with. We understood that our individual happiness could not exist without family harmony. How interesting that my white-skinned, Anglo family understood the old Ubuntu philosophy: "I am what I am because of who we all are."

Q What did you learn about self-sufficiency and independence? How do you feel when you need to ask someone for help?

Adjusting my understanding of what's fair.

ANOTHER PARTICULARLY STUBBORN hard-drive attitude I've had to wrestle with is the idea that "fair means equal." This attitude fits nicely with the myth of meritocracy. When I believed that all Americans had an equal chance at getting an A, getting a job, or getting a house in a nice neighborhood, giving some people "help" sounded unfair. Again, I couldn't see the help I'd received as a member of the dominant racial group.

Yet once I recognized the imbalance of resources and access historically given to white people, my ideas changed. Suddenly things like affirmative action and housing subsidies, which had once sounded like unfair programs that helped people I assumed simply weren't helping themselves, made sense. Once I understood that limiting all but one or two college spots to white people only, giving land grants to white people only, offering citizenship to white people only, and parceling out GI Bill education and housing subsidies mostly to white people only, I understood that programs seeking to right the imbalance and level a long-unlevel playing field were equitable.

The best explanation I ever heard about the difference between equality and equity came from a principal I'd gone to for advice about how to explain the "special" accommodations I was offering one student to his classmates. When the other students said, "That's not fair! How come I don't get rewards? How come I don't get to take breaks?" I didn't have the language to describe the situation to them without making the student being accommodated sound weak. My attempts to quell their sense of unfairness by saying, "He needs it, and you don't," weren't working.

"It's the difference between equality and equity," the principal began.

I drew a blank. "Um, can you say more?"

"Sure. Here's a great way to explain it to kids. Ask them what they'd do if there was a test that involved writing their answer on a line on the board— a line five feet above the ground."

I thought for a minute. Several of my students would be too short to reach the line. "Well, some of them couldn't reach it, so that wouldn't be fair, right?"

"Unfair, or *inequitable*." She paused before continuing. "'Equality' means giving every student exactly the same thing to meet the same expectation. 'Equity' means both holding people of differing needs to a single expectation and giving them what they need to achieve it." In other words, it's a way to level the playing field.

My favorite example of equity in action tells the story of the Montgomery County Public Schools (MCPS) in Maryland. The school system has 140,000 students and 202 schools. Like urban school districts across the country, Montgomery County's schools found themselves grappling with the achievement gap, the phenomenon in which student achievement patterns and dropout rates closely track racial lines. Under the leadership of superintendent Jerry Weast, the district took on the achievement gap with a stunningly bold approach.

In an effort to explicitly name the issue of racial and economic disparities, Mr. Weast mapped out the lower and higher achieving schools by zones. "Green Zone" schools were in higher-income, predominantly white neighborhoods and considered among the nation's best public schools. "Red Zone" schools were in high-minority, low-income neighborhoods and, typical of national patterns, suffered from low achievement and high dropout rates. Mr. Weast's goal was not only to bring the Red schools up to the Green schools' level of achievement but to raise the educational standards for everyone, Green schools included.

To identify the barriers to achievement, create buy-in, and develop strategies and goals, Mr. Weast cast the net wide, seeking input and support from every stakeholder imaginable: students, parents, teachers, support staff, bus drivers, secretaries, lunch servers, board members, union leaders, government officials, and civic and community leaders. With broad community input and support, MCPS implemented a strategy based on equity, allocating more resources to the Red Zone schools than to the Green Zone schools in order to provide the students who were lagging with the extra support and time they would need to catch up.

Using measurements such as school, college, and workforce readiness, literacy and math benchmarks, state exam scores, and graduation rates, MCPS set specific goals. Weast's initiative, rolled out in 2000, has made significant progress but still has a ways to go. Not surprisingly, the first goals to be reached were in the younger grades and within the on-grade expectations. The achievement gap in the higher grades and in Advanced Placement classes has proven more difficult to close. The gap in the drop-out rate, however, has been reduced across the board, giving me hope that over time the gap will continue to reduce, as the younger students move through the educational system.

When I analyze how Jerry Weast worked, I noticed that he did not impose his ideas on others as much as he used his position of power to involve and empower people at all levels of the system and surrounding communities. In fact, at every turn he replaced a status quo "white" attitude or behavior with an alternative approach, effectively flattening the traditional hierarchy. It's interesting to think about how acting in ways beyond the white culture facilitates the creation of racial equity. Here are a few examples of how Mr. Weast acted beyond white cultural norms to create a racially equitable plan:

- He replaced conflict avoidance with explicit conversation and conflict resolution.
- He sought knowledge gained from both formal education and life experience by soliciting input from everyone, from data analysts to bus drivers.
- He worked with white communities to examine their degree of comfort and entitlement relative to communities of color.
- Instead of acting on a sense of urgency, he took the time necessary to include multiple perspectives, develop collaborations and consensus, and think about long-term impacts.
- By replacing competitiveness with a sense of community and collaboration, he allowed the entire district to feel part of a whole, not like 202 schools fighting school by school for limited resources.
- He allowed people to free themselves from emotional restraint by encouraging them to speak their minds passionately. In fact, the book chronicling the process, *Leading for Equity: The Pursuit of Excellence in Montgomery County Public Schools*, speaks openly about how emotional it got at times.

- He replaced judgment with curiosity by intensely investigating root causes of systemic barriers. Mr. Weast himself even rode the school bus to see what he could learn from that part of students' experience.

If I lived in Montgomery County, my children would have been in a Green Zone school. Could I have been convinced to have my county's resources shifted from my child's school to a Red Zone school if I didn't understand the achievement gap's historical roots? I can't know for sure, but I think it may have been a hard concept for me to embrace. Again, I would have seen it as an unfair advantage being given to people who I thought weren't doing enough for themselves. In retrospect I can see that the way I trotted my kids off to one after-school activity after another had a lot to do with the time and money whiteness had afforded me. I now understand that the less equality there is, the more efforts to create equity are needed.

 Which of the following special-by-race programs have benefited you in your life? How?
- white-only or white-dominated neighborhood
- white-only or white-dominated country club
- other types of white-only or white-dominated social clubs
- legacy at a private school
- legacy at an institution of higher education
- lending rates for white people

How habits that seem so innocuous to me can alienate people of color.

UNTIL I BECAME AWARE of how my internalized white ways of thinking and acting interfered with my best intentions to bridge the racial divide, I was like a bull in a china shop. What passed for normal in my white world had the potential to alienate people of color. Until I understood this problem, I moved clumsily around people of color, creating unintentional slights, reinforcing the white stereotype, and perpetuating the kind of mistrust and misunderstanding that fuels racism.

My introduction to this reality, a huge piece of the undoing-racism puzzle, came a year into my journey when I attended the White Privilege Conference, a national forum for people interested in exploring and addressing the ways in which beliefs and behaviors normalized in a white-dominated culture affect outcomes in America's classrooms, media, sports, religious communities, social and medical services, and businesses. The 1,500-person conference, about 85 percent white, is thick with educators, pastors, and social workers.

At the request of one of my mentors, Barbara Beckwith, I'd agreed to not only attend the conference but assist her in a workshop she would be leading. In the shuttle from the airport to the conference center, Barbara and I learned that conference founder and director Dr. Eddie Moore had asked to meet with all workshop presenters that afternoon to set the tone for the conference. I immediately felt a sense of being a fraud, as I, who a year earlier hadn't even known the term "white privilege," was being asked to an insiders' meeting. As soon as we got ourselves settled, Barbara and I picked up our name tags and headed to the orientation. As I pinned on my name tag that identified me as a "presenter," I felt even worse.

When we walked into the room, I felt stunned as Barbara gave an enthusiastic "Hi Eddie!" to a young black man. I looked at his name tag. Sure enough, this wasn't just any Eddie; this was Eddie Moore, *the* Eddie Moore.

How could a black guy be running a conference about white privilege? I wondered. I kept my thoughts to myself but couldn't wait to get Barbara's take.

As the orientation began, Dr. Moore leaned forward, put his elbows on his knees, took a deep breath, and said something along the lines of, "Listen folks, we have such a big responsibility here. We want everyone to feel comfortable and taken care of. We need to be sure no one's trying to put himself or herself above anyone else. One of the ways we can do that is by not going around thinking we're experts, or trying to figure out who's the better antiracist." I felt so relieved. Thinking I had to act like an expert had been stressing me out.

Dr. Moore went on: "You know, I wanted the name tags to say 'facilitator,' not 'presenter,' because that's what I'm hoping you all will be doing. This conference isn't about lecturing or being the expert in the room. It's about leading focused co-learning. The heart of the conference is our workshops, and they're about sharing what we know and learning from what we don't."

A presenter in the room offered this: "One thing I like to say when I start a workshop is that when it comes to racism, everyone has something to teach and something to learn." I was feeling better about my nonexpert status by the minute. This was my kind of conference. The fact that just being me, with all I did know and did not know, was okay felt liberating.

"And this is hard to say, but I gotta say it," Dr. Moore continued. "This conference is killing our colleagues of color." I felt a rush of confusion. *What does that mean?* "The white culture is showing up left and right," he said, "and it's killing my brothers and sisters." I still had no idea what he could be referring to. "Please, please, catch yourself," he pleaded. "Catch your white brothers and sisters, and help them. Don't fall into the kind of thinking and acting that hurts people of color."

I couldn't wait to get Barbara alone and ask her what he was talking about and how it could be that a black guy ended up founding a conference about white privilege. It unnerved me to think that the conference abounded with the very unintentional slights and oversights we were supposedly all here to address. What might I inadvertently do to offend a person of color over the next few days? The rough-cut workshop where I had been called out for my unwelcome white behavior had taught me just how easily that could happen. But I didn't know how much I didn't know about what white behavior looked like.

When we left the orientation, I whispered to Barbara, "What kind of things is he talking about? How are people being hurt?"

"Oh you know, white people acting all professional and talking about this degree or that degree. Stuff like that."

Okay. I felt relieved. With no degree in anything related to racism, there'd be little chance I'd fall into that trap. Then I admitted to Barbara that I'd made the assumption Eddie was a white guy.

"Ha! You're not alone. A lot of people are surprised when they first meet him." Though I didn't say it, I still wondered what it meant that a black man had founded a conference for white people. A few days later, it would all make sense.

On the next day, the first official day of the conference, we broke for lunch. Barbara and I and the swarm of conference attendees headed to a large room with round tables in the center and long tables stacked with box lunches along the side. We picked up our boxes and sat down at a table with a single black man already eating his lunch. As I unpacked my box, I glanced up at our tablemate. Our name tags included our first and last names in large letters, and the town or city from which we'd traveled in smaller letters beneath. Eager to make conversation, I tried to break the ice.

"So Henry, what do you do for work in Chicago?"

The conversation went on from there. We chatted with Henry and the assortment of other people who eventually filled our table. I thought it had been a lunch without incident.

As we walked away, Barbara said, "You remember how you asked Henry right off the bat what he did for work?"

Uh-oh, I thought. "Yes," I said.

"That's one of those things I've learned can drive people of color crazy."

I felt dumbstruck. Not only had I never heard this, but I couldn't imagine how that could possibly be offensive. It was the standard first question at a professional conference, wasn't it?

"What?" I stopped in my tracks. "Why?"

"I know," Barbara put her hand on my arm and shook her head. "This is why it's so tricky. It's the first question you ask in a white setting, right? 'What do you do?'"

"Yes." I pictured my father, my uncles, and my white coworkers greeting each other with a hearty handshake and a "So what do you do, Tim?" If there were a top-ten list of icebreaker questions in my world, this would be on it.

"Well, for people of color," Barbara explained, "it can easily be felt as you questioning someone's credentials. And frankly, most cultures around the world don't rank what you do for work as a hot topic of conversation. This glorification of professional status is a white culture thing."

"Oh my God," I nodded. "I get it."

Barbara smiled at me and leaned closer. "There's more. There's a tendency in the white culture to need to label someone, to identify them, before you can relate to them. Like when people say, 'What are you?' meaning, 'Are you Korean or Japanese or Chinese or what?' It really bothers people of color. For them it's like, 'Why do you need to know that? Can't you just relate to me without needing to put me in a box?' So I always try to stick with something we have in common—like today, a good question might have been, 'What workshop did you go to this morning?'"

Though I could immediately see the logic in what Barbara was saying, I also questioned how much a seemingly small exchange mattered. I wondered if perhaps these white antiracists were taking things a little too far. What took me much longer to see was the connection between my tip-of-the-iceberg behaviors and the underlying belief system that drove them. Though, at the time, asking someone, "So what do you do for work?" felt as normal and polite as saying please and thank you, I now see a clear connection to my boxes and ladders mindset. I needed to be able to fit someone in a box in order to engage with them. My social skills were based on finding out where people lived, worked, had grown up, and had gone to school so I could place them in a social context, not get to know them as individuals.

Questions like "So what do you do for work?" are what people of color consider to be "microaggressions," seemingly minor interactions that trigger a stress response. Often they are so subtle that the person of color can't even describe why it bothers them. Even in the white world well-intended questions and comments can have a negative impact on someone. A friend of mine who was struggling to get pregnant spoke to me about how she dreaded the question "So when are you and Charlie going to start your family?" The pain she was already experiencing with their infertility issues seared her as she'd smile and made up an excuse about timing. Another friend who is gay told me about how awkward it was to have acquaintances ask if he were married. Though he'd come out to his family, he wasn't interested in sharing his sexual orientation in his professional circles. Yet when he'd try to get out of the conversation with a quick no, people would often say, "A good-looking guy like you?" and then turn to their spouse and say something like, "Hey honey, don't we know some nice young girl to fix Mark up with?" Then he felt his choice was to either tell them he was in a relationship with a man or go out on a dead-end date.

It's still hard for me not to start a conversation with "So what do you do for work?" My hardwired attitude is just dying for that easy (for me) way into a conversation. But I'm taking the practice seriously. I try not to start with that question, or any other social locator questions, not even in all-white settings. Aren't there more interesting aspects of a person than what they do for work? And why do I need to know if someone's married or planning on becoming a parent? That's the kind of stuff people will tell me if and when they want to. Practicing staying away from social location questions is getting me out of small-talk autopilot and forcing me to think about where I am, whom I'm with, and how I can best connect to the moment and person at hand. It makes my interactions more authentic.

If you're now thinking, "Oh my God, I'm more afraid than ever of being in a racially mixed group of people!" remember this: Part of becoming multicultural means letting go of the need to be perfect, or even polite, as you've known it. It means being willing to be authentic and to stay engaged when it gets uncomfortable. Even the most seasoned white racial justice educators and activists will tell you that they still rely on those around them to point out the ways in which their white-grown perspective or behavior might be interfering with their best intentions. The key is to keep learning and always take feedback when it's offered.

Though the White Privilege Conference made me feel like a fish out of water, the perspective I gained forever changed me. Three days later, as I shook Dr. Moore's hand and said good-bye, I understood how it could be possible that the White Privilege Conference be led by a person of color—indeed, I realized that it must be. The whole point of the conference is for white people like me to gain objectivity about the white culture in order to suspend our own reality long enough to take in another. The feedback people of color and white antiracists have offered me has gone from feeling like hot coals under my feet to cool water running through my hands. I am grateful for every insight about how I unintentionally enact alienating ideas and behaviors, so I can move more gracefully across racial cultures. Could there be any greater irony than having once thought myself raceless only to discover that not only do I have a race, but nearly all my thoughts and actions are born of the culture in which it's embedded? I know now that I am not raceless; in fact, I am a living, breathing expression of the white culture.

Q Make a list of five conversation starters that have nothing to do with identifying a person by where they're from, what they do for work, or any other sorting and ranking criteria. For example, think about how you'd feel asking or being asked, "So what was the most interesting thing that happened in your day today?"

OUTER WORK

There is no social change fairy.
There is only the change made
by the hands of individuals.

—Winona LaDuke

When it comes to racism, there's no such thing as neutral.

UNDERSTANDING MY INTERNALIZED TENDENCIES as a white person is just a start. The ultimate goal is to interrupt, advocate, and educate without doing more harm than good—something I am in danger of doing every day. As a racial justice advocate, I need to become aware of my own racialized tendencies as well as find ways to interrupt racism when I see it in the world around me. I've learned that when it comes to race, there's no such thing as neutral: either I'm intentionally and strategically working against it, or I'm aiding and abetting the system. As historian and activist Howard Zinn said, "You can't be neutral on a moving train."

As I started to wrap my head around this concept, I noticed parallels with the antibullying training I'd received as a teacher. The exact same words are used: "There's no such thing as neutral." Today's antibullying pedagogy describes three distinct roles: (1) bullies, (2) victims, and (3) bystanders. Traditionally the approach has been to reprimand the bully and console the victim while ignoring the bystanders, those who witness but neither partake in nor stand up to the bullying. More recently, however, educators and psychologists recognized that the real power rests in empowering bystanders to become allies in the fight to eliminate childhood bullying.

Typical bullying in an elementary school happens in cubby rooms and far corners of the playground, away from adult eyes but within sight of other kids. In my experience, kids who've felt powerless and ashamed as bystanders are relieved to be encouraged and learn strategies for intervening. Only once they are clear about the dynamics and their role as allies can they come together and have a positive impact on the whole community by mitigating the feelings of fear, guilt, anxiety, and anger that are the lifeblood of bullying. It's a case of peer pressure at its best.

If racism were a person, they would definitely be a bully. Racism intimidates and silences. It commits violence. As Coretta Scott King said, "In this society violence against poor people and minority groups is routine. I remind you that starving a child is violence; suppressing a culture is violence; neglecting schoolchildren is violence; discrimination against a working man is violence; ghetto house is violence; ignoring medical needs is violence; contempt for equality is violence; even a lack of will power to help humanity is a sick and sinister form of violence." And though her words were spoken in 1969, they remain true today.

Opportunities abound for white people to move out of the bystander role and into the ally role in an effort to prevent racism from getting fueled and refueled every day, across every sector, and in every state, city, and town. Unlike playground bullying, racism does not offer up a single person to point to and deal with. The worst racism operates silently and often unknowingly in people's hearts and minds. It gets embedded in our institutions through small and large choices during policy creation and everyday behaviors: The teacher who insists, "This is the way we do things," without seeking information about the origins of a student's behavior. The mall developers who say, "Reroute the buses from *that* neighborhood away from our mall," without thinking through the impact on the rerouted. The police department that directs its officers to spend more time patrolling black and brown neighborhoods, instead of recognizing that there is no difference in drug use rates across the color line, only a difference in who gets away with it. The employer who hires the person around whom he "just somehow feels more comfortable" without considering the business potential in hiring someone from a culture different from his.

Like the kid on the playground, white people often are the ones to be in the position to see the problem in action—policies being developed, hiring strategies being planned, or even racist jokes being tossed around. All of these are moments when we have a choice: Do I remain a bystander and stay silent? Or do I become an ally and ask the hard questions about how this might affect the range of people in our community or organization? Do I dare ask explicitly if it will further advantage white people while simultaneously disadvantaging people of color? Do I dare suggest that because we are a group of all or mostly white people, we cannot possibly be thinking and acting on behalf of those who are not living the white experience?

The powerlessness and isolation I felt as a bystander (which I didn't even realize I was) have been replaced by a sense of empowerment that comes with feeling there's a critical role for me in dismantling racism. But here's the catch: it's trickier than one would think to take on the role of ally and not be, well, too white. I should not be in the role to take over, dominate, or be an expert. The role is not for me to swoop in and "fix." The white ally role is a supporting one, not a leading one.

I also have to be careful not to replace the idea that "I'm a good person" with "I'm a good ally" and therefore think I am not susceptible to screwing up and don't need guidance from people of color and other white allies. I will always have to check my privilege, my perceptions, and my behaviors as I try to work in alliance with people of all colors in the struggle to interrupt, advocate, and educate. Much like pursuing good physical health, working to be an effective ally means making a commitment and working on it. It seems just as I think I've got it, a racialized current event or interpersonal exchange reminds me just how much I need to seek perspective and support from others who understand the dynamics of racism. It's a lifelong commitment.

 What might prevent you from stepping out of the bystander role and into the ally role? Make a list of your reasons. What do you notice as you look at this list? What might you do to overcome the obstacles you've listed?

Sharing the burden of racism.

SOMEWHERE EARLY IN THIS JOURNEY, a man of color signed a note to me, "In solidarity, James." The word "solidarity" jolted me. Here he'd just extended to me the honor of being "in" something with him, and I was feeling uncomfortable about it. It made me feel like a fraud and a jerk. Why did I have such a strong reaction to that word?

As I reflected on my jumbled feelings, I realized that along with the terms "antiracist" and "activist," the word "solidarity" had lived in my imagination as a radical ideal and piece of vocabulary best left to rebellious, armband-wearing, angry people. Recently I looked up the definition of "solidarity" and found descriptors such as "union," "fellowship," "common responsibilities and interests." In a thesaurus I found the antonyms "enmity, hate, hatred, partiality, unhealthiness, unsoundness." How on earth did a concept as compassionate and life affirming as solidarity get misconstrued in my head as angry and aggressive?

So what does solidarity really look like? Here's a great example. Years ago I heard a story about an elementary school girl whose classmates had teased her and pointed at her bald head; she had lost her hair as a result of chemotherapy. The girl's teacher tried to explain to the class that Suzy had leukemia and was receiving chemotherapy. The teacher also tried to convey to the students Suzy's courage in enduring the medical treatments and their side effects while also maintaining her academic schedule. Still, the teasing continued. After a few days of trying to get her students to understand the cruelty of their teasing, Suzy's teacher took a different tack, showing up at school one day with a scarf tied around her head. She stood quietly before the class, removed the scarf, and revealed her own bald head—shaved clean the night before. As the class sat in stunned silence, she explained that as long as Suzy had to live without a full head of hair, she would too. Within a few days all of Suzy's classmates had also shaved their heads.

I find it interesting that in the past, when I was able to fully grasp this teacher's powerful act, I would have bristled had someone used the word "solidarity" to describe it. When I think of the example Suzy's teacher offered by replacing the disempowering behavior of bullying with the empowering behavior of solidarity, I realize how much I've lost by not understanding these concepts earlier.

In the same way Suzy's teacher stepped up to demonstrate that Suzy was not alone, white people have the opportunity to be in solidarity with people of color. There are many ways I'm learning to do this. Some are small. For instance, because my friend Bill doesn't feel comfortable collecting his newspaper from the driveway unless he's fully dressed, I am practicing changing out of my PJs before taking out the garbage or fetching the paper. I no longer open food packages in the grocery store to take the edge off my hunger, something for which friends of color have been brought to the manager's desk. If I get stopped for speeding, I no longer try to sweet talk my way out it; I put my hands on the steering wheel and do exactly what the officer tells me to do. When I hand over my credit card, I automatically hand over my driver's license with it. All of these things require me to do what my friends of color feel is standard practice for them yet is very new to me. None of these will change the world, but they serve to keep alive in me a sense of purpose.

As for what solidarity looks like in a racial and/or systemic context, consider the Montgomery County Public Schools example (pp. 207–9). In that case, a huge range of perspectives was sought before any policies were created. In the end, the predominantly white communities became invested in doing what was right for the whole county, not just for their children or their town. The white superintendent and the white towns' school communities stood in solidarity with the historically marginalized towns' school communities.

In addition to being prepared to stand up against institutional and political decisions that advantage white people while simultaneously disadvantaging people of color, I need to commit to bringing a new level of care into my relationships with colleagues and friends of color. Before this journey, I didn't understand how easy it is to screw up in this department and how vigilant I would need to be. In the film *Mirrors of Privilege: Making Whiteness Visible*, a black woman describes her feelings about friendships with white people. "For you, wanting to be my friend is like a simple stroll across the room. For me, it's like crawling on my hands and knees across a room of broken glass." Putting in extra effort in recognition of this inequity is something I'm learning to do—which doesn't mean it's easy.

One Friday afternoon, in year 1 of my journey, I'd been enjoying a new friendship with Rebecca, a black woman whose daughter played field hockey with my daughter. We gravitated toward one another on the sidelines at games and talked about everything from our kids to their schools to politics to racism. After the last game of the season, as we were standing in the field house, I asked Rebecca if her daughter was planning to do a winter sport. Instead of using her daughter's name, however, I used the name of the one other black girl on the team. The second I said it, I questioned myself, wondering, *Oh my God, what is her name?* I had known her name before the conversation, but now I was so flustered I couldn't even straighten myself out. In the moment before she gently corrected me, a look flashed across Rebecca's face that let me know I'd mixed up the names. Though I continued to chat as if it were no big deal, inside I was horrified. I knew how much mistaken identity means to black people.

As I drove home, I felt sick. I'd just jeopardized my status as a "safe" white person in Rebecca's life. On top of that, I was chairing the school's diversity committee, organizing workshops about racism, writing a book about race, and I'd just mixed up two black girls. The weight of my offense sat on my heart like an eight-ton elephant. I vacillated between the pain of knowing I'd hurt my new friend and the discomfort of having humiliated myself. I knew I had to face up to my blunder.

When I got home, Bruce was in the kitchen preparing dinner, all chipper and ready to hand me a beer.

"Welcome to the weekend," he crooned, arms outstretched for a big hug.

I walked straight past the kitchen into the living room. "Oh my God," I dropped my bag and started pacing around with my head in my hands. "I just did the stupidest thing." I told him the story.

"What's the big deal? I mix up the white girls all the time. They all look alike, for Christ's sake, in their ponytails and fleece jackets."

It's true, I also mix up my daughters' white friends from time to time. But as a result of America's uneven playing field, experiences across color lines can't be compared, and trying to do so is insulting. The context is entirely different. Mistaken identity, especially in the black community, carries unspeakable history. If I didn't understand its backstory, I too would have underestimated the seriousness of mixing up two people of color.

It starts with understanding the phenomenon of "own-race bias." Because white people have dominated my life in terms of interpersonal relationships, schoolmates, neighbors, colleagues, TV shows, movies, media images, and history books, I am exceeding familiar with the full range of white faces. Not so with people of color. Because of exposure I am more able to identify people within my own race than in other racial groups.

What's interesting is that this is often less true for people of color, because most are all too familiar with white faces. Whereas I can chose to live in a white world, most people of color can't isolate themselves within their racial group because the white group controls the resources needed to build a life. Everyone in America is exposed to the same white-dominated world of media and politics. White is the face of the dominant culture, where bosses, government officials, and teachers can make or break one's ability to achieve.

The long history of white people mistaking one black person for another is one of those unintended consequences of racism that deepens the divide. Mistaken identity has caused everything from a "Do my coworkers even know who I am?" feeling of invisibility among people of color to false accusations resulting in retaliation, incarceration, and death. In 1971, for instance, five white eyewitnesses positively identified five black men, labeled the Quincy Five, as perpetrators of a murder in Tallahassee. Despite a lack of any physical evidence, the five were charged with murder based on the accounts of five live witnesses, all of whom insisted these were the guys. Years later, the five were exonerated when a new trial introduced physical evidence pointing to three other black men. Mistaking one person of color for another is a red-hot button, and when I screwed up with Rebecca's daughter, I knew it. I explained all of this to Bruce and then asked to be left alone to call Rebecca and apologize.

"But what if she didn't even notice it?" he asked. "Then aren't you creating an issue out of nothing?"

"It's not sitting right with me," I said. "I doubt it's sitting right with her." I closed myself in my bedroom, the school directory in hand, and stared at the phone. I paced, imagining how to apologize. I finally settled on being as direct as possible. I dialed and waited.

"Hi, it's Debby, " I said when she answered. We'd never spoken on the phone before. "Listen, I feel sick about mixing up Janet and Nicky."

"Oh it's okay. It's no big deal," she said. I didn't buy it.

"Well, I feel like it was a really stupid white-person thing to do, and I'm so sorry if it hurt you."

There was a long pause.

"I wish you could talk to my coworker," she said. We both laughed. She told me how she'd been struggling with a white coworker who repeatedly made racist remarks and then chastised Rebecca for suggesting the comments were racist. We went on to have a long conversation about a wide range of topics. We were on solid ground again, and I felt it. If I ever mix up two people of color again, I hope I'll have the courage to fess up and apologize sooner. I still regret my friend had to sit with my unintended slight for the few hours she did.

Tolerating the discomfort of owning up to my blunder gave me the opportunity to share the discomfort caused by racism and send the message: "This situation stinks, but I want to be in it with you so I can get out of it with you." By holding myself accountable for what I knew was a misstep, I was able to stand in solidarity with Rebecca.

Vernā Myers, a black attorney, has worked since 1992 with white law firms that are scratching their heads about their lack of success in attracting and retaining lawyers of color. She's learned how microaggressions on the part of white employees have driven away employees of color. At a talk I attended, Vernā gave an example of how a "polite" behavior can play out for a person of color. She told a story about an Asian lawyer largely ignored by his coworkers. When she asked his firm's white lawyers what they thought might be behind this behavior she discovered that they couldn't pronounce his name, so they avoided him. They didn't want to be rude.

Vernā is a fabulous public speaker and as funny as any of my favorite stand-up comedians: Steve Martin, Chris Rock, Jay Leno, and Jerry Seinfeld. So try imagining that kind of humor and tone as you hear what Vernā then said to the crowd full of Boston attorneys.

"Not want to have to learn his name? Are you kidding me? That's what this is about? Man, we black folks have been learning *everything* about you for years! We know your TV shows; we know your hair products; we know your names; we know how you like to do things. We have to! Is it really that much to ask to meet us halfway?"

I don't think it's too much to ask to meet another person halfway. Best of all, it is something I can do because it's in my control. Surely I, living on the advantaged side of the racial equation, can expand myself to be a part of a more inclusive and united America. All things considered, it feels like a fairly small request to meet people of color on common ground by sharing the burden of being uncomfortable and out of my element.

Q Think of an issue in your own community (town, school, workplace, religious organization) that has been raised by people of color. How would you approach people who are focused on the problem? How would you go about being in solidarity with them? What could you offer?

Why "tolerance" and "celebrating diversity" set the bar too low.

SHARING THE BURDEN of social discomfort is not simply a matter of helping someone else feel good. It's about leveling the playing field in pursuit of nurturing individual and collective potential. My colleague Vernā Myers puts it this way: "diversity is being invited to the party; inclusion is being asked to dance." Have you ever been invited to a party but not known many people and not been reached out to and included? I have. It makes me wish I'd never accepted the invitation. Hiring an employee or admitting a student of color and then "tolerating" them and/or "celebrating" their food and holidays without understanding their cultural norms in the context of the dominant culture is a setup for underachievement. Too often the result is discomfort and disengagement on the part of the person of color, which results in poor performance, which then gets blamed on the person of color, not on the dominant culture's lack of awareness or inability to be truly inclusive and multicultural.

An article written by Harvard Business School professors David Thomas and Robin Ely titled "Making Difference Matter: A New Paradigm for Managing Diversity" addresses the need for strategies beyond simply adding people of color to one's team in order to bring in "insider information" or to speak to same-race clients. Thomas and Ely point out that members of groups outside of America's dominant culture "bring different, important, and competitively relevant knowledge and perspective about how to actually do work—how to design processes, reach goals, frame tasks, create effective teams, communicate ideas, and lead."

The article made me think about all the times I've heard educators say, "We need to have more teachers of color so our kids of color have adults they can relate to." Never have I heard someone say, "You know, we really need to get some educators and administrators from different cultures in here to help us think about our processes and curriculum in fresh ways."

Nor have I ever heard anyone suggest it might be good for white students to build relationships with authority figures of color.

The article also shed light on how assimilation thinking had led me astray in my early efforts to diversify organizations. When I brought people of color to the board or staff, my thinking was that their best role was to speak for and be a bridge to their race. Seeing people of color in that limited role prevented me from integrating their full range of potential into the organization. This shift in paradigm is what Thomas and Ely describe as moving from assimilation (my way or the highway) or differentiation (let's celebrate our differences) to integration—the more mature understanding that differences are powerful tools that can be used to strengthen the whole.

One of my favorite examples of how difference can work across cultures is a thwarted but brilliant effort by a mixed-blood Cherokee named Sequoyah. In 1821 he took the English example of a written language and applied it to his own unwritten one by creating an eighty-six-character alphabet. Because each character matched a specific sound in the Cherokee language, formerly illiterate Cherokees were able to learn the alphabet in a single day and learn to read and write their language in a single week. The invention was never supported by white Christian missionaries working with Native people because they feared that learning to read and write in their own language might preclude Native Americans from learning English. Also fundamental was the premise that destroying Native cultures was a necessary step in retaining English dominance.

While teaching first and second grade students to read the English language, I found its symbol-to-sound correlations could be quite irrational. Here's a two-consonant blend, now a three-consonant blend. Here *A* sounds this way; here it sounds that way. Follow it with a *U*, and it sounds totally different. Put an *O* before it, and it becomes silent. Sometimes I felt stupid trying to explain the English language to a six-year-old. I felt they were spot-on when they'd say, "This makes no sense. Who decided to make this so complicated, anyway?" They're right. Think of the resources America spends on teaching its children to read and write such a complex language system. I appreciate Sequoyah's approach, and I have to wonder, had Americans been in a "making differences matter" mindset in 1821, how might Sequoyah's contribution have been put to use in the English language? What if American linguists had been willing to add or drop letters in the name of creating a more user-friendly version of the English language?

The idea of cultivating and drawing on multiple competencies seems to me the very essence of humanity: discovering and using all our tools to maximize the potential of the group and its individuals. What if instead of "winner take all" in a world of haves and have nots, a society of thriving people expanded the pie for everyone? Who in our currently marginalized populations might rise to find the cure for cancer, bring a novel approach to environmental concerns, invent the next great American commodity, or be the teacher who reaches a child no one else can?

Being competent in multiple ways serves everyone. Not only does this kind of psychic stretching create better communities; it creates better people. As I learned about making differences matter across racial lines, I thought back to a lesson I'd learned at Simmons College Graduate School of Management, in an MBA program designed by and for women. The program put front and center the need for women to understand male corporate culture (which I now would call *white* male corporate culture) in order to thrive professionally. The deans contended that, whether by socialization or hard wiring, men flourished in hierarchical cultures while women tended to do best in collaborative settings. Dean Anne Jardim summed it up with the phrase "Men build ladders; women build webs." The deans urged us neither to abandon our female inclination to build webs nor to minimize the value of hierarchy. Instead, they argued, learn to value both approaches and to know when to apply one over the other.

Though the ideal in a hierarchical organization is that everyone, regardless of ladder rung, will work for the good of the company, too often personal temptation takes over. It's also a lot easier to step on someone when the illusion of disconnectedness (boxes and ladders) is maintained. The web approach encourages connections and relationships both horizontally and vertically in the hierarchical organization, creating a more inclusive environment, where more employees feel as invested in the organization as in their rank within it. The web creates a level of stability and accountability that pure hierarchy may not. Successful companies, the deans argued, knew when to use which approach.

In order to harvest the full range of any given group's talents, people must first feel included, appreciated, and free to speak their minds. Freedom of speech, however, becomes meaningful only when those on the receiving end truly know how to listen.

Have you ever been to an event that celebrated diversity? What did you learn about the various cultures' belief systems? Did the event give you insight into how a person from that culture might feel, given their cultural values and habits, if they tried to engage in an organization steeped in values and habits from the dominant white culture?

Listening both to bear witness and to learn.

IN THE FILM *White Privilege 101: Getting In on the Conversation*, a black inter-viewee talks about how people tend to speak *at* each other, not *to* or *with* each other. At one point he says, "You know what we need? We need a listening revolution." I agree! Though authentic and curious questioning and listen-ing is an amazing tool for learning and healing, I know I've been socialized to talk at someone, prove a point, or show off how much I know.

I marvel at astute listeners and feel particularly inspired by organiza-tions and institutions that are integrating listening-based programs. One of my favorite examples is the use of restorative justice as an alternate approach to crime and punishment. Drawing on ancient practices from Native Amer-ican and other cultures around the globe, the practice of restorative justice allows the whole community to understand the offense and its impact and take part in repairing the harm done. It's not necessarily the right tool for every crime, but it seems to me to be an excellent one to have in the toolbox.

Across America, police departments and school systems are increasingly adding restorative justice to their methodology. I heard a great anecdote from my niece, who was working at a Boston public middle school when a food fight broke out in the cafeteria. At the end of the upset thirty kids were fingered as offenders. Food prepared by cafeteria workers was scattered and smeared on floors, walls, and tables. Custodians were left to clean up the mess. In my day all thirty kids would have been suspended, isolated at home for a few days, and given a stiff talking-to by the principal. I'm guessing the offenders might even have gained peer status for their connection to such a high-profile event. The opportunity to understand the impact on the community would have been lost, as would the chance to strengthen bonds across age, role, class, and positions of power.

Instead of using the suspension method, the school organized a series of restorative justice "circles," in which a combination of offenders, students hit by food, cafeteria workers, custodians, administrators, and teachers participated. Each circle (literally people sitting in chairs arranged in a circle) provided individuals the chance to convey to the offenders the impact their actions had had on them. It also gave the offenders a chance to say their piece. There's a recognition that community healing means everyone has a chance to heal, offenders included.

Through the circles the community worked together to develop a logical consequence, ultimately "sentencing" each of the thirty offenders to after-school cafeteria cleanup duty for several weeks. I like that the cafeteria workers and custodians got to witness the offenders doing the dirty work of cleaning up while being given a reprieve from it themselves. I like that the offenders were both burdened through the consequence and given the opportunity to repair their reputations through a drawn-out public display of repaid labor. I'm guessing that in the end the offenders had ample opportunity to reflect on their behavior and perhaps even build bonds with the cafeteria workers and custodians. What a contrast to being sent into isolation for a few days.

The principles of restorative justice resonate deeply with me because they embody the idea that collective well-being is inseparable from individual well-being. Using missteps as moments to learn and become stronger empowers individuals and communities to hold one another accountable through strengthening relationships, not by punitive, silencing divisiveness.

The listening principle can also be applied proactively. A diversity director from a private school shared this story. To balance out the many dinners held at the school for parents who'd donated money or served as volunteers, he'd encouraged the headmaster to create a special event for people who fit neither profile. He'd heard increasing reports of parents and students feeling undervalued and silenced by their own sense of not belonging. To his credit, the headmaster not only listened but sent out an invitation to all six hundred enrolled families, making no assumptions about who did and did not feel the sense of belonging so vital for collective well-being. The invitation read, "You Are Invited to an I Don't Feel Like I Belong Party." The invitation went on to explain that it had come to the headmaster's attention that there were unspoken ways in which people felt uncomfortable at the school. "Let's make the unspeakable speakable by joining together for a community dinner where we start to learn how to create a more welcoming school." Over three hundred families attended.

People were invited to stand and speak about the ways in which they felt outside of the school's norm and how it affected their ability to add their voice to school issues, as well as their child's ability to learn and form friendships. People spoke of feeling judged for having too much money or too little money, for living a lifestyle too urban, too suburban, too Jewish, too Muslim, too Catholic. People worried that their car was too flashy, too rusty, too old, too new. Parents of color felt they were on a different planet, invisible, unwelcome, unwanted. Parents who'd not attended private school themselves felt awkward, unsure of how to navigate the system. The list went on; the night went on.

What if an entire town took on the charge of exploring how its entrenched white culture might be threatening its future? What if that town engaged in a community-wide conversation in which white folks asked its most marginalized citizens, "What can we do differently to be a more welcoming and inclusive town?" Guess which American town is doing just this. Are you sitting down? Winchester, Massachusetts, my own leafy green, once whiter than white, affluent suburban hometown.

In a stunning full-circle moment, I found myself hearing a woman at a Boston workshop say something that sounded like "the Winchester Multicultural Network." I walked closer and paused. I had to know if I'd heard it right.

"I'm sorry to interrupt, but can I ask what group you were just talking about?"

"Sure," a woman answered, the group widening its circle to allow me in. "We were just talking about an event we went to the other night at the Winchester Multicultural Network."

"Winchester where?" I asked, unable to form a full sentence as I tried to compute the possibility that my white Winchester could have anything to do with multiculturalism.

"Winchester," she repeated. I still must have looked blank. "The town?"

"I know," I said, coming back to my senses. "I grew up there."

"Have you been back lately? They are doing great stuff."

Not long after this conversation, I found myself driving out to Winchester to meet with the organization's board as they planned their twentieth-anniversary celebration—a town-wide forum, a listening forum. Called "Winchester in Transition," the gathering featured a panel

of community members to help the town gauge its progress in transition-
ing from exclusive to inclusive. A woman with a physical disability, a Chinese mother, a Palestinian man, an African American history teacher, and a
lesbian wife and mother told personal anecdotes of lives in which differences could not be hidden. You could have heard a pin drop as each person spoke. When the last person had spoken, the microphone got passed
around the room of 120 people, mostly white, who had their own stories
to tell of hiding their sexual orientation, of feeling isolated because of a
disabled child at home, of feeling judged and boxed in.

When I believed that leaders knew best, the top-down, authoritative
model made sense. I used to feel irritated when people couldn't just buck up
and go with the program. Now that I understand the human toll that results
when a few at the top are allowed to define what's best for the collective, I
recognize the immense value in making room for all to hear and be heard.
Whether it's individuals listening one-on-one, or events organized for the
purpose of collective listening, allowing people to define their own realities
is a critical component of creating equity.

Q Challenge yourself in the next conversation you're part of to ask more
questions than you typically would and refrain from offering your own
opinion. Take note of where the conversation goes.

Using the topic of race as a relationship builder, not buster.

KNOWING THAT SPEAKING ONE'S TRUTH and listening to others' truth is a crucial step in racial healing is one thing. Having the language to pull it off is another. Because I spent a lifetime not knowing how to talk about race, learning how was no small task. I envision a day when people can talk about race with terminology and ease that reflect an advanced understanding of race and its impact on American society. Children, not yet as laden with racial baggage as I am, have proven to me just how normal it can be.

In my first year of teaching I was placed in Ms. Edwards's classroom. As we prepared for our students' first day of school, she handed me a stack of white poster board and said, "Could you go cut these into twenty-four-inch by eighteen-inch pieces? They're for our self-portrait project." She paused and looked up at me. "Do you remember when Emily did this?" My daughter Emily had been taught by Ms. Edwards, a middle-aged white woman, in first grade. I thought about Emily's vibrant self-portrait, big and bold with not a spot left unpainted.

"Not only do I remember it; it's still hanging on the family room wall," I answered.

"Really? Do you remember what her skin color recipe was?"

I looked at her blankly, unsure if I'd heard her correctly.

"Look at this," she said excitedly as she walked over and opened a cabinet door revealing ten bottles of tempura paint ranging in color from creamy white to dark brown.

"Oh, so everyone gets to pick their own color?" I asked, wondering who would choose to be that peachy pink bottle.

"No," she whispered, her eyes sparkling, "they mix however many paints they need to match their own unique skin color." She looked straight into my eyes. "This is amazing. Wait till you see how it works."

When the day came to do the project, Ms. Edwards instructed everyone to start working on their portraits by outlining their bodies and painting their clothes and hair. "But don't do the parts where your skin is showing until you've met with me to figure out your skin color recipe." She spoke the words "skin color recipe" as matter-of-factly as if she were saying "pencil" or "backpack."

One by one the kids went over to the paint area with Ms. Edwards and pointed to bottles they thought might contribute to their color. Watching her let them swirl together various paint blobs and compare the color on the palette to the color of their arm stirred something in me. Even more intriguing was watching them stride back to their classmates to reveal their recipes and compare color swatches, talking about skin color like it was no big deal.

"What are you?" one might say to a classmate, holding out the index card bearing a paint swatch on one side and the written recipe on the other.

"Two parts coffee, one part cinnamon, and one part peach. What are you?"

"Almond and peach, half and half."

They'd hold their arms against the paint color they'd mixed to show off their likeness to the color they'd blended. They compared their own skin tones to classmates' skin tones by holding their forearms side by side. *What a no-nonsense way of talking about skin color*, I thought.

I loved the project and the way Ms. Edwards recorded the recipes so that throughout the year when kids were painting they could portray themselves in realistic, self-selected tones. One outcome of the project was the way it allowed kids to think about and describe each other. One day on the playground a girl came racing across the hardtop to tell me someone had fallen from the climbing structure and hurt herself. By the time she got to me we could see another teacher hovering over the injured girl, obstructing her from my view.

"Nellie, what's wrong? Who is it?" I asked, wondering if it were a student from our class and if I should be scurrying over there myself.

Out of breath and still shaken she said, "It's Julia. You know? From the other class?" I wasn't sure who Julia was and it must have shown on my face.

Nellie helped me out. "You know, the one who's peach-almond colored with chestnut hair? She wears that flowered jacket?"

The more I understand race, the more I appreciate the skin color recipe project. In contrast to my youth where "flesh"-colored pencils and Band-Aids adhered to one skin color recipe, this variety of skin tones and hues made sense from both a visual and an intellectual perspective. Can children taught to see skin colors as a combination of shared colors also swallow a myth that all "black people" are this way or all "white people" are that way? I wonder if they will suffer less from the kind of black-and-white, either/or thinking that I developed.

Learning to speak about racism is a core element of a course I now co-facilitate, "White People Challenging Racism: Moving from Talk to Action" (WPCR), housed at the Cambridge Center for Adult Education. I first came to know the five-week course as a student. I have to chuckle as I think back to my anticipation of the first class. Still stuck in either/or thinking, my assumption had been that I was taking it so that I could make the monumental leap from being a nice girl to a pissed-off activist. The idea of stepping into this role made me nervous, but hey, if this is what it took to right the wrongs I was learning about, I figured I had no choice. When I arrived at class the first night, I remember taking note of the fact that neither the cofacilitators leading the class nor the students looked anything like what I'd expected. They looked, well, like regular people. I relaxed a bit.

About halfway through the first class, cofacilitators Barbara and Mark handed out little slips of white paper, explaining that we'd be doing some role playing. I broke into a cold sweat. *Role playing?* I didn't feel ready for this. Weren't they going to first teach me to be bitchy and savvy? Tough and full of all the answers?

"Okay, now we're going to break into pairs and practice. We want to hone our skills at speaking up when a typical racist comment comes up. Pair up and decide which one of you will go first," she said, as if we were about to do something as benign as decorate cookies. I thought about who was on either side of me and panicked. I had just met both of them. Still attached to my self-image, I really wasn't up for making an ass of myself in the first class. The woman beside me smiled and said, "I guess it's us."

"By the way," Barbara explained, "these scenarios are real comments that people who've taken this class have shared with us." She looked around and asked one person to volunteer to read the scenario we'd all be role playing. A young woman across the room raised her hand and read:

"My boyfriend, Ramón, is from the Dominican Republic. We visit my brother every couple of months. My brother, who's in the produce business, persists in calling my boyfriend Romaine (like the lettuce), as if he didn't know better. No matter how many times I mention how annoying this is to Ramón and me, my brother doesn't seem to get it. I don't know what to do to clearly and firmly get the point across that this is disrespectful."

Holy shit, I thought. *How am I supposed to respond to that?*

"Do you want to go first?" offered my young partner. "Why don't you play the sister? I'll be the brother," she suggested.

I took it, read it one more time, and choked back my fear. I got all puffy and angry like I thought an antiracist activist should. "I am so mad at you! How dare you call my boyfriend "Romaine," like the head of lettuce!" I said, like a tantrumming three-year-old.

My partner, responding in full character, smirked at me and taunted, "What's the matter? Can't you take a little joke? Why are you so serious all of a sudden?"

I cringed. If someone in my family said that I'd just shut down. I leaned over and whispered to her, "I hate role playing. I really don't see how this is going to help."

I looked around the room and saw the other pairs engaged in animated conversations. I thought maybe they'd finished their role playing and were talking about current events or something. But as I listened I heard "Ramón" or "Romaine" and knew they were managing to keep their conversations going. They went on for *five* minutes.

"Okay, let's stop here," Mark said. "Who found something that worked?"

"I played the role of the brother," a man said, "and my sister totally disarmed me when she said it was changing the way she felt about me. I mean, how can you argue with that? It felt like I actually *was* the brother and I didn't want to lose my sister's respect."

Another student said, "I was playing the sister, and he [she pointed to her partner] was really stubborn and tough. But when I gently reminded him of the way he'd been teased with a nickname as a kid, his whole demeanor changed."

Wait a minute, I remember thinking. *These conversations aren't aggressive*. This *I can do!* None of the table-slapping, foot-stomping, you're-wrong-and-I'm-right attitude I'd imagined figured into their strategies.

Far from my old understanding—that conversations serve as a stage on which to prove one's self-worth through witty banter, biographical data, or the recall of facts—authentic dialogues about race (or any other complex idea, for that matter) make mutual learning, not winning or losing, the goal.

The kinds of conversations practiced in the WPCR class are not to be confused with the courageous conversations I wrote about earlier. Courageous conversations involve people of all colors coming together for the express purpose of exploring the borderlands where racial cultures collide and collude. In contrast, WPCR prepares students for the kind of conversations that typically arise in white-only settings. Now that race is in the front of my mind, I find it extraordinary how frequently comments are made— either in jest, in judgment, or out of curiosity—that provide an opening for an everyday conversation about race.

As we played out our scenarios in the WPCR course, the cofacilitators would remind us, "The important thing is to keep the conversation going." We made lists on the board of what kinds of words and behaviors would keep a conversation moving and what would shut it down. I've learned that the way to be effective is to explore the topic with the "racial offender." Though conversations like these (as opposed to the pissed-off activist ones I'd imagined) are more in keeping with who I am, they are still challenging. For a girl who was taught to keep conversation pleasant and upbeat, this is unfamiliar territory. Having been advised by my parents never to discuss politics or religion in polite company, I often feel I'm violating a social code—and I suppose I am. It's taken me hours of practice to learn not to fall into old patterns. Occasionally I still find myself fighting the urge to change the subject.

Increasingly I am able to go into these conversations free of the need to make a particular point or make myself look good. I am humbled by the collective intelligence that emerges when people use conversation to deepen understanding. I've freed myself from the rigid notion that I have, or will ever have, all the answers. I've also let go of the belief that answers are fixed in time and space. Even when I hit a conversational dead end and feel defensive or fed up, I've found out that by rethinking that moment later on, I'm better prepared for the next conversation. It's a learning process, one with clear results. Slowly but surely I've developed the kind of questioning and listening skills that make me not only a better racial justice advocate but a better parent, wife, teacher, friend, and colleague.

The implications for this kind of personal transformation are tremendous. While I'm conditioning myself to be a change agent in the creation of a more inclusive culture, I am awakening in myself lost pieces of my own humanity. As I free myself from stringent rules and forced outcomes,

I am discovering once again the curiosity, creativity, and compassion that I tamped down over the course of my upbringing. Conversations about race are allowing me to build bridges not only to other people but to forgotten parts of myself as I trade out bravado, security, and status for vulnerability, faith, and connection.

Q Make a list of five ways to shut a conversation down. Next make a list of five ways to keep a conversation going.

RECLAIMING MY HUMANITY

Race is not a cause, it's a part of becoming fully human.

—Billie Mayo

Reclaiming my human family, reclaiming myself.

I THINK THE MOMENT MY MOTHER told me of the Indians'
alcohol-soaked demise was when my soul first cracked, letting in a sip
of cognitive dissonance that would be added to over the years. For my
entire life a part of me has been reaching toward lost truths, missing details
between what I was told and what I felt, information that would still the
rumblings in my consciousness. I couldn't have known at the age of five
that by thinking a fellow human being less human, I made myself less
human, or that by disconnecting from my human family I began the process of disconnecting from my natural intuition and ability to love, relying
more and more on what I was told and less and less on what I felt.

Racism's ultimate grip on me came not just from my conditioning to
ignore it but from the inverse story that I was told about it. As I picked up
the notion that race and racism belonged to other people, my mind was
trained 180 degrees away from the harsh reality that racism is a problem
created by white people and *blamed* on people of color. The problem is not
simply that racism wasn't discussed. Messages supporting a contradictory
story were pushed on me, a story that placed disproportionate value on
individualism, intellect, and bravado.

By being taught to buck up and compete in a world of individual players,
I learned to silence feelings of vulnerability, curiosity, and compassion. As
those parts of me withered, the void filled with assumption and judgment.
In the same way my white town presumably protected me from people who
could undermine my safety or financial stability, my buck-up attitude presumably protected me from my own vulnerability. Allowing myself to feel
anger, grief, or confusion was tantamount to saying I was weak. Admitting
vulnerability felt like letting go of my ladder rung and plummeting, landing
who knows where.

Ironically, only when I tapped into my own vulnerability did I rediscover
my inner strength and start listening to my own voice, the one that for years

had been trying to tell me something wasn't right. My vulnerability also became the birthplace for the courage I needed to put this book out into the world, as part of an effort to embolden other white Americans to reconsider their ideas about race, racism, and their role in it.

In Father Gregory Boyle's book *Tattoos on the Heart*, the author shares intimate stories of his work to support teenage gang members trying to break free from their gang culture. In exploring what he calls "restorative love," he shares poet Galway Kinnell's line, "Sometimes it is necessary to reteach a thing its loveliness." I find it curious that as much as "inner-city" black and brown kids, devastated by racism, need to be retaught their loveliness, so do I. Racism demands an artificial and divisive construction of humanity, in terms of how I make sense of others and also how I envision myself.

"When we relearn our loveliness," Father Boyle elaborates, "we begin to foster tenderness for our own human predicament. A spacious and undefended heart finds room for everything you are and carves enough space for everyone else." This is the heart of the matter, isn't it? Sitting right in front of us are the seeds of our own salvation: each other.

One of the most heart-wrenching episodes in my life was watching my father in his final days of life, plagued with regret. In that last month he wore on his body and face the leaded weight of deep depression—a shocking change in demeanor from his usual state. His blue eyes became dull, and his once animated brows sagged. The lean muscles that had long made him appear younger than his actual age alternately seized and slackened. As he lay in frozen, silent despondence, I gently tried to get at what was on his mind.

"Dad, are you okay?" I asked repeatedly. Typical of his lifelong tendency not to focus on himself or his feelings, he would ignore my question and ask me something like, "How was the drive up here?" He was barely able to croak it out through gritted teeth. We were as far from "okay" as we could be, yet depression wasn't in our family lexicon, so I'd follow his lead and change the topic.

My siblings and I tried to imagine what was behind his state of mind. Was it simply an effect of the anesthesia from recent surgery? We'd heard about postoperative depression. Was he worried about my mother? He was used to visiting her in the nursing home daily. We tried to assure him we were taking care of his house, our mother, his bills, everything. Nothing seemed to help. We wondered together if we should get him a prescription for antidepressants. One day, sitting in the chair beside his bed, I leaned in and with new urgency begged him to tell me what was bothering him.

Slowly lifting his hand to his forehead, he began rubbing it hard. After a while he managed to say in a low monotone, "I didn't do enough."

Instead of making room for him to follow up, or consider what he'd said, I jumped in: "That's ridiculous! You filled every minute of every day. You are the most hardworking person I know!" There was a long silence. My heart pounded as the sense of regret filled the room. I wanted to douse it, fix it, bring back his lively spirit.

"I don't mean that," he said in a half-whisper. "I mean I could have helped people who really needed it." He turned over. I felt paralyzed and heartsick and useless.

I'll never know what he was thinking about, though I will always wonder if it included an episode that occurred between us in the 1970s. One evening, when I walked into the living room to get help with a math assignment, I glimpsed my father seated in a chair, head in hands, my mother squatting beside him with her hand on his shoulder. Engrossed in their conversation, they didn't notice me standing by the door. As he spoke into his hands, shaking his head from side to side, short muffled phrases like "makes me sick" and "impossible position" and "good family" and "Debby's friend" and "damn it" came through.

Unable to contain my curiosity any longer, I asked, "What's going on?" They both looked up, shocked that I was there.

"Nothing. Your father had a hard day at work," my mother said.

I didn't buy it. I walked closer and pestered my father until he finally told me that a Jewish family had applied to the country club, and the board was divided over whether or not to let them in.

"Do I know them?"

"I don't think so," he said, getting up from the chair and turning to shuffle papers around his desk, his back to me.

I got angry and demanded to be told who the family was. My father explained that "for reasons of confidentiality" he couldn't tell me. That sounded official, so I tried a different tactic.

"What does being Jewish have to do with anything?"

"It's complicated, Deb."

"Well, you'd let in a Jewish family, wouldn't you?"

Silence.

"Dad, you'll make sure they get in, right?"

My mother, who'd left the room, came back in looking worried. "Deb, leave Daddy alone. He needs to think about this by himself."

I left. And never brought it up again. As far as I know, no Jewish families joined the club during my teenage years. I can only imagine the conflict he felt over choosing to take a stand or acquiesce to group opinion. Was this incident isolated, or were there other, even many other moments when he knew inequity and injustice were in motion and he didn't take a stand? What did he see? What did he hear? What did he know? What did he ignore? And how did that affect him? My guess is that in the world of corporate law, country clubs, and Boston institutions, going against the status quo must have felt too threatening to a man providing for a wife and five children living a high-class white life, especially when his own mother had invested so much in his social climb. His love for fellow human beings he may have wanted to use his privilege to reach out to was outweighed by his fear of losing his privilege by doing so.

Thinking back to his words near the end of his life, "I didn't do enough," I will forever regret my inability to respond more skillfully to his anguish, regardless of what it revolved around. I had not yet learned to have courageous conversations or to approach a situation as a listener and not a fixer. I had not yet learned the power of bearing witness to a fellow human being needing to release a private pain.

That was my final conversation with my dad. At seven o'clock the next night he dropped dead as a nurse moved him from his chair to his bed. In an instant a pulmonary embolism seized his broken heart. My sister reported that his last day had been one of his bluest. The father I adored left this world consumed with regret—and perhaps with oceans of secrets between us.

Lord knows I don't ever want to find myself at the end of my life, my body spent, wishing back time so I could love more deeply or do more to leave the world a better place. Here, in midlife, it would be easy to stay in my comfort zone, wishing and hoping for change from the great beyond or some fantasy political leader. There's no question that transforming myself from compliant white person into increasingly aware white ally has been uncomfortable. I have not taken the easy route. Yet as my mother used to say, "The easy way isn't always the best way." Of course, she was referring to things like taking the extra time to sift the flour or lace up my skates properly, but I'll take those words in this situation. I don't know what track my life, or American life, will take exactly, but I know this: social evolution is inevitable; it's how we guide it that's up for grabs. If taking part in transforming the bully requires the discomfort inherent in growth and change, I'm on board. I used to say I wanted my epitaph to read, "Good Person." Now I think I'd prefer something like "Faced the Bully."

I can't give away my privilege. I've got it whether I want it or not. What I can do is use my privilege to create change. I can speak up without fear of bringing down my entire race. I can suggest change with less chance of losing my job. If I lose my job, I have a white husband who can support me because he's a white man who had access to education and now has access to employment. If my husband's job gets targeted because I speak up against racism, I have an extended circle of white family and friends who would advocate for us. At least I think they would. I believe America is rich with white people clamoring to demonstrate their moral courage and be a part of change that creates the kind of world we can feel good about leaving to our children. We have a choice to make: resist change and keep alive antiquated beliefs about skin color, or outgrow those beliefs and make real the equality we envision.

Self-examination and the courage to admit to bias and unhelpful inherited behaviors may be our greatest tools for change. Allowing ourselves to be vulnerable enough to expose our ignorance and insecurities takes courage. And love. I believe the most loving thing a person, or a group of people, can do for another is to examine the ways in which their own insecurities and assumptions interfere with others' ability to thrive. Please join me in opening your heart and mind to the possibility that you—yes, even well-intentioned you—have room to change and grow, so that you can work with people of all colors and ethnicities to co-create communities that can unite, strengthen, and prosper.

TELL ME WHAT TO DO!

The good news is that everyone can do something to loosen racism's hold on America. The bad news is that unless you set yourself up for success, trying to do something helpful can actually perpetuate racism. Take time to learn and engage with the problem in order to lower the chances of making the same mistakes I did.

LEARN

Books

Myers, Vernā A. *Moving Diversity Forward: How to Go From Well-Meaning to Well-Doing.* Chicago: American Bar Association, 2011.

———. *What If I Say the Wrong Thing? 25 Habits for Culturally Effective People.* Chicago: American Bar Association, 2013.

Takaki, Ronald. *A Different Mirror: A History of Multicultural America.* New York: Back Bay Books, 2008.

Tochluk, Shelly. *Witnessing Whiteness: The Need to Talk About Race and How to Do It.* Lanham, MD: Rowman & Littlefield, 2009.

Films

Cracking the Codes: The System of Racial Inequity, directed by Shakti Butler. Oakland, CA: World Trust Educational Services, 2012. 75 minutes. Cost: $50–$350, depending on intended use.

Race: The Power of an Illusion. Produced by Larry Adelman. San Francisco: California Newsreel, 2003. 3 hours. Cost: $25–$195, depending on intended use.

White Like Me. Produced by Tim Wise. Northampton, MA: Media Education Foundation, 2013. 68 minutes. Cost: $150–$275, depending on intended use.

Websites

Race: The Power of an Illusion, www.pbs.org/race. Extensive supplementary material related to the three-part PBS documentary.

Witnessing Whiteness, witnessingwhiteness.com. Free workshop agendas and curriculum resources.

For additional resources, see my website: debbyirving.com.

ENGAGE

Prepare yourself to adopt an "I don't know what I don't know" attitude. The sooner you can become comfortable with seeking what you don't know, as opposed to proving what you do, the more you will learn and the more effective you'll become as a racial justice advocate. When you talk to friends and colleagues of color, share what you're learning about whiteness, but don't expect them to educate you. Find a racially mixed group in your community already doing this work. Their wisdom and support will be crucial to your learning and your contribution of time, talent, and resources. As with joining any group, fit matters. Take time to get to know who's doing what in your community. Is there a racial justice organization? Does an organization you're already interested in do social or racial justice work? Find a group and a role that feel just right so that you stay committed.

DONATE

Race Forward

"Race Forward's mission is to build awareness, solutions and leadership for racial justice by generating transformative ideas, information and experiences. We define racial justice as the systematic fair treatment of people of all races, resulting in equal opportunities and outcomes for all and we work to advance racial justice through media, research, and leadership development. Offices in New York, Chicago, and Oakland." For more information, see Race Forward's website: www.raceforward.org.

White Privilege Conference (WPC) Fund

"The WPC provides a challenging, collaborative and comprehensive experience. We strive to empower and equip individuals to work for equity and justice through self and social transformation." For more information, see WPC's website: whiteprivilegeconference.com.

For additional suggestions, see my website: debbyirving.com.

SPUR RACIAL AWARENESS AND EDUCATION

Purchase books and films for your local library, community center, religious organization, workplace, or school. Films can be pricey, so consider hosting a fundraiser or chipping in with others to make the purchase.

TAKE A COURSE

Most universities and colleges offer courses in race and identity. See if you can audit one.

ACKNOWLEDGMENTS

First of all, a general and heartfelt thanks to the hundreds of racial justice educators, learners, and activists whose questions, ideas, stories, and challenges drove my racial identity awakening. If not for you, there would have been no racial justice community in which to immerse myself and learn.

Initial thanks go to Nelda Barron, whose brilliantly choreographed curriculum is responsible for penetrating my white lens. Thanks, too, to Wheelock College for continuing to make "Racial and Cultural Identity" a required course. Special thanks to Wheelock professor Debbie Samuels-Peretz and my "Racial and Cultural Identity" classmates, all of whom contributed to the start of my journey.

Huge thanks to Paul Marcus of Community Change Inc. and Barbara Beckwith of White People Challenging Racism, who held my hand from start to finish. Knowing I could count on your wise counsel as I learned, questioned, and struggled though regrets, false summits, embarrassments, and achievements gave me the foundational support and camaraderie I needed.

Angela Giudice, I can't thank you enough for inserting yourself into the process. Just as I thought my book ready for publication, Angela, a seasoned racial justice educator, offered to read it. Over the next two years, eighty-two hour-long coaching sessions with Angela deepened my understanding of my own racialization. Several of *Waking Up White*'s most compelling revelations are due to my work with Angela.

A special thanks to Dr. Eddie Moore Jr., founder and director of the White Privilege Conference (WPC), and the WPC community for modeling what it looks like to face uncomfortable truths with compassion and skill.

To my fellow Winsor Parent Network for Diversity Forum committee members—Stephanie Bode Ward, Barbara Deck, Yvonne Dumornay, Bill Hughes, Vivek Pandit, Lynn Randall, Pankaj Tandon, Kasumi Verdine, and

Hong Xu—thank you for your hours of collaborative conversation, planning, and analysis.

Thanks to friends and colleagues who have supported me by sending me books, films, tips, articles, and contacts, or shared with me their own work: Joyce Allen-Beckford, Maggie Anderson, Donna Bivens, Stacy Blake-Beard, Manikka Bowman, Janelle Bradshaw, Julian Braxton, Lisa Ceremsak, James DeWolf Perry, Jay Fedigan, Sarah Fiarman, Phil Fogelman, Bill Gardiner, Jennifer Garvey Berger, Janet Gillespie, Trudy Glidden, Wendy Jane Grossman, Kathy-Ann Hart, David Howse, Norma Johnson, Paul Kivel, Trishia Lichauco, Iesha Martin, Michael Martin, Billie Mayo, Peggy McIntosh, Georgianna Melendez, Charles Modiano, Ann Moritz, Cheryl Munroe, Vernā Myers, Susan Naimark, Natalie Nathan, Nitin Nohria, Paula Parnagian, Carolyn Peter, Gianpiero Petriglieri, Tom Shapiro, Deborah Shariff, James Sherley, William "Smitty" Smith, David Thomas, Sandy Thompson, Shelly Tochluk, Phyllis Unterschuetz, Russ Vernon-Jones, Larry Ward, Phoebe Williams, Tim Wise, and Jeff Young. Thank you all.

To perfect strangers I sat next to on airplanes and buses and in waiting rooms of doctors' offices: thank you for engaging so spontaneously in conversations about your own experiences with racism. Your eagerness demonstrated to me just how prevalent among white people is the urge to better understand racism.

While I spent hours in conversation, learning from people of various ages and backgrounds about their experiences with racism, I also grounded myself in the education and analysis offered by trainers who've been doing this work for decades: Crossroads Antiracism Organizing and Training, the People's Institute for Survival and Beyond, Race Forward, VISIONS Inc., and the White Privilege Conference. Thank you for your racial justice education offerings.

Thanks to the many readers who reviewed all or parts of *Waking Up White* versions 1 through 9: Fabrizia Adang, Mecky Adnani, Barbara Allen, Joyce Allen-Beckford, Sarah Baker, Barbara Beckwith, Claire Berman, Stacy Blake-Beard, Claire Blumenfeld, Stephanie Bode Ward, Taylor Bodman, Chris Bossie, Diane Brancazio, Peggy Burnieika, Rob Burnieika, Michelle Chalmers, Willa Chamberlain, Karen Coleman, Sara Cornell, Brian Corr, Jennifer Costa, Annette Cournoyer, Barbara Deck, Brooke Deterline, Kelly DeWolfe, Helen Dunn, Elizabeth Edwards, Christine Emello, Lana Ewing, Natali (Tali) Freed, Bill Gardiner, Jennifer Garvey Berger, Trudy Glidden,

Josie Green, Christa Haberstroh, Sarah Halter Hahesy, Calley Hastings, Bill Hughes, Emily Hummel, Julia Irvine Madore, Dale Irving, Walter Irving, Norma Johnson, Paul Johnson, Marta Kagan, Rebekah Kane, Cleve Kapala, Kathleen Kelly, Martha Clarke Kiley, Bobby Kittredge, Lucia Kittredge, Esu Lackey, Trishia Lichauco, Molly Liddell, Kendall Lord, Ellen Madigan, Anna Madigan Jenoski, TJ Manning, Mary Manson, Catherine Matejcek, Paul Marcus, Michael Martin, Billie Mayo, Marc McGovern, Ann Moritz, Vernā Myers, Susan Naimark, Karla Nicholson, Sean T. O'Sullivan, Joe Petner, Marianna Pierce, Cathy Putnam, Fred Putnam, John Rabinowitz, Lynn Randall, Elizabeth Rettig McCarthy, Marc Russell, Tyler Schaeffer, Eleanor Scianella, Stephanie Seller, Tom Shapiro, Pat Shine, Molly Simmons, Sheila Sinclair, Kent Smith, Lenny Smith, Herb Tyson, and Cynthia Williams. Each of you offered some unique piece of feedback that contributed both to my own understanding of racial issues and to the final version of the book.

To my beloved cohort of "White People Challenging Racism: Moving from Talk to Action" cofacilitators: you are the best colleagues a person could ask for. Thank you, Barbara Beckwith, Natali (Tali) Freed, Denise Garcia, Adam Gibbons, Pamela Goldstein, Lisa Graustein, Xochi Kountz, Stewart Lanier, Danilo Morales, Stella Panzarella, Stephen Pereira, Mark Schafer, and Jennifer Yanco.

Finally, in addition to learning about racism, my journey required learning how to write and publish a book. For writing support and training I thank Grub Street. What a stroke of luck to have one of the country's premier writers' communities right here in my hometown of Boston. To Kate Victory Hannisian of Blue Pencil Consulting, thank you for the "book therapy" and for understanding what I was trying to do before I understood it myself. To Mark Fischer and Joe Finder, thank you for believing in my project and supporting my publishing efforts.

To the team who at long last helped birth this book, thank you! Beth Wright, Ann Delgehausen, and Zan Ceeley of Trio Bookworks: never in my wildest dreams did I imagine a team that would both know my subject matter and make the publishing process so rich and fun. To Brad Norr, thank you for translating my words into visual imagery, and most of all for the book cover that says it all. To my publicist and longtime friend, Martha Clarke Kiley, thank you for helping me figure out how to take my book from concept to media channels to readers' bedside tables. Thanks to all of you for understanding the urgency of my message and the need for it to drive the project.

I'd also like to extend a thank-you to Oprah Winfrey and Elizabeth Gilbert, both of whom modeled for me the power of plain English, authenticity, and personal stories to create change. You'll find all three elements from start to finish in *Waking Up White*.

Special thanks to my sister Lucia Kittredge for her exceptional support and desire to learn along with me. To my other siblings—Emily Hummel, Bobby Kittredge, and Diane Kittredge—as well as several of my Pierce cousins, thank you for your interest in my work and for reminding me how lucky I am to be from a family in which pushing boundaries and having difficult conversations in the name of social change is allowed. Thank you all for suggesting that my parents, no longer here to speak for themselves, would be proud of me.

Last, and certainly not least, I will try to convey the gratitude I feel for my husband, Bruce, and daughters, Emily and Jane, who had little choice but to come on this journey with me. Thank you for allowing me to shed old beliefs and adopt new ones even when it affected our relationships, time together, and family resources. Thank you for stepping out of your comfort zones with me in the name of social change. May we continue to change and grow as a family for many years to come.

NOTES ON SOURCES

INTRODUCTION

xiii **invention and perpetuation of the idea of white superiority:** For more
on race as a human-made invention that's been codified and made real
in terms of lived experience, see the website for the PBS documentary
Race: The Power of an Illusion, www.pbs.org/race/000_General/000_00-Home
.htm, and the website *Race: Are We So Different?*, American Anthropological
Association, 2011, www.understandingrace.org/home.html.

1   WHAT WASN'T SAID

3 **"Whatever happened to all the Indians?":** In my childhood culture, the
term "Indian" was commonly used to describe North America's indigenous people. I had no understanding that this term, assigned by white
Europeans, was offensive to many indigenous people then and now. In
meeting people of indigenous heritage throughout this journey, I've
learned there's a great variety of preferred language. I now ask people how
they identify themselves.

4 **not so much incorrect as incomplete:** Chimamanda Ngozi Adichie, "The
Danger of a Single Story," TED Talk, July 2009, www.ted.com/talks/chima
manda_adichie_the_danger_of_a_single_story.html.

4 **how disease brought by our ancestors:** Ojibwa, "American Indians and
European Diseases," *Native American Netroots*, November 12, 2011, www
.nativeamericannetroots.net/diary/1142/american-indians-and-european
-diseases.

5 **stripping them of the languages, customs, beliefs:** For more on the deculturalization of American Indians at the hands of white European settlers,
see Russell Thornton, *American Indian Holocaust and Survival: A Population History
Since 1492* (1987; reprint, Norman: University of Oklahoma Press, 1990).

3   RACE VERSUS CLASS

13   **white Anglo-Saxon Protestant (WASP):** Despite the fact the term "WASP" is an obnoxious one for many, I choose to use it throughout the book because it is core to my identity.

14   **a story told by John Hope Franklin:** John Hope Franklin, *Mirror to America: The Autobiography of John Hope Franklin* (New York: Farrar, Straus and Giroux, 2005), 340.

4   OPTIMISM

17   **the postwar baby boom:** "The Baby Boomer Generation [Born 1946–1964]," Value Options: Putting People First, no date, www.eapexpress.com /spotlight_YIW/baby_boomers.htm.

19   **the documentary *Cracking the Codes*:** Shakti Butler, *Cracking the Codes: The System of Racial Inequality*, DVD, 75 mins. (Oakland, CA: World Trust Educational Services, 2012).

7   THE GI BILL

32   **the focus turns to the GI Bill:** "The House We Live In," episode 3, *Race: The Power of an Illusion*, DVD, produced by Llewellyn M. Smith (San Francisco: California Newsreel, 2003). For more information, including a series transcript, see the documentary's website: www.pbs.org/race.

33   **one million black GIs:** William H. Smith and Ellen Ternes, *The Invisible Soldiers: Unheard Voices*, DVD, directed by Jonathan J. Nash (Sudbury, MA: WHS Media, 2004).

33   **program tilted heavily in favor of white people:** The Social Security Act of 1935 excluded agricultural and domestic workers, most of whom were African Americans, contributing to the racial wealth gap still widening today.

34   **whose equity grew steadily over time:** *The Possessive Investment in Whiteness: How White People Profit from Identity Politics* (Philadelphia: Temple University Press, 1998).

35   **Realtors are low-lives:** Since my father's death, my husband has become a realtor. They are not *all* low-lives!

36   **epidermal gold card:** My term is inspired by a quote by Manning Marable from his book *Black Liberation in Conservative America* (Boston: South End, 1997): "Whiteness in a racist, corporate-controlled society is like having

the image of an American Express card . . . stamped on one's face: immediately you are 'universally accepted'" (22–23).

8 RACIAL CATEGORIES

38   **the film documents a racially mixed class:** "The Difference Between Us," episode 1, *Race: The Power of an Illusion*, DVD, produced by Christine Herbes-Sommers (San Francisco: California Newsreel, 2003).

9 WHITE SUPERIORITY

42   **race as a "social construct" and a "human invention":** These terms are frequently used in connection with race. See, for example, "The Difference Between Us," episode 1, *Race: The Power of an Illusion*, DVD, produced by Christine Herbes-Sommers (San Francisco: California Newsreel, 2003), and the website *Race: Are We So Different?*, American Anthropological Association, 2011, www.understandingrace.org/home.html. For more on the evolution of racial categories in general and whiteness in particular, see Nell Irvin Painter, *The History of White People* (New York: Norton, 2010).

43   **Chardin's take on skin color:** See Sir John Chardin, *Travels in Persia, 1673–1677* (New York: Dover, 1988). Nell Irvin Painter refers to Chardin's travel writings in her essay "Why White People Are Called 'Caucasian,'" in *Collective Degradation: Slavery and the Construction of Race*, Proceedings of the Fifth Annual Gilder Lehrman Center International Conference at Yale University, November 7–8, 2003, www.yale.edu/glc/events/race/Painter.pdf.

43   **the steam engine and the gun:** Jared Diamond (host), *Guns, Germs, and Steel*, DVD, directed by Cassian Harrison and Tim Lamber (London: Lion Television, 2005). For more information see the documentary's website: www.pbs.org/gunsgerms steel.

43   **culture in which parents push their children to achieve:** Monica Ly, "Asians + Math," *AsiaXpress*, January 6, 2008, asiaxpress.com/Articles /2008 /jan/math/1.html; Julianne Hing, "Asian Americans Respond to Pew: We're Not Your Model Minority," *Colorlines*, June 21, 2012, colorlines.com /archives/2012/06/pew_asian_american_study.html; Amy Chua, *Battle Hymn of the Tiger Mother* (New York: Penguin, 2011).

43   **Kenyan runners:** Adharanand Finn, "Why Are Kenyans the Fastest Runners?" *Huffington Post*, May 18, 2012, www.huffingtonpost.com /adharanand-finn/post_3393_b_1527065.html; Brendan Koerner,

"Why Are Kenyans Fast Runners?" *Slate*, November 3, 2003, www.slate. com/articles/news_and_politics/explainer/2003/11/why_are_kenyans fast_runners.html; Weldon Johnson, "Kenyan Distance Running Part I: Kenya, the Land of Opportunity," LetsRun.com, March 2007, www .letsrun.com/news/2007/03/kenyan-distance-running-part-i-kenya -the-land-of-opportunity/.

44   **Like a fish unable to recognize:** The metaphor of whiteness being as invisible to white people as water is invisible to fish is frequently used in the racial justice movement.

44   **pigment of the imagination:** I first saw this term on a T-shirt at the White Privilege Conference.

44   **black in America and white in Brazil:** Roland Soong, "Racial Classifications in Latin America," *Zona Latina*, August 15, 1999, www.zonalatina.com /Zldata55.htm.

10   THE MELTING POT

46   **"white ethnics":** Adalberto Aguirre Jr. and Jonathan H. Turner, *American Ethnicity: The Dynamics and Consequences of Discrimination*, 3rd ed. (Boston: McGraw-Hill, 2001).

46   **17.3 million people immigrated:** John Simkin, "Immigration 1820–1920," Spartacus Educational, June 2013, www.spartacus.schoolnet.co.uk /USAES1920S.htm.

46   **utterly unattainable unless one is white:** A major source for my understanding of the issue of who historically could and couldn't be white in the United States is "The Story We Tell," episode 2, *Race: The Power of an Illusion*, DVD, produced by Tracy Heather Strain (San Francisco: California Newsreel, 2003).

47   **English conquest of North America:** Joel Spring, *Deculturalization and the Struggle for Equality: A Brief History of the Education of Dominated Cultures in the United States*, 6th ed. (Boston: McGraw-Hill, 2007), 5.

48   **the Carlisle Indian School:** "In the White Man's Image," season 4, episode 12, *The American Experience*, DVD, directed by Christine Lesiak (Boston: American Experience, 1992), available online at www.youtube.com/ watch?v=14RifPPh1YU; *Invisible*, DVD, produced by Gunnar Hansen, David Westphal, and James Eric Francis (Northeast Harbor, Maine: Episcopal Diocese of Maine & Acadia Film Video, 2005); *Our Spirits Don't Speak*

English: Indian Boarding School, DVD, produced by Steven Heape (Dallas: Rich-Heape Films, 2008).

48   **long hair has spiritual significance:** Ojibwa, "Long Hair," *Native American Net-roots*, July 26, 2010, www.nativeamericannetroots.net/diary/601/long-hair.

49   **"language, religion, family structure:** Charla Bear, "American Indian Boarding Schools Haunt Many," National Public Radio, May 2008, www .npr.org/templates/story/story.php?storyId=16516865.

49   **the 1854 *Types of Mankind*:** Josiah Clark Nott, *Types of Mankind: Or, Ethnological Researches Based Upon the Ancient Monuments, Paintings, Sculptures, and Crania of Races, and Upon Their Natural, Geographical, Philological and Biblical History* (Philadelphia: Lippincott, Grambo, 1854).

50   **the Naturalization Act of 1790:** "An Act to Establish an Uniform Rule of Naturalization," 1790, Harvard University Library, pds.lib.harvard.edu /pds/view/5596748 (a scan of the original act). Note that "white" and "good" are both highly subjective terms, giving those in power the ultimate power to grant citizenship or not.

50   **Hawaiian businessman Takao Ozawa:** To learn more about the Supreme Court's rulings over Takao Ozawa, Bhagat Singh Thind, and other petitioners, see "The House We Live In," episode 3, *Race: The Power of an Illusion*, DVD, produced by Llewellyn M. Smith (San Francisco: California Newsreel, 2003).

52   **World War II internment camp:** "Personal Justice Denied: Report of the Commission on Wartime Relocation and Internment of Civilians," National Park Service, 1982, www.nps.gov/history/history/online_ books/personal _justice_denied/.

11   HEADWINDS AND TAILWINDS

54   **skin color symbolism + favoritism + power = systemic racism:** My formula is inspired by one used by many antiracism educators: race + power = racism.

55   **In his book *Outliers*:** Malcolm Gladwell, *Outliers: The Story of Success* (New York: Little, Brown, 2008).

56   **ABC News *Nightline* video:** *Nightline: Update—The Color Line and the Bus Line*, DVD, produced by Ted Koppel (New York: ABC News, 2009).

60   **Tom Shapiro, author:** Thomas M. Shapiro, *The Hidden Cost of Being African American: How Wealth Perpetuates Inequality* (New York: Oxford University Press, 2004);

Melvin L. Oliver and Thomas M. Shapiro, *Black Wealth/ White Wealth: A New Perspective on Racial Inequality*, 10th anniversary ed. (New York: Routledge, 2006).

60   **2011 headline:** Rakesh Kochhar, Richard Fry, and Paul Taylor, "Wealth Gaps Rise to Record Highs Between Whites, Blacks, Hispanics—Twenty-to-One," Pew Research Social & Demographic Trends, July 26, 2011, www .pewsocialtrends.org/2011/07/26/wealth-gaps-rise-to-record-highs -between-whites-blacks-hispanics/.

12   ICEBERGS

64   **Sociologist Kenneth Cushner explains:** Kenneth Cushner, *Beyond Tourism: A Practical Guide to Meaningful Educational Travel* (Lanham, MD: ScarecrowEducation, 2004), 40.

66   **"right, good, and beautiful.":** This phrase is from Dr. Valerie Batts, executive director and cofounder of VISIONS Inc.

66   **a traveling exhibit, *Race: Are We So Different?*:** Developed by the American Anthropological Association in collaboration with the Science Museum of Minnesota, *Race* is the first nationally traveling exhibition to tell the stories of race from biological, cultural, and historical points of view. To learn more about the exhibit, including its touring schedule, see *Race: Are We So Different?*, American Anthropological Association, 2011, www.understand-ing race.org /home.html.

67   **Frederick Hoffman:** Frederick L. Hoffman, *Race Traits and Tendencies of the American Negro* (New York: Macmillan, 1896).

13   INVISIBILITY

69   **cueing up a video:** Christopher Chabris and Daniel Simons, "The Original Selective Attention Task," *The Invisible Gorilla*, 2010, www.theinvisible gorilla.com/videos.html. Try also watching the second video, "The Monkey Business Illusion."

70   **In 1988 Dr. Peggy McIntosh:** Peggy McIntosh, "White Privilege: Unpacking the Invisible Knapsack," *Peace and Freedom Magazine* (July/August 1989): 10–12. In addition to serving as an American studies and women's studies professor at Wellesley College, Dr. McIntosh is a world-renowned speaker and writer on the topic of racism and other forms of oppression. She is also the founder and codirector of the National SEED (Seeking Educational Equity and Diversity) Project on Inclusive Curriculum. Her essay "White Privilege:

Unpacking the Invisible Knapsack" is considered by many white people to be a catalyst for their "waking up" process. Though Dr. McIntosh's original paper listed forty-six examples, a subsequent list, published without her permission, bumped the number up to a tidy fifty by taking four examples from a separate list she'd created regarding heterosexual privilege. Dr. McIntosh prefers that her original list be used and invites readers to email her at mmcintosh@wellesley.edu for copies. See debbyirving.com/peggy-mcintosh-articles for a list of Dr. McIntosh's articles on white privilege.

72   **Diane Sawyer did an investigative report:** "True Colors," *Primetime Live*, produced by Diane Sawyer (New York: ABC News, 1992). The report is available online in two parts: www.youtube.com/watch?v=YyL5EcAwB9c and www.youtube.com/watch?v=gOS3BBmUxvs.

73   **workshop titled "Reproducing Whiteness":** David S. Owen, "Reproducing Whiteness: A Framework for Understanding the Mechanics of Whiteness," presentation at the twelfth annual White Privilege Conference, Minneapolis, April 13–16, 2011.

73   **workshop, led by Crossroads:** Contact Crossroads Antiracism Organizing & Training, PO Box 309, Matteson IL 60443-0309, phone: 708.503.0804, info@crossroadsantiracism.org.

14   ZAP!

79   **white people's casual ignorance:** To learn more about the impact of white people's ignorance, see Norma Johnson, "A Poem for My White Friends: I Didn't Tell You," *White Privilege Conference Journal* 3, no. 1 (2013), www.wpcjournal.com/article/view/11842.

16   LOGOS AND STEREOTYPES

86   **processing the millions of pieces of information:** Ben Thomas, "Web Portals and Mouse Mazes: How Your Brain Sorts the World," *Huffington Post*, April 29, 2013, www.huffingtonpost.com/ben-thomas/web-portals-and-mouse-maz_b_2674543.html.

86   **Samuel Ichiye Hayakawa writes:** Samuel Ichiye Hayakawa, *Language in Thought and Action* (London: Allen & Unwin, 1952).

87   **low-number license plates:** In some parts of the United States, low-number plates indicate either a connection to someone in power who pulled strings or an inherited number, passed down through the family.

In the inherited case, the lower the number, the longer one's family has
been an established, car-buying American family. Along with the antiques,
paintings, and silver, the low-number plate is a family heirloom.

87   **Sociologist Allan Johnson's writings:** Allan G. Johnson, *The Forest and the Trees:*
Sociology as Life, Practice, and Promise (Philadelphia: Temple University Press,
1997), 39–40, 44–45.

87   **the PBS documentary People Like Us:** *People Like Us: Social Class in America* (TV
documentary), directed by Alex Kurzman (New York: Center for New
American Media, 2001).

88   **African slaves' easy-to-identify dark skin:** To learn more about the history
of slavery see "Background Readings: History," *Race: The Power of an Illusion*, PBS,
2003, www.pbs.org/race/000_About/002_04-background-02.htm. See
also Nell Irvin Painter, *The History of White People* (New York: Norton, 2010).

89   **Dr. Martin Luther King's advice:** To read Dr. Martin Luther King's full
"I Have a Dream" speech from the 1963 March on Washington, see
www.archives.gov/press/exhibits/dream-speech.pdf.

90   **"I'd been walking the streets:** Claude M. Steele, *Whistling Vivaldi: And*
Other Clues to How Stereotypes Affect Us (New York: Norton, 2010), 6.

17   MY GOOD PEOPLE

95   **the term "cultural fantasy":** Nell Irvin Painter, *The History of White People*
(New York: Norton, 2010), x.

18   COLOR-BLIND

101   **"I couldn't believe it:** *White Privilege 101: Getting In on the Conversation*, DVD,
directed by Adam Burke (Colorado Springs: Matrix Center for the Advancement of Social Equity and Inclusion, 2004).

101   **In his article "The Right Hand of Privilege,":** Steven Jones, "The Right
Hand of Privilege," Jones & Associates Consulting, 2003, www.jonesand
associatesconsulting.com/The_Right_Hand_of_Privilege_ThoughtPaper
.pdf.

19   MY GOOD LUCK

104   **How could I afford to live on $12,000 a year:** To put my 1984 salary and

rent in context, the 2014 equivalent of $12,000 is about $30,000 (thirty years at 3 percent annual inflation); the 2014 equivalent of $143 is $347 (thirty years at 3 percent annual inflation).

104 **rent-controlled apartment buildings:** Patricia Cantor, "25 Years Ago Tenants Organized, Formed Coalitions, Took to the Streets, and Won Rent Control in Massachusetts," National Housing Institute, March/April 1995, www.nhi.org/online/issues/80/massrent.html.

20 MY ROBIN HOOD SYNDROME

107 **called "dysfunctional rescuing,":** Valerie Batts, "Is Reconciliation Possible? Lessons from Combating 'Modern Racism,'" VISIONS Inc., 2002, visions-inc.org/wp-content/uploads/Is-Reconciliation-Possible .pdf, 15.

25 BELONGING

138 **the term "entitlement gap":** Susan Naimark, *The Education of a White Parent: Wrestling with Race and Opportunity in the Boston Public Schools* (Amherst, MA: Levellers, 2012), 53–55.

138 **the story of a parent meeting:** Susan Naimark, "Teachable Moments Not Just for Kids," *Rethinking Schools* (summer 2009), www.rethinkingschools .org/restrict.asp?path=archive/23_04/mome234.shtml.

141 **Studies have shown that parent involvement:** Science News, "Parental Involvement Strongly Impacts Student Achievement," *Science Daily*, May 28, 2008, www.sciencedaily.com/releases/2008/05/080527123852.htm; Karen Mapp, "Making the Connection Between Families and Schools," *Harvard Education Letter* 13, no. 5 (September/October 2007), www.hepg.org /hel/article/356.

26 SURVIVING VERSUS THRIVING

143 **a spontaneous experiment in 1968:** "A Class Divided," season 3, episode 9, *Frontline*, directed by William Peters (New York: Frontline and Yale University Films, 1985).

145 **"psychological disfigurement.":** Andrea Stuart, *Sugar in the Blood: A Family's Story of Slavery and Empire* (New York: Knopf, 2013), 212.

28   I AM THE ELEPHANT

150   **the invisible veil of privilege:** The idea of privilege as invisible is often credited to Peggy McIntosh, although she recognizes a connection between her use of the term "invisible" and how Ralph Ellison used it in his 1952 novel *Invisible Man*, which traces the life of a black man in 1950s America. As for the term "veil of privilege," I first heard it at the following presentation: Steven Jones, "How to Make the Invisible Visible: Tools for Pulling Back the Veil of Privilege," lege," presentation to the Twenty-Second National Association of Independent Schools (NAIS) People of Color Conference, Denver, December 3–5, 2009.

150   **a two-contestant running race:** My road race analogy depicts the privilege side of racism. To see a short film using a running race to depict the discrimination side of racism, watch *Unequal Opportunity Race*, produced by Kimberlé Crenshaw and Luke Harris, YouTube video, 4:04, African American Policy Forum, www.youtube.com/watch?v=eBb5TgOXgNY.

29   INTENT AND IMPACT

162   **hide behind my intent:** I learned the concept of hiding behind my intent from Vernā A. Myers, *Moving Diversity Forward: How to Go from Well-Meaning to Well-Doing* (Chicago: American Bar Association, 2011), 50.

30   FEELINGS AND THE CULTURE OF NICENESS

170   **the book *Too Good for Her Own Good*:** Claudia Bepko and Jo-Ann Krestan, *Too Good for Her Own Good: Breaking Free from the Burden of Female Responsibility* (New York: Harper & Row, 1990).

171   **puts the blame on the complainer:** William Ryan, *Blaming the Victim*, rev. and updated ed. (New York: Vintage Books, 1976).

31   COURAGEOUS CONVERSATIONS

172   **Courageous Conversations:** See Glenn E. Singleton and Curtis Linton, eds., *Facilitator's Guide to Courageous Conversations About Race* (Thousand Oaks, CA: Corwin, 2007), and Beverly Daniel Tatum, *"Why Are All the Black Kids Sitting Together in the Cafeteria?" and Other Conversations About Race* (New York: Basic Books, 1997).

176   "Truth without love is brutality: Warren W. Wiersbe, *On Being a Leader for God* (Grand Rapids, MI: Baker Books, 2011), 39.

33   PERCEPTION AND FEAR

180   Reconstructing my racial identity: To learn more about white identity development theory as developed by Janet H. Helms, see "Racial Identity Development," Unitarian Universalist Association of Congregations, no date, www.uua.org/documents/gardinerwilliam/whiteness/racial_identity_dev .pdf.

180   "monstrous, hairy and pale skinned": Ronald Takaki, *A Different Mirror: A History of Multicultural America* (New York: Back Bay Books, 2008), 23.

180   in some African American novels: Barbara Beckwith quotes them in *What Was I Thinking? Reflecting on Everyday Racism* (Roselle, NJ: Inquiring Minds, 2009).

182   anti-Obama actions sought to redraw the lines: "Racial Slurs Continue Against Obama Despite Historic Achievement," *Fox News*, March 30, 2009, www.foxnews.com/politics/2009/03/30/racial-slurs-continue-obama -despite-historic-achievement/; Frank Bohn, "Guns Sales Surge After Obama's Election," CNN, November 11, 2008, www.cnn.com/2008 /CRIME/11/11/obama.gun.sales/.

182   "more perfect union,": Constitution of the United States, National Archives, www.archives.gov/exhibits/charters/constitution_transcript. html.

182   NPR-hosted roundtable conversation: Michele Norris, "York Voters Express Post-Election Hopes, Fears," National Public Radio, October 24, 2008, www .npr.org/templates/story/story.php?storyId=96086423.

183   Dr. Martin Luther King's concept: "Beloved Community" is a term first coined in the early days of the twentieth century by the philosopher-theologian Josiah Royce, who founded the Fellowship of Reconciliation. Dr. Martin Luther King Jr., a member of the Fellowship of Reconciliation, popularized the term by including it as one of the six principles of nonviolence. See "The King Philosophy," The King Center, 2012, www.theking center.org/king-philosophy.

184   Imagine a country: This end-of-chapter exercise was inspired by Paul Marcus of Community Change, who uses it in his presentation "Living in the Matrix and Its Implications for Understanding Racism and Privilege." He adapted the exercise from Patti DeRosa of Change Works Consulting.

34　BECOMING MULTICULTURAL

187　**the New York Times published an article:** Guy Deutscher, "Does Your Language Shape How You Think?" *New York Times Magazine*, August 26, 2010, www.nytimes.com/2010/08/29/magazine/29language-t.html?page wanted=all.

188　**better equipped with strategies to cope:** Dani Monroe, *Untapped Talent: Unleashing the Power of the Hidden Workforce* (New York: Palgrave Macmillan, 2013).

35　IF ONLY YOU'D BE MORE LIKE ME

192　**Peggy McIntosh explained to me:** Peggy McIntosh's "hard drive" metaphor is from a personal email exchange, October 20, 2012.

36　THE DOMINANT WHITE CULTURE

194　**list of dominant white culture behaviors:** Though many lists have been created, they're strikingly similar. Mine is heavily influenced by a version I learned in a training with Undoing Racism: The People's Institute for Survival and Beyond; see www.pisab.org.

37　BOXES AND LADDERS

200　**the borderlands where people from different cultures:** Robette Anne Dias and Chuck Ruelhle, "The Borderlands," Crossroads Ministry, no date, www .crossroadsantiracism.org/wp-content/themes/crossroads/PDFs/The Borderlands.pdf.

38　THE RUGGED INDIVIDUAL

201　**Interdependence is our lifeblood:** Kendra Cherry, "Hierarchy of Needs: The Five Levels of Maslow's Hierarchy of Needs," About.com, no date, http:// psychology.about.com/od/theoriesofpersonality/a/hierarchyneeds.htm.

202　**Encouraging students to reason together:** Anuradha A. Gokhale, "Collaborative Thinking Enhances Critical Thinking," *Virginia Tech Journal of Technology Education* (fall 1995), http://scholar.lib.vt.edu/ejournals/JTE/v7n1 /gokhale.jte-v7n1.html?ref=Sawos.Org.

202   **African American students perform better:** "Cooperative Learning,"
Diversifying Economic Quality: A Wiki for Instructors and Departments,
no date, www.diversifyingecon.org/index.php/Cooperative_learning.

202   **collective orientation:** To learn more about how cultural values develop
out of survival needs based on climate and geography, see the work of
Dr. Edwin Nichols on Robert S. Wright's website, www.robertswright.ca
/CulturalCompetenceAdjudicativeBoards20100427.pdf.

39   EQUALITY STARTS WITH EQUITY

207   **a stunningly bold approach:** Stacey M. Childress, Denis P. Doyle, and
David A. Thomas, *Leading for Equity: The Pursuit of Excellence in Montgomery County
Public Schools* (Cambridge, MA: Harvard Education Press, 2009).

208   **The gap in the dropout rate:** Donna St. George, "In Montgomery Schools,
Achievement Gap Widens in Some Areas, Drawing Criticism," *Washington
Post*, March 12, 2013.

40   BULL IN A CHINA SHOP

213   **what people of color consider to be "microaggressions,":** Tori DeAngelis,
"Unmasking 'Racial Micro Aggressions,'" *American Psychological Association* 40,
no. 2 (2009), www.apa.org/monitor/2009/02/microaggression.aspx.

41   FROM BYSTANDER TO ALLY

219   **historian and activist Howard Zinn:** Howard Zinn, *You Can't Be Neutral on a
Moving Train: A Personal History of Our Times* (Boston: Beacon, 2002).

220   **As Coretta Scott King said:** "Coretta Scott King on Poverty," A View from
the Cave: Reporting on International Aid and Development, June 3, 2011,
www.aviewfromthecave.com/2011/06/coretta-scott-king-on-poverty.html.

220   **Opportunities abound for white people:** See, for example, John Raible,
"Checklist for White Allies Against Racism," State University of New York,
Cortland, 1994, johnraible.files.wordpress.com/w007/05/revised-2009
-checklist-for-allies.pdf.

221   **I will always have to check my privilege:** Melissa McEwan, "On the Fixed
State Ally Model vs. Process Model Ally Work," Shakesville, April 3, 2013,
www.shakesville.com/2013/04/on-fixed-state-ally-model-vs-process.html.

42 SOLIDARITY AND ACCOUNTABILITY

223 the Montgomery County Public Schools example: Stacey M. Childress, Denis P. Doyle, and David A. Thomas, *Leading for Equity: The Pursuit of Excellence in Montgomery County Public Schools* (Cambridge, MA: Harvard Education Press, 2009).

223 In the film Mirrors of Privilege: *Mirrors of Privilege: Making Whiteness Visible*, DVD, directed by Shakti Butler and Rick Butler (Oakland, CA: World Trust Educational Services, 2006).

225 the phenomenon of "own-race bias.": Kathleen L. Hourihan, Assron S. Benjamin, and Xiping Liu, "A Cross-Race Effect in Metamemory: Predictions of Face Recognition Are More Accurate for Members of Our Own Race," *Science Direct: Journal of Applied Research in Memory and Cognition* (September 2012), www.sciencedirect.com/science/article/pii/S2211368112000630; Christian A. Meissner and John C. Brigham, "Thirty Years of Investigating the Own-Race Bias in Memory for Faces," *Psychology, Public Policy, and Law* 7, no. 1 (2001): 3–35.

43 FROM TOLERANCE TO ENGAGEMENT

228 "diversity is being invited to the party: Chapter 1 in Vernā A. Myers, *Moving Diversity Forward: How to Go from Well-Meaning to Well-Doing* (Chicago: American Bar Association, 2011).

228 An article written by Harvard Business School professors: David A. Thomas and Robin J. Ely, "Making Differences Matter: A New Paradigm for Managing Diversity," *Harvard Business Review* (September 1996), http://hbr.org/1996/09/making-differences-matter-a-new-paradigm-for-managing-diversity/ar/1.

229 In 1821 he took the English example: Joel Spring, *Deculturalization and the Struggle for Equality: A Brief History of the Education of Dominated Cultures in the United States*, 6th ed. (Boston: McGraw-Hill, 2007), 26–28.

230 "Men build ladders: Dean Jardim said this during a class at Simmons Graduate School of Management in 1990.

44 LISTENING

232 In the film White Privilege 101: *White Privilege 101: Getting In on the Conversation*, DVD, directed by Adam Burke (Colorado Springs: Matrix Center for the Advancement of Social Equity and Inclusion, 2004).

232 **restorative justice as an alternate approach:** To learn more about restorative justice, see the website for Suffolk University's Center for Restorative Justice: http://suffolk.edu/college/centers/15970.php.

234 **"the Winchester Multicultural Network.":** To learn more about the Winchester Multicultural Network, see its website: www.wmcn.org.

45 NORMALIZING RACE TALK

236 **skin color recipe:** The skin color recipe project was created by Carolyn Callender, a Haggerty School teacher.

238 **a course I now cofacilitate:** To learn more about the course "White People Challenging Racism: Moving from Talk to Action," see its website: www.wpcr-boston.org.

46 WHOLE AGAIN

246 **My vulnerability also became the birthplace:** The idea of vulnerability as a "birthplace" for courage comes from the work of Brene Brown. Learn more at www.brenebrown.com.

246 **Father Gregory Boyle's book:** Gregory Boyle, *Tattoos on the Heart: The Power of Boundless Compassion* (New York: Free Press, 2010), 87.

CPSIA information can be obtained
at www.ICGtesting.com
Printed in the USA
BVHW080431140219
540169BV00003B/270/P